W9-DDJ-426

WITHDRAWN

MISS PEREGRINE'S HOME
FOR PECULIAR CHILDREN

Miss Peregrine's Home for Peculiar Children

Ransom Riggs

THORNDIKE PRESS
A part of Gale, Cengage Learning

GALE
CENGAGE Learning·

Detroit • New York • San Francisco • New Haven, Conn • Waterville, Maine • London

GALE
CENGAGE Learning®

Recommended for Middle Readers.
Copyright © 2011 by Ransom Riggs.
Thorndike Press, a part of Gale, Cengage Learning.

ALL RIGHTS RESERVED
Thorndike Press® Large Print The Literacy Bridge.
The text of this Large Print edition is unabridged.
Other aspects of the book may vary from the original edition.
Set in 16 pt. Plantin.

LIBRARY OF CONGRESS CATALOGING-IN-PUBLICATION DATA

Riggs, Ransom.
    Miss Peregrine's Home for Peculiar Children / by Ransom Riggs. —
Large print ed.
      p. cm.
      "Thorndike Press Large Print The Literacy Bridge"—Copyright p.
    Summary: A horrific family tragedy sends sixteen-year-old Jacob
journeying to a remote island off the coast of Wales, where he discovers
the crumbling ruins of an old orphanage that was home to children
who were more than just peculiar, but possibly dangerous—and who
may still be alive. Illustrated with vintage found photographs.
    ISBN 978-1-4104-5023-4 (hardcover) — ISBN 1-4104-5023-6 (hardcover)
    1. Large type books. [1. Supernatural—Fiction. 2. Grandfathers—Fiction.
3. Orphanages—Fiction. 4. Wales—Fiction. 5. Large type books.] I. Title.
PZ7.R4423Mi 2012
[Fic]—dc23   2012012884

Published in 2012 by arrangement with Quirk Productions, Inc.

Printed in Mexico
7 8 9 10 11 12 20 19 18 17 16

SLEEP IS NOT, DEATH IS NOT;
WHO SEEM TO DIE LIVE.
HOUSE YOU WERE BORN IN,
FRIENDS OF YOUR SPRING-TIME,
OLD MAN AND YOUNG MAID,
DAY'S TOIL AND ITS GUERDON,
THEY ARE ALL VANISHING,
FLEEING TO FABLES,
CANNOT BE MOORED.
— *Ralph Waldo Emerson*

PROLOGUE

I had just come to accept that my life would be ordinary when extraordinary things began to happen. The first of these came as a terrible shock and, like anything that changes you forever, split my life into halves: Before and After. Like many of the extraordinary things to come, it involved my grandfather, Abraham Portman.

Growing up, Grandpa Portman was the most fascinating person I knew. He had lived in an orphanage, fought in wars, crossed oceans by steamship and deserts on horseback, performed in circuses, knew everything about guns and self-defense and surviving in the wilderness, and spoke at least three languages that weren't English. It all seemed unfathomably exotic to a kid who'd never left Florida, and I begged him to regale me with stories whenever I saw him. He always obliged, telling them like secrets that could be entrusted only to me.

When I was six I decided that my only chance of having a life half as exciting as Grandpa Portman's was to become an explorer. He encouraged me by spending afternoons at my side hunched over maps of the world, plotting imaginary expeditions with trails of red pushpins and telling me about the fantastic places I would discover one day. At home I made my ambitions known by parading around with a cardboard tube held to my eye, shouting, "Land ho!" and "Prepare a landing party!" until my parents shooed me outside. I think they worried that my grandfather would infect me with some incurable dreaminess from which I'd never recover — that these fantasies were somehow inoculating me against more practical ambitions — so one day my mother sat me down and explained that I couldn't become an explorer because everything in the world had already been discovered. I'd been born in the wrong century, and I felt cheated.

I felt even more cheated when I realized that most of Grandpa Portman's best stories couldn't possibly be true. The tallest tales were always about his childhood, like how he was born in Poland but at twelve had been shipped off to a children's home in Wales. When I would ask why he had to leave his parents, his answer was always the same: because the monsters were after him. Poland was simply rotten with them, he said.

"What *kind* of monsters?" I'd ask, wide-eyed. It became a sort of routine. "Awful hunched-over ones with rotting skin and black eyes," he'd say. "And they walked like this!" And he'd shamble after me like an old-time movie monster until I ran away laughing.

Every time he described them he'd toss in some lurid new detail: they stank like putrefying trash; they were invisible except for their shadows; a pack of squirming tentacles lurked inside their mouths and could whip out in an instant and pull you into their powerful jaws. It wasn't long before I had trouble falling asleep, my hyperactive imagination transforming the hiss of tires on wet pavement into labored breathing just outside my window or shadows under the door into twisting gray-black tentacles. I was scared of the monsters but thrilled to imagine my grandfather battling them and surviving to tell the tale.

More fantastic still were his stories about life in the Welsh children's home. It was an enchanted place, he said, designed to keep kids safe from the monsters, on an island where the sun shined every day and nobody ever got sick or died. Everyone lived together in a big house that was protected by a wise old bird — or so the story went. As I got older, though, I began to have doubts.

"What *kind* of bird?" I asked him one afternoon at age seven, eyeing him skeptically across the card table where he was letting me win at Monopoly.

"A big hawk who smoked a pipe," he said.

"You must think I'm pretty dumb, Grandpa."

He thumbed through his dwindling stack of orange and blue money. "I would never think that about you, Yakob." I knew I'd offended him because the Polish accent he could never quite shake had come out of hiding, so that *would* became *vood* and *think* became *sink*. Feeling guilty, I decided to give him the benefit of the doubt.

"But why did the monsters want to hurt you?" I asked.

"Because we weren't like other people. We were peculiar."

"Peculiar how?"

"Oh, all sorts of ways," he said. "There was a girl who could fly, a boy who had bees living inside him, a brother and sister who could lift boulders over their heads."

It was hard to tell if he was being serious.

Then again, my grandfather was not known as a teller of jokes. He frowned, reading the doubt on my face.

"Fine, you don't have to take my word for it," he said. "I got pictures!" He pushed back his lawn chair and went into the house, leaving me alone on the screened-in lanai. A minute later he came back holding an old cigar box. I leaned in to look as he drew out four wrinkled and yellowing snapshots.

The first was a blurry picture of what looked like a suit of clothes with no person in them. Either that or the person didn't have a head.

"Sure, he's got a head!" my grandfather said, grinning. "Only you can't see it."

"Why not? Is he invisible?"

"Hey, look at the brain on this one!" He raised his eyebrows as if I'd surprised him with my powers of deduction. "Millard, his name was. Funny kid. Sometimes he'd say, 'Hey Abe, I know what you did today,' and he'd tell you where you'd been, what you had to eat, if you picked your nose when you thought nobody was looking. Sometimes he'd follow you, quiet as a mouse, with no clothes on so you couldn't see him — just watching!" He shook his head. "Of all the things, eh?"

He slipped me another photo. Once I'd

11

had a moment to look at it, he said, "So? What do you see?"

"A little girl?"

"And?"

"She's wearing a crown."

He tapped the bottom of the picture. "What about her feet?"

I held the snapshot closer. The girl's feet weren't touching the ground. But she wasn't jumping — she seemed to be floating in the air. My jaw fell open.

"She's flying!"

"Close," my grandfather said. "She's levitating. Only she couldn't control herself too well, so sometimes we had to tie a rope around her to keep her from floating away!"

My eyes were glued to her haunting, doll-like face. "Is it real?"

"Of course it is," he said gruffly, taking the picture and replacing it with another, this one of a scrawny boy lifting a boulder. "Victor and his sister weren't so smart," he said, "but boy were they strong!"

"He doesn't *look* strong," I said, studying the boy's skinny arms.

"Trust me, he was. I tried to arm-wrestle him once and he just about tore my hand off!"

But the strangest photo was the last one. It was the back of somebody's head, with a face painted on it.

I stared at the last photo as Grandpa Portman explained. "He had two mouths, see? One in the front and one in the back. That's why he got so big and fat!"

"But it's fake," I said. "The face is just painted on."

"Sure, the *paint*'s fake. It was for a circus show. But I'm telling you, he had two mouths. You don't believe me?"

I thought about it, looking at the pictures and then at my grandfather, his face so earnest and open. What reason would he have to lie?

"I believe you," I said.

And I really did believe him — for a few years, at least — though mostly because I wanted to, like other kids my age wanted to believe in Santa Claus. We cling to our fairy tales until the price for believing them becomes too high, which for me was the day in second grade when Robbie Jensen pantsed me at lunch in front of a table of girls and announced that I believed in fairies. It was just deserts, I suppose, for repeating my grandfather's stories at school but in those humiliating seconds I foresaw the moniker "fairy boy" trailing me for years and, rightly or not, I resented him for it.

Grandpa Portman picked me up from

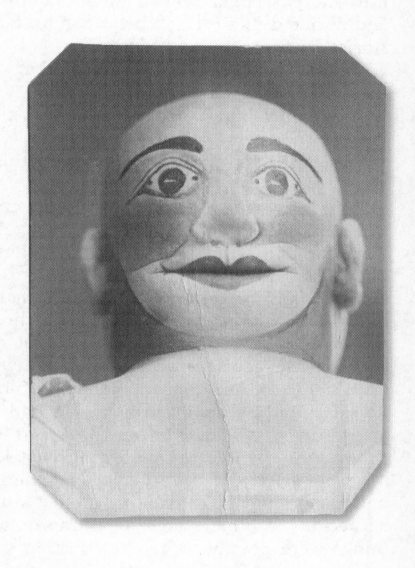

school that afternoon, as he often did when both my parents were working. I climbed into the passenger seat of his old Pontiac and declared that I didn't believe in his fairy stories anymore.

"What fairy stories?" he said, peering at me over his glasses.

"You know. The stories. About the kids and the monsters."

He seemed confused. "Who said anything about fairies?"

I told him that a made-up story and a fairy tale were the same thing, and that fairy tales were for pants-wetting babies, and that I knew his photos and stories were fakes. I expected him to get mad or put up a fight, but instead he just said, "Okay," and threw the Pontiac into drive. With a stab of his foot on the accelerator we lurched away from the curb. And that was the end of it.

I guess he'd seen it coming — I had to grow out of them eventually — but he dropped the whole thing so quickly it left me feeling like I'd been lied to. I couldn't understand why he'd made up all that stuff, tricked me into believing that extraordinary things were possible when they weren't. It wasn't until a few years later that my dad explained it to me: Grandpa had told him some of the same stories when he was a kid, and they weren't lies, exactly, but exaggerated versions of the truth — because the story of Grandpa Portman's childhood wasn't a fairy tale at all. It was a horror story.

My grandfather was the only member of his family to escape Poland before the Second World War broke out. He was twelve years old when his parents sent him into the arms of strangers, putting their youngest son on a train to Britain with nothing more than a suitcase and the clothes on his back. It was a one-way ticket. He never saw his mother or father again, or his older brothers, his cousins, his aunts and uncles. Each one would be dead before his sixteenth birthday, killed by the monsters he had so narrowly escaped. But these weren't the kind of monsters that had tentacles and rotting skin, the kind a seven-year-old might be able to wrap his mind around — they were monsters with human faces, in crisp uniforms, marching in lockstep, so banal you don't recognize them for what they are until it's too late.

Like the monsters, the enchanted-island story was also a truth in disguise. Compared to the horrors of mainland Europe, the children's home that had taken in my grandfather must've seemed like a paradise, and so in his stories it had become one: a safe haven of endless summers and guardian angels and magical children, who couldn't *really* fly or turn invisible or lift boulders, of course. The peculiarity for which they'd been hunted was simply their Jewishness. They were orphans of war, washed up on that little island in a tide of blood. What made them amazing wasn't that they had miraculous powers; that they had escaped the ghettos and gas chambers was miracle enough.

I stopped asking my grandfather to tell me stories, and I think secretly he was relieved. An air of mystery closed around the details of his early life. I didn't pry. He had been through hell and had a right to his secrets. I felt ashamed for having been jealous of his life, considering the price he'd paid for it, and I tried to feel lucky for the safe and unextraordinary one that I had done nothing to deserve.

Then, a few years later, when I was fifteen, an extraordinary and terrible thing happened, and there was only Before and After.

CHAPTER ONE

I spent the last afternoon of Before constructing a 1/10,000-scale replica of the Empire State Building from boxes of adult diapers. It was a thing of beauty, really, spanning five feet at its base and towering above the cosmetics aisle, with jumbos for the foundation, lites for the observation deck, and meticulously stacked trial sizes for its iconic spire. It was almost perfect, minus one crucial detail.

"You used Neverleak," Shelley said, eyeing my craftsmanship with a skeptical frown. "The sale's on Stay-Tite." Shelley was the store manager, and her slumped shoulders and dour expression were as much a part of her uniform as the blue polo shirts we all had to wear.

"I thought you said Neverleak," I said, because she had.

"Stay-Tite," she insisted, shaking her head regretfully, as if my tower were a crippled racehorse and she the bearer of the pearl-handled pistol. There was a brief but awkward silence in which she continued to shake her head and shift her eyes from me to the tower and back to me again. I stared blankly at her, as if completely failing to grasp what she was passive-aggressively implying.

"Ohhhhhh," I said finally. "You mean you want me to do it over?"

"It's just that you used Neverleak," she repeated.

"No problem. I'll get started right away." With the toe of my regulation black sneaker I nudged a single box from the tower's foundation. In an instant the whole magnificent structure was cascading down around us, sending a tidal wave of diapers crashing across the floor, boxes caroming off the legs of startled customers, skidding as far as the automatic door, which slid open, letting in a rush of August heat.

Shelley's face turned the color of ripe pomegranate. She should've fired me on the spot, but I knew I'd never be so lucky. I'd been trying to get fired from Smart Aid all summer, and it had proved next to impossible. I came in late, repeatedly and with the flimsiest of excuses; made shockingly incorrect change; even misshelved things on purpose, stocking lotions among laxatives and birth control with baby shampoo. Rarely had I worked so hard at anything, and yet no matter how incompetent I pretended to be, Shelley stubbornly kept me on the payroll.

Let me qualify my previous statement: It was next to impossible for *me* to get fired from Smart Aid. Any other employee would've been out the door a dozen minor infractions ago. It was my first lesson in politics. There are three Smart Aids in Englewood, the small, somnolent beach town where I live. There are twenty-seven in Sarasota County, and one hundred and fifteen in all of Florida, spreading across the state like some untreatable rash. The reason I couldn't be fired was that my uncles owned every single one of them. The reason I couldn't quit was that working at Smart Aid as your first job had long been a hallowed family tradition. All my campaign of self-sabotage had earned me was an unwinnable feud with Shelley and the deep and abiding resentment of my coworkers — who, let's face it, were going to resent me anyway, because no matter how many displays I knocked over or customers I shortchanged, one day I was going to inherit a sizable chunk of the company, and they were not.

Wading through the diapers, Shelley poked her finger into my chest and was about to say something dour when the PA system interrupted her.

"Jacob, you have a call on line two. Jacob, line two."

She glared at me as I backed away, leaving her pomegranate-faced amid the ruins of my tower.

The employee lounge was a dank, windowless room where I found the pharmacy assistant, Linda, nibbling a crustless sandwich in the vivid glow of the soda machine. She nodded at a phone screwed to the wall.

"Line two's for you. Whoever it is sounds *freaked.*"

I picked up the dangling receiver.

"Yakob? Is that you?"

"Hi, Grandpa Portman."

"Yakob, thank God. I need my key. Where's my key?" He sounded upset, out of breath.

"What key?"

"Don't play games," he snapped. "You know what key."

"You probably just misplaced it."

"Your father put you up to this," he said.

24

"Just tell me. He doesn't have to know."

"Nobody put me up to anything." I tried to change the subject. "Did you take your pills this morning?"

"They're coming for me, understand? I don't know how they found me after all these years, but they did. What am I supposed to fight them with, the goddamned butter knife?"

It wasn't the first time I'd heard him talk like this. My grandfather was getting old, and frankly he was starting to lose it. The signs of his mental decline had been subtle at first, like forgetting to buy groceries or calling my mother by my aunt's name. But over the summer his encroaching dementia had taken a cruel twist. The fantastic stories he'd invented about his life during the war — the monsters, the enchanted island — had become completely, oppressively real to him. He'd been especially agitated the last few weeks, and my parents, who feared he was becoming a danger to himself, were seriously considering putting him in a home. For some reason, I was the only one who received these apocalyptic phone calls from him.

As usual, I did my best to calm him down. "You're safe. Everything's fine. I'll bring over a video for us to watch later, how's that sound?"

"No! Stay where you are! It's not safe here!"

"Grandpa, the monsters aren't coming for you. You killed them all in the war, remember?" I turned to face the wall, trying to hide my end of this bizarre conversation from Linda, who shot me curious glances while pretending to read a fashion magazine.

"Not all of them," he said. "No, no, no. I killed a lot, sure, but there are always more." I could hear him banging around his house, opening drawers, slamming things. He was in full meltdown. "You stay away, hear me? I'll be fine — cut out their tongues and stab them in the eyes, that's all you gotta do! If I could just find that goddamned *KEY!*"

The key in question opened a giant locker in Grandpa Portman's garage. Inside was a stockpile of guns and knives sufficient to arm a small militia. He'd spent half his life collecting them, traveling to out-of-state gun shows, going on long hunting trips, and dragging his reluctant family to rifle ranges on sunny Sundays so they could learn to shoot. He loved his guns so much that sometimes he even slept with them. My dad had an old snapshot to prove it: Grandpa Portman napping with pistol in hand.

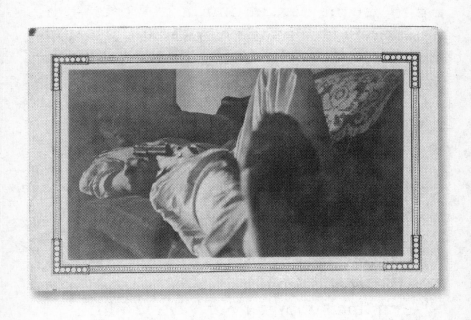

When I asked my dad why Grandpa was so crazy about guns, he said it sometimes happened to people who used to be soldiers or who had experienced traumatic things. I guess that after everything my grandfather had been through, he never really felt safe anywhere, not even at home. The irony was, now that delusions and paranoia were starting to get the best of him, it was true — he wasn't safe at home, not with all those guns around. That's why my dad had swiped the key.

I repeated the lie that I didn't know where it was. There was more swearing and banging as Grandpa Portman stomped around looking for it.

"Feh!" he said finally. "Let your father have the key if it's so important to him. Let him have my dead body, too!"

I got off the phone as politely as I could and then called my dad.

"Grandpa's flipping out," I told him.

"Has he taken his pills today?"

"He won't tell me. Doesn't sound like it, though."

I heard my dad sigh. "Can you stop by and make sure he's okay? I can't get off work right now." My dad volunteered part-time at the bird rescue, where he helped rehabilitate snowy egrets hit by cars and pelicans that had swallowed fishhooks. He was an amateur ornithologist and a wannabe nature writer — with a stack of unpublished manuscripts to prove it — which are real jobs only if you happen to be married to a woman whose family owns a hundred and fifteen drug stores.

Of course, mine was not the realest of jobs either, and it was easy to ditch whenever I felt like it. I said I would go.

"Thanks, Jake. I promise we'll get all this Grandpa stuff sorted out soon, okay?"

All this Grandpa stuff. "You mean put him in a home," I said. "Make him someone else's problem."

"Mom and I haven't decided yet."

"Of course you have."

"Jacob . . ."

"I can handle him, Dad. Really."

"Maybe now you can. But he's only going to get worse."

"Fine. Whatever."

I hung up and called my friend Ricky for a ride. Ten minutes later I heard the unmistakable throaty honk of his ancient Crown Victoria in the parking lot. On my way out I broke the bad news to Shelley: her tower of Stay-Tite would have to wait until tomorrow.

"Family emergency," I explained.

"Right," she said.

I emerged into the sticky-hot evening to find Ricky smoking on the hood of his battered car. Something about his mud-encrusted boots and the way he let smoke curl from his lips and how the sinking sun lit his green hair reminded me of a punk, redneck James Dean. He was all of those things, a bizarre cross-pollination of subcultures possible only in South Florida.

He saw me and leapt off the hood. "You fired yet?" he shouted across the parking lot.

"Shhhh!" I hissed, running toward him. "They don't know my plan!"

Ricky punched my shoulder in a manner meant to be encouraging but that nearly snapped my rotator cuff. "Don't worry, Special Ed. There's always tomorrow."

He called me Special Ed because I was in a few gifted classes, which were, technically speaking, part of our school's special-education curriculum, a subtlety of nomenclature that Ricky found endlessly amusing. That was our friendship: equal parts irritation and cooperation. The cooperation part was an unofficial brains-for-brawn trade agreement we'd worked out in which I helped him not fail English and he helped me not get killed by the roided-out socio-

30

paths who prowled the halls of our school. That he made my parents deeply uncomfortable was merely a bonus. He was, I suppose, my best friend, which is a less pathetic way of saying he was my only friend.

Ricky kicked the Crown Vic's passenger door, which was how you opened it, and I climbed in. The Vic was amazing, a museum-worthy piece of unintentional folk art. Ricky bought it from the town dump with a jar of quarters — or so he claimed — a pedigree whose odor even the forest of air-freshener trees he'd hung from the mirror couldn't mask. The seats were armored with duct tape so that errant upholstery springs wouldn't find their way up your ass. Best of all was the exterior, a rusted moonscape of holes and dents, the result of a plan to earn extra gas money by allowing drunken partygoers to whack the car with a golf club for a buck a swing. The only rule, which had not been rigorously enforced, was that you couldn't aim at anything made of glass.

The engine rattled to life in a cloud of blue smoke. As we left the parking lot and rolled past strip malls toward Grandpa Portman's house, I began to worry about what we might find when we got there. Worstcase scenarios included my grandfather running naked in the street, wielding a hunting rifle, foaming at the mouth on the front lawn, or lying in wait with a blunt object in hand. Anything was possible, and that this would be Ricky's first impression of a man I'd spoken about with reverence made me especially nervous.

The sky was turning the color of a fresh bruise as we pulled into my grandfather's subdivision, a bewildering labyrinth of interlocking cul-de-sacs known collectively as Circle Village. We stopped at the guard gate to announce ourselves, but the old man in the booth was snoring and the gate was open, as was often the case, so we just drove in. My phone chirped with a text from my dad asking how things were going, and in the short time it took me to respond, Ricky managed to get us completely, stunningly lost. When I said I had no idea where we were, he cursed and pulled a succession of squealing U-turns, spitting arcs of tobacco juice from his window as I scanned the neighborhood for a familiar landmark. It wasn't easy, even though I'd been to visit my grandfather countless times growing up, because each house looked like the next: squat and boxy with minor variations, trimmed with aluminum siding or dark seventies wood, or fronted by plaster colonnades that seemed almost delusionally aspirational. Street signs, half of which had turned a blank and blistered white from sun exposure, were little help. The only real landmarks were bizarre and colorful lawn ornaments, of which Circle Village was a veritable open-air museum.

Finally I recognized a mailbox held aloft by a metal butler that, despite his straight back and snooty expression, appeared to be crying tears of rust. I shouted at Ricky to turn left; the Vic's tires screeched and I was flung against the passenger door. The impact must've jarred something loose in my brain, because suddenly the directions came rushing back to me. "Right at the flamingo orgy! Left at the multiethnic roof Santas! Straight past the pissing cherubs!"

When we turned at the cherubs, Ricky slowed to a crawl and peered doubtfully down my grandfather's block. There was not a single porch light on, not a TV glowing behind a window, not a Town Car in a carport. All the neighbors had fled north to escape the punishing summer heat, leaving yard gnomes to drown in lawns gone wild and hurricane shutters shut tight, so that each house looked like a little pastel bomb shelter.

"Last one on the left," I said. Ricky tapped

the accelerator and we sputtered down the street. At the fourth or fifth house, we passed an old man watering his lawn. He was bald as an egg and stood in a bathrobe and slippers, spraying the ankle-high grass. The house was dark and shuttered like the rest. I turned to look and he seemed to stare back — though he couldn't have, I realized with a small shock, because his eyes were a perfect milky white. *That's strange,* I thought. *Grandpa Portman never mentioned that one of his neighbors was blind.*

The street ended at a wall of scrub pines and Ricky hung a sharp left into my grandfather's driveway. He cut the engine, got out, and kicked my door open. Our shoes hushed through the dry grass to the porch.

I rang the bell and waited. A dog barked somewhere, a lonely sound in the muggy evening. When there was no answer I banged on the door, thinking maybe the bell had stopped working. Ricky swatted at the gnats that had begun to clothe us.

"Maybe he stepped out," Ricky said, grinning. "Hot date."

"Go ahead and laugh," I said. "He's got a better shot than we do any night of the week. This place is crawling with eligible widows." I joked only to calm my nerves. The quiet made me anxious.

I fetched the extra key from its hiding place in the bushes. "Wait here."

"Hell I am. Why?"

"Because you're six-five and have green hair and my grandfather doesn't know you and owns lots of guns."

Ricky shrugged and stuck another wad of tobacco in his cheek. He went to stretch himself on a lawn chair as I unlocked the front door and stepped inside.

Even in the fading light I could tell the house was a disaster; it looked like it'd been ransacked by thieves. Bookshelves and cabinets had been emptied, the knicknacks and large-print *Reader's Digest*s that had filled them thrown across the floor. Couch cushions and chairs were overturned. The fridge and freezer doors hung open, their contents melting into sticky puddles on the linoleum.

My heart sank. Grandpa Portman had really, finally lost his mind. I called his name — but heard nothing.

I went from room to room, turning on lights and looking anywhere a paranoid old man might hide from monsters: behind furniture, in the attic crawlspace, under the workbench in the garage. I even checked inside his weapons cabinet, though of course it was locked, the handle ringed by scratches where he'd tried to pick it. Out on the lanai, a gallows of unwatered ferns swung browning in the breeze; while on my knees on the astroturfed floor I peered beneath rattan benches, afraid what I might discover.

I saw a gleam of light from the backyard.

Running through the screen door, I found a flashlight abandoned in the grass, its beam pointed at the woods that edged my grandfather's yard — a scrubby wilderness of sawtoothed palmettos and trash palms that ran for a mile between Circle Village and the next subdivision, Century Woods. According to local legend, the woods were crawling with snakes, raccoons, and wild boars. When I pictured my grandfather out there, lost and raving in nothing but his bathrobe, a black feeling welled up in me. Every other week there was a news story about some geriatric citizen tripping into a retention pond and being devoured by alligators. The worst-case scenario wasn't hard to imagine.

I shouted for Ricky and a moment later he came tearing around the side of the house. Right away he noticed something I hadn't: a long mean-looking slice in the screen door. He let out a low whistle. "That's a helluva cut. Wild pig coulda done it. Or a bobcat maybe. You should see the claws on them things."

A peal of savage barking broke out nearby. We both started then traded a nervous glance. "Or a dog," I said. The sound triggered a chain reaction across the neighborhood, and soon barks were coming from every direction.

"Could be," Ricky said, nodding. "I got a .22 in my trunk. You just wait." And he walked off to retrieve it.

The barks faded and a chorus of night insects rose up in their place, droning and alien. Sweat trickled down my face. It was dark now, but the breeze had died and somehow the air seemed hotter than it had all day.

I picked up the flashlight and stepped toward the trees. My grandfather was out there somewhere, I was sure of it. But where? I was no tracker, and neither was Ricky. And yet something seemed to guide me anyway — a quickening in the chest; a whisper in the viscous air — and suddenly I couldn't wait another second. I tromped into the underbrush like a bloodhound scenting an invisible trail.

It's hard to run in a Florida woods, where every square foot not occupied by trees is bristling with thigh-high palmetto spears and nets of entangling skunk vine, but I did my best, calling my grandfather's name and sweeping my flashlight everywhere. I caught a white glint out of the corner of my eye and made a beeline for it, but upon closer inspection it turned out to be just a bleached and deflated soccer ball I'd lost years before.

I was about to give up and go back for Ricky when I spied a narrow corridor of freshly stomped palmettos not far away. I stepped into it and shone my light around; the leaves were splattered with something dark. My throat went dry. Steeling myself, I began to follow the trail. The farther I went, the more my stomach knotted, as though my body knew what lay ahead and was trying to warn me. And then the trail of the flattened brush widened out, and I saw him.

My grandfather lay facedown in a bed of creeper, his legs sprawled out and one arm twisted beneath him as if he'd fallen from a great height. I thought surely he was dead. His undershirt was soaked with blood, his pants were torn, and one shoe was missing. For a long moment I just stared, the beam of my flashlight shivering across his body. When I could breathe again I said his name, but he didn't move.

I sank to my knees and pressed the flat of my hand against his back. The blood that soaked through was still warm. I could feel him breathing ever so shallowly.

I slid my arms under him and rolled him onto his back. He was alive, though just barely, his eyes glassy, his face sunken and white. Then I saw the gashes across his mid-section and nearly fainted. They were wide and deep and clotted with soil, and the ground where he'd lain was muddy from blood. I tried to pull the rags of his shirt over the wounds without looking at them.

I heard Ricky shout from the backyard. "I'M HERE!" I screamed, and maybe I should've said more, like *danger* or *blood,* but I couldn't form the words. All I could think was that grandfathers were supposed to die in beds, in hushed places humming with machines, not in heaps on the sodden reeking ground with ants marching over them, a brass letter opener clutched in one trembling hand.

A letter opener. That was all he'd had to defend himself. I slid it from his finger and he grasped helplessly at the air, so I took his hand and held it. My nail-bitten fingers twinned with his, pale and webbed with purple veins.

"I have to move you," I told him, sliding one arm under his back and another under his legs. I began to lift, but he moaned and went rigid, so I stopped. I couldn't bear to hurt him. I couldn't leave him either, and there was nothing to do but wait, so I gently brushed loose soil from his arms and face and thinning white hair. That's when I noticed his lips moving.

His voice was barely audible, something less than a whisper. I leaned down and put my ear to his lips. He was mumbling, fading in and out of lucidity, shifting between English and Polish.

"I don't understand," I whispered. I repeated his name until his eyes seemed to focus on me, and then he drew a sharp breath and said, quietly but clearly, "Go to the island, Yakob. Here it's not safe."

It was the old paranoia. I squeezed his hand and assured him we were fine, he was going to be fine. That was twice in one day that I'd lied to him.

I asked him what happened, what animal had hurt him, but he wasn't listening. "Go to the island," he repeated. "You'll be safe there. Promise me."

"I will. I promise." What else could I say?

"I thought I could protect you," he said. "I should've told you a long time ago . . ." I could see the life going out of him.

"Told me what?" I said, choking back tears.

"There's no time," he whispered. Then he raised his head off the ground, trembling with the effort, and breathed into my ear: "Find the bird. In the loop. On the other side of the old man's grave. September third, 1940." I nodded, but he could see that I didn't understand. With his last bit of strength, he added, "Emerson — the letter. Tell them what happened, Yakob."

With that he sank back, spent and fading. I told him I loved him. And then he seemed to disappear into himself, his gaze drifting past me to the sky, bristling now with stars.

A moment later Ricky crashed out of the underbrush. He saw the old man limp in my arms and fell back a step. "Oh man. Oh Jesus. Oh *Jesus*," he said, rubbing his face with his hands, and as he babbled about finding a pulse and calling the cops and did you see anything in the woods, the strangest feeling came over me. I let go of my grandfather's body and stood up, every nerve ending tingling with an instinct I didn't know I had. There was something in the woods, all right — I could feel it.

There was no moon and no movement in the underbrush but our own, and yet somehow I knew just when to raise my flashlight and just where to aim it, and for an instant in that narrow cut of light I saw a face that seemed to have been transplanted directly from the nightmares of my childhood. It stared back with eyes that swam in dark liquid, furrowed trenches of carbon-black flesh loose on its hunched frame, its mouth hinged open grotesquely so that a mass of long eel-like tongues could wriggle out. I shouted something and then it twisted and was gone, shaking the brush and drawing Ricky's attention. He raised his .22 and fired, *pap-pap-pap-pap,* saying, "What was that? What the hell was that?" But he hadn't seen it and I couldn't speak to tell him, frozen in place as I was, my dying flashlight flickering over the blank woods. And then I must've blacked out because he was saying *Jacob, Jake, hey Ed areyouokayorwhat,* and that's the last thing I remember.

CHAPTER TWO

I spent the months following my grand-father's death cycling through a purgatory of beige waiting rooms and anonymous offices, analyzed and interviewed, talked about just out of earshot, nodding when spoken to, repeating myself, the object of a thousand pitying glances and knitted brows. My parents treated me like a breakable heirloom, afraid to fight or fret in front of me lest I shatter.

I was plagued by wake-up-screaming nightmares so bad that I had to wear a mouth guard to keep from grinding my teeth into nubs as I slept. I couldn't close my eyes without seeing it — that tentacle-mouth horror in the woods. I was convinced it had killed my grandfather and that it would soon return for me. Sometimes that sick panicky feeling would flood over me like it did that night and I'd be sure that nearby, lurking in a stand of dark trees, beyond the next car in a parking lot, behind the garage where I kept my bike, it was waiting.

My solution was to stop leaving the house. For weeks I refused even to venture into the driveway to collect the morning paper. I slept in a tangle of blankets on the laundry room floor, the only part of the house with no windows and also a door that locked from the inside. That's where I spent the day of my grandfather's funeral, sitting on the dryer with my laptop, trying to lose myself in online games.

I blamed myself for what happened. *If only I'd believed him* was my endless refrain. But I hadn't believed him, and neither had anyone else, and now I knew how he must've felt because no one believed me, either. My version of events sounded perfectly rational until I was forced to say the words aloud, and then it sounded insane, particularly on the day I had to say them to the police officer who came to our house. I told him everything that had happened, even about the creature, as he sat nodding across the kitchen table, writing nothing in his spiral notebook. When I finished all he said was, "Great, thanks," and then turned to my parents and asked if I'd "been to see anyone." As if I wouldn't know what that meant. I told him I had another statement to make and then held up my middle finger and walked out.

My parents yelled at me for the first time in weeks. It was kind of a relief, actually — that old sweet sound. I yelled some ugly things back. That they were glad Grandpa Portman was dead. That I was the only one who'd really loved him.

The cop and my parents talked in the driveway for a while, and then the cop drove off only to come back an hour later with a man who introduced himself as a sketch artist. He'd brought a big drawing pad and asked me to describe the creature again, and as I did he sketched it, stopping occasionally to ask for clarifications.

"How many eyes did it have?"

"Two."

"Gotcha," he said, as if monsters were a perfectly normal thing for a police sketch artist to be drawing.

As an attempt to placate me, it was pretty transparent. The biggest giveaway was when he tried to give me the finished sketch.

"Don't you need this for your files or something?" I asked him.

He exchanged raised eyebrows with the cop. "Of course. What was I thinking?"

It was totally insulting.

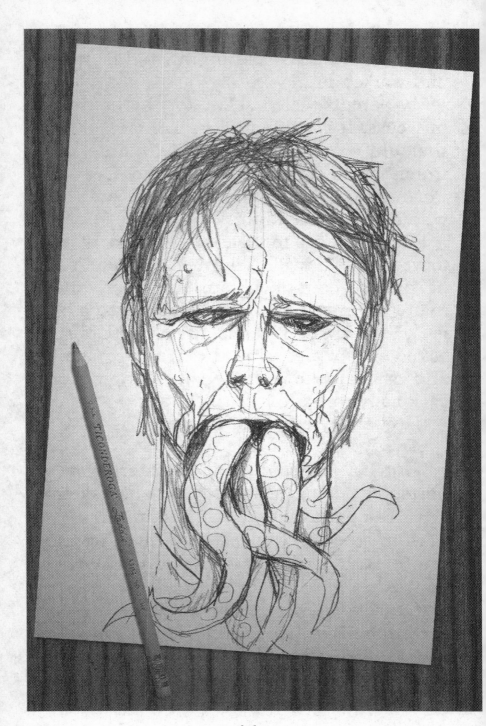

46

Even my best and only friend Ricky didn't believe me, and he'd been there. He swore up and down that he hadn't seen any creature in the woods that night — even though I'd shined my flashlight right at it — which is just what he told the cops. He'd heard barking, though. We both had. So it wasn't a huge surprise when the police concluded that a pack of feral dogs had killed my grandfather. Apparently they'd been spotted elsewhere and had taken bites out of a woman who'd been walking in Century Woods the week before. All at night, mind you. "Which is exactly when the creatures are hardest to see!" I said. But Ricky just shook his head and muttered something about me needing a "brain-shrinker."

"You mean head-shrinker," I replied, "and thanks a lot. It's great to have such supportive friends." We were sitting on my roof deck watching the sun set over the Gulf, Ricky coiled like a spring in an unreasonably expensive Adirondack chair my parents had brought back from a trip to Amish country, his legs folded beneath him and arms crossed tight, chain-smoking cigarettes with a kind of grim determination. He always seemed vaguely uncomfortable at my house, but I could tell by the way his eyes slid off me whenever he looked in my direc-

47

tion that now it wasn't my parents' wealth that was making him uneasy, but me.

"Whatever, I'm just being straight with you," he said. "Keep talking about monsters and they're gonna put you away. Then you really will be Special Ed."

"Don't call me that."

He flicked away his cigarette and spat a huge glistening wad over the railing.

"Were you just smoking and chewing tobacco at the same time?"

"What are you, my mom?"

"Do I *look* like I blow truckers for food stamps?"

Ricky was a connoisseur of your-mom jokes, but this was apparently more than he could take. He sprang out of the chair and shoved me so hard I almost fell off the roof. I yelled at him to get out, but he was already going.

It was months before I'd see him again. So much for having friends.

Eventually, my parents did take me to a brain-shrinker — a quiet, olive-skinned man named Dr. Golan. I didn't put up a fight. I knew I needed help.

I thought I'd be a tough case, but Dr. Golan made surprisingly quick work of me. The calm, affectless way he explained things was almost hypnotizing, and within two sessions he'd convinced me that the creature had been nothing more than the product of my overheated imagination; that the trauma of my grandfather's death had made me see something that wasn't really there. It was Grandpa Portman's stories that had planted the creature in my mind to begin with, Dr. Golan explained, so it only made sense that, kneeling there with his body in my arms and reeling from the worst shock of my young life, I had conjured up my grandfather's own bogeyman.

There was even a name for it: acute stress reaction. "I don't see anything cute about it," my mother said when she heard my shiny new diagnosis. Her joke didn't bother me, though. Almost anything sounded better than *crazy.*

Just because I no longer believed the monsters were real didn't mean I was better, though. I still suffered from nightmares. I was twitchy and paranoid, bad enough at interacting with other people that my parents hired a tutor so that I only had to go to school on days I felt up to it. They also — finally — let me quit Smart Aid. "Feeling better" became my new job.

Pretty soon, I was determined to be fired from this one, too. Once the small matter of my temporary madness had been cleared up, Dr. Golan's function seemed mainly to consist of writing prescriptions. Still having nightmares? I've got something for that. Panic attack on the school bus? This should do the trick. Can't sleep? Let's up the dosage. All those pills were making me fat and stupid, and I was still miserable, getting only three or four hours of sleep a night. That's why I started lying to Dr. Golan. I pretended to be fine when anyone who looked at me could see the bags under my eyes and the way I jumped like a nervous cat at sudden noises. One week I faked an entire dream journal, making my dreams sound bland and simple, the way a normal person's should be. One dream was about going to the dentist. In another I was flying. Two nights in a row, I told him, I'd dreamed I was naked in school.

Then he stopped me. "What about the creatures?"

I shrugged. "No sign of them. Guess that means I'm getting better, huh?"

Dr. Golan tapped his pen for a moment and then wrote something down. "I hope you're not just telling me what you think I want to hear."

"Of course not," I said, my gaze skirting the framed degrees on his wall, all attesting to his expertness in various subdisciplines of psychology, including, I'm sure, how to tell when an acutely stressed teenager is lying to you.

"Let's be real for a minute." He set down his pen. "You're telling me you didn't have the dream even *one* night this week?"

I'd always been a terrible liar. Rather than humiliate myself, I copped to it. "Well," I muttered, "maybe one."

The truth was that I'd had the dream *every* night that week. With minor variations, it always went like this: I'm crouched in the corner of my grandfather's bedroom, amber dusk-light retreating from the windows, pointing a pink plastic BB rifle at the door. An enormous glowing vending machine looms where the bed should be, filled not with candy but rows of razor-sharp tactical knives and armor-piercing pistols. My grandfather's there in an old British army uniform, feeding the machine dollar bills, but it takes a lot to buy a gun and we're running out of time. Finally, a shiny .45 spins toward the glass, but before it falls it gets stuck. He swears in Yiddish, kicks the machine, then kneels down and reaches inside to try and grab it, but his arm gets caught. That's when they come, their long black tongues slithering up the outside of the glass, looking for a way in. I point the BB gun at them and pull the trigger, but nothing happens. Meanwhile Grandpa Portman is shouting like a crazy person — *find the bird, find the loop, Yakob vai don't you understand you goddamned stupid yutzi* — and then the windows shatter and glass rains in and the black tongues are all over us, and that's generally when I wake up in a puddle of sweat, my heart doing hurdles and my stomach tied in knots.

Even though the dream was always the same and we'd been over it a hundred times, Dr. Golan still made me describe it in every session. It's like he was cross-examining my subconscious, looking for some clue he might have missed the ninety-ninth time around.

"And in the dream, what's your grandfather saying?"

"The same stuff as always," I said. "About the bird and the loop and the grave."

"His last words."

I nodded.

Dr. Golan tented his fingers and pressed them to his chin, the very picture of a thoughtful brain-shrinker. "Any new ideas about what they might mean?"

"Yeah. Jack and shit."

"Come on. You don't mean that."

I wanted to act like I didn't care about the last words, but I did. They'd been eating away at me almost as much as the nightmares. I felt like I owed it to my grandfather not to dismiss the last thing he said to anyone in the world as delusional nonsense, and Dr. Golan was convinced that understanding them might help purge my awful dreams. So I tried.

Some of what Grandpa Portman had said made sense, like the thing about wanting me to go to the island. He was worried that the monsters would come after me, and thought the island was the only place I could escape them, like he had as a kid. After that he'd said, "I should've told you," but because there was no time to tell me whatever it was he should've told me, I wondered if he hadn't done the next best thing and left a trail of bread crumbs leading to someone who *could* tell me — someone who knew his secret. I figured that's what all the cryptic-sounding stuff about the loop and the grave and the letter was.

For a while I thought "the loop" could be a street in Circle Village — a neighborhood that was nothing but looping cul-de-sacs — and that "Emerson" might be a person my grandfather had sent letters to. An old war buddy he'd kept in touch with or something.

Maybe this Emerson lived in Circle Village, in one of its loops, by a graveyard, and one of the letters he'd kept was dated September third, 1940, and that was the one I needed to read. I knew it sounded crazy, but crazier things have turned out to be true. So after hitting dead-ends online I went to the Circle Village community center, where the old folks gather to play shuffleboard and discuss their most recent surgeries, to ask where the graveyard was and whether anyone knew a Mr. Emerson. They looked at me like I had a second head growing out of my neck, baffled that a teenaged person was speaking to them. There was no graveyard in Circle Village and no one in the neighborhood named Emerson and no street called Loop Drive or Loop Avenue or Loop anything. It was a complete bust.

Still, Dr. Golan wouldn't let me quit. He suggested I look into Ralph Waldo Emerson, a supposedly famous old poet. "Emerson wrote his fair share of letters," he said. "Maybe that's what your grandfather was referring to." It seemed like a shot in the dark, but, just to get Golan off my back, one afternoon I had my dad drop me at the library so I could check it out. I quickly discovered that Ralph Waldo Emerson had indeed written lots of letters that had been

54

published. For about three minutes I got really excited, like I was close to a breakthrough, and then two things became apparent: first, that Ralph Waldo Emerson had lived and died in the 1800s and therefore could not have written any letters dated September third, 1940, and, second, that his writing was so dense and arcane that it couldn't possibly have held the slightest interest for my grandfather, who wasn't exactly an avid reader. I discovered Emerson's soporific qualities the hard way, by falling asleep with my face in the book, drooling all over an essay called "Self-Reliance" and having the vending-machine dream for the sixth time that week. I woke up screaming and was unceremoniously ejected from the library, cursing Dr. Golan and his stupid theories all the while.

The last straw came a few days later, when my family decided it was time to sell Grandpa Portman's house. Before prospective buyers could be allowed inside, though, the place had to be cleaned out. On the advice of Dr. Golan, who thought it would be good for me to "confront the scene of my trauma," I was enlisted to help my dad and Aunt Susie sort through the detritus. For a while after we got to the house my dad kept taking me aside to make sure I was okay. Surprisingly, I seemed to be, despite the scraps of police tape clinging to the shrubs and the torn screen on the lanai flapping in the breeze; these things — like the rented Dumpster that stood on the curb, waiting to swallow what remained of my grandfather's life — made me sad, not scared.

Once it became clear I wasn't about to suffer a mouth-frothing freak-out, we got down to business. Armed with garbage bags we proceeded grimly through the house, emptying shelves and cabinets and crawl spaces, discovering geometries of dust beneath objects unmoved for years. We built pyramids of things that could be saved or salvaged and pyramids of things destined for the Dumpster. My aunt and father were not sentimental people, and the Dumpster pile was always the largest. I lobbied hard to keep certain things, like the eight-foot stack of water-damaged *National Geographic* magazines teetering in a corner of the garage — how many afternoons had I spent poring over them, imagining myself among the mud men of New Guinea or discovering a cliff-top castle in the kingdom of Bhutan? — but I was always overruled. Neither was I allowed to keep my grandfather's collection of vintage bowling shirts ("They're embarrassing," my dad claimed), his big band and swing 78s ("Someone will pay good money for those"), or the contents of his massive, still-locked weapons cabinet ("You're kidding, right? I hope you're kidding").

I told my dad he was being heartless. My aunt fled the scene, leaving us alone in the study, where we'd been sorting through a mountain of old financial records.

"I'm just being practical. This is what happens when people die, Jacob."

"Yeah? How about when *you* die? Should I burn all your old manuscripts?"

He flushed. I shouldn't have said it; mentioning his half-finished book projects was definitely below the belt. Instead of yelling at me, though, he was quiet. "I brought you along today because I thought you were mature enough to handle it. I guess I was wrong."

"You *are* wrong. You think getting rid of all Grandpa's stuff will make me forget him. But it won't."

He threw up his hands. "You know what? I'm sick of fighting about it. Keep whatever you want." He tossed a sheaf of yellowed papers at my feet. "Here's an itemized schedule of deductions from the year Kennedy was assassinated. Go have it framed!"

I kicked away the papers and walked out, slamming the door behind me, and then waited in the living room for him to come out and apologize. When I heard the shredder roar to life I knew he wasn't going to, so I stomped across the house and locked myself in the bedroom. It smelled of stale air and shoe leather and my grandfather's slightly sour cologne. I leaned against the wall, my eyes following a trail worn into the carpet between the door and the bed, where a rectangle of muted sun caught the edge of a box that poked out from beneath the bedspread. I went over and knelt down and pulled it out. It was the old cigar box, enveloped in dust — as if he'd left it there just for me to find.

Inside were the photos I knew so well: the invisible boy, the levitating girl, the boulder lifter, the man with a face painted on the back of his head. They were brittle and peeling — smaller than I remembered, too — and looking at them now, as an almost adult, it struck me how blatant the fakery was. A little burning and dodging was probably all it took to make the "invisible" boy's head disappear. The giant rock being hoisted by that suspiciously scrawny kid could have easily been made out of plaster or foam. But these observations were too subtle for a six-year-old, especially one who wanted to believe.

Beneath those photos were five more that Grandpa Portman had never shown me. I wondered why, until I looked closer. Three were so obviously manipulated that even a kid would've seen through them: one was a laughable double exposure of a girl "trapped" in a bottle; another showed a "levitating" child, suspended by something hidden in the dark doorway behind her; the third was a dog with a boy's face pasted crudely onto it. As if these weren't bizarre enough, the last two were like something out of David Lynch's nightmares: one was an unhappy young contortionist doing a frightening backbend; in the other a pair of freakish twins were dressed in the weirdest costumes I'd ever seen. Even my grandfather, who'd filled my head with stories of tentacle-tongued monsters, had realized images like these would give any kid bad dreams.

Kneeling there on my grandfather's dusty floor with those photos in my hands, I remembered how betrayed I'd felt the day I realized his stories weren't true. Now the truth seemed obvious: his last words had been just another sleight of hand, and his last act was to infect me with nightmares

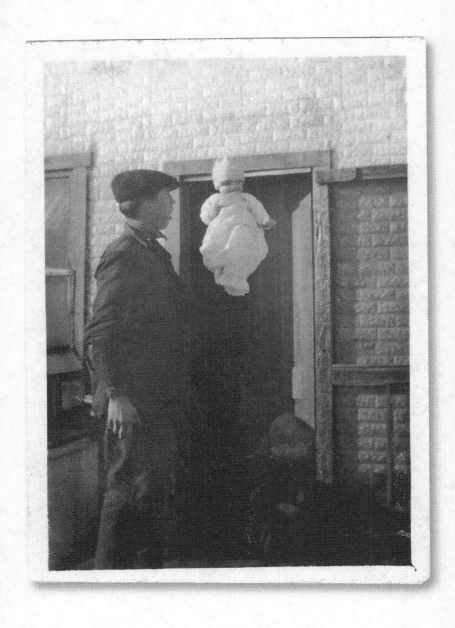

61

63

and paranoid delusions that would take years of therapy and metabolism-wrecking medications to rout out.

I closed the box and brought it into the living room, where my dad and Aunt Susie were emptying a drawer full of coupons, clipped but never used, into a ten-gallon trash bag.

I offered up the box. They didn't ask what was inside.

"So that's it?" Dr. Golan said. "His death was meaningless?"

I'd been lying on the couch watching a fish tank in the corner, its one golden prisoner swimming in lazy circles. "Unless you've got a better idea," I said. "Some big theory about what it all means that you've haven't told me. Otherwise . . ."

"What?"

"Otherwise, this is just a waste of time."

He sighed and pinched the bridge of his nose as if trying to dispel a headache. "What your grandfather's last words meant isn't my conclusion to draw," he said. "It's what *you* think that matters."

"That is such psychobabble bullshit," I spat. "It's not what I *think* that matters; it's what's true! But I guess we'll never know, so who cares? Just dope me up and collect the bill."

I wanted him to get mad — to argue, to insist I was wrong — but instead he sat poker faced, drumming the arm of his chair with his pen. "It sounds like you're giving up," he said after a moment. "I'm disappointed. You don't strike me as a quitter."

"Then you don't know me very well," I replied.

I could not have been less in the mood for a party. I'd known I was in for one the moment my parents began dropping unsubtle hints about how boring and uneventful the upcoming weekend was sure to be, when we all knew perfectly well I was turning sixteen. I'd begged them to skip the party this year because, among other reasons, I couldn't think of a single person I wanted to invite, but they worried that I spent too much time alone, clinging to the notion that socializing was therapeutic. So was electroshock, I reminded them. But my mother was loath to pass up even the flimsiest excuse for a celebration — she once invited friends over for our cockatiel's birthday — in part because she loved to show off our house. Wine in hand, she'd herd guests from room to overfurnished room, extolling the genius of the architect and telling war stories about the construction ("It took *months* to get these sconces from Italy").

We'd just come home from my disastrous session with Dr. Golan. I was following my dad into our suspiciously dark living room as he muttered things like "What a shame we didn't plan anything for your birthday" and "Oh well, there's always next year," when all the lights flooded on to reveal streamers, balloons, and a motley assortment of aunts, uncles, cousins I rarely spoke to — anyone my mother could cajole into attending — and Ricky, whom I was surprised to see lingering near the punch bowl, looking comically out of place in a studded leather jacket. Once everyone had finished cheering and I'd finished pretending to be surprised, my mom slipped her arm around me and whispered, "Is this okay?" I was upset and tired and just wanted to play *Warspire III: The Summoning* before going to bed with the TV on. But what were we going to do, send everyone home? I said it was fine, and she smiled as if to thank me.

"Who wants to see the new addition?" she sang out, pouring herself some chardonnay before marching a troupe of relatives up the stairs.

Ricky and I nodded to each other across the room, wordlessly agreeing to tolerate the other's presence for an hour or two. We hadn't spoken since the day he nearly shoved me off the roof, but we both understood the importance of maintaining the illusion of having friends. I was about to go talk to him when my uncle Bobby grabbed me by the elbow and pulled me into a corner. Bobby was a big barrel-chested guy who drove a big car and lived in a big house and would eventually succumb to a big heart attack from all the foie gras and Monster Thickburgers he'd packed into his colon over the years, leaving everything to my pothead cousins and his tiny quiet wife. He and my uncle Les were copresidents of Smart Aid, and they were always doing this — pulling people into corners for conspiratorial chats, as if plotting a mob hit rather than complimenting the hostess on her guacamole.

"So, your mom tells me you're really turning the corner with, uh . . . on this whole Grandpa thing."

My thing. No one knew what to call it.

"Acute stress reaction," I said.

"What?"

"That's what I had. Have. Whatever."

"That's good. Real good to hear." He waved his hand as if putting all that unpleasantness behind us. "So your mom and I were thinking. How'd you like to come up to Tampa this summer, see how the family business works? Crack heads with me at HQ for a while? Unless you love stocking shelves!" He laughed so loudly that I took an involuntary step backward. "You could even stay at the house, do a little tarpon fishing with me and your cousins on the weekends." He then spent five long minutes describing his new yacht, going into elaborate, almost pornographic detail, as if that alone were enough to close the deal. When he finished, he grinned and stuck out his hand for me to shake. "So whaddaya think, J-dogg?"

I guess it was designed to be an offer I couldn't refuse, but I'd have rather spent the summer in a Siberian labor camp than live with my uncle and his spoiled kids. As for working at Smart Aid HQ, I knew it was a probably inevitable part of my future, but I'd been counting on at least a few more summers of freedom and four years of college before I had to lock myself in a corporate cage. I hesitated, trying to think of a graceful way out. Instead what I said was, "I'm not sure my psychiatrist would think it's such a great idea right now."

His bushy eyebrows came together. Nodding vaguely, he said, "Oh, well, sure, of course. We'll just play it by ear then, pal, how's that sound?" And then he walked off without waiting for an answer, pretending to see someone across the room whose elbow he needed to grab.

My mother announced that it was time to open presents. She always insisted I do this in front of everyone, which was a problem because, as I may have mentioned already, I'm not a good liar. That also means I'm not good at feigning gratitude for regifted CDs of country Christmas music or subscriptions to *Field and Stream* — for years Uncle Les had labored under the baffling delusion that I am "outdoorsy" — but for decorum's sake I forced a smile and held up each unwrapped trinket for all to admire until the pile of presents left on the coffee table had shrunk to just three.

I reached for the smallest one first. Inside was the key to my parents' four-year-old luxury sedan. They were getting a new one, my mom explained, so I was inheriting the old one. My first car! Everyone *oohed* and *aahed,* but I felt my face go hot. It was too much like showing off to accept such a lavish present in front of Ricky, whose car cost less than my monthly allowance at age twelve. It seemed like my parents were always trying to get me to care about money, but I didn't, really. Then again, it's easy to say you don't care about money when you have plenty of it.

The next present was the digital camera I'd begged my parents for all last summer. "Wow," I said, testing its weight in my hand. "This is awesome."

"I'm outlining a new bird book," my dad said. "I was thinking maybe you could take the pictures."

"A new book!" my mom exclaimed. "That's a phenomenal idea, Frank. Speaking of which, whatever happened to that last book you were working on?" Clearly, she'd had a few glasses of wine.

"I'm still ironing out a few things," my dad replied quietly.

"Oh, I *see*." I could hear Uncle Bobby snickering.

"Okay!" I said loudly, reaching for the last present. "This one's from Aunt Susie."

"Actually," my aunt said as I began tearing away the wrapping paper, "it's from your grandfather."

I stopped midtear. The room went dead quiet, people looking at Aunt Susie as if she'd invoked the name of some evil spirit. My dad's jaw tensed and my mom shot back the last of her wine.

71

"Just open it and you'll see," Aunt Susie said.

I ripped away the rest of the wrapping paper to find an old hardback book, dog-eared and missing its dust jacket. It was *The Selected Works of Ralph Waldo Emerson.* I stared at it as if trying to read through the cover, unable to comprehend how it had come to occupy my now-trembling hands. No one but Dr. Golan knew about the last words, and he'd promised on several occasions that unless I threatened to guzzle Drano or do a backflip off the Sunshine Skyway bridge, everything we talked about in his office would be held in confidence.

I looked at my aunt, a question on my face that I didn't quite know how to ask. She managed a weak smile and said, "I found it in your grandfather's desk when we were cleaning out the house. He wrote your name in the front. I think he meant for you to have it."

God bless Aunt Susie. She had a heart after all.

"Neat. I didn't know your grandpa was a reader," my mom said, trying to lighten the mood. "That was thoughtful."

"Yes," said my dad through clenched teeth. "Thank you, Susan."

I opened the book. Sure enough, the title

page bore an inscription in my grandfather's shaky handwriting.

I got up to leave, afraid I might start crying in front of everyone, and something slipped out from between the pages and fell to the floor.

I bent to pick it up. It was a letter.

Emerson. The letter.

I felt the blood drain from my face. My mother leaned toward me and in a tense whisper asked if I needed a drink of water, which was Mom-speak for *keep it together, people are staring.* I said, "I feel a little, uh . . ." and then, with one hand over my stomach, I bolted to my room.

The letter was handwritten on fine, unlined paper in looping script so ornate it was almost calligraphy, the black ink varying in tone like that of an old fountain pen. It read:

Dearest Abe,

I hope this note finds you safe & in the best of health. It's been such a long time since we last received word from you! But I write not to admonish, only to let you know that we still think of you often & pray for your well-being. Our brave, handsome Abe!

73

THE

SELECTED WORKS OF RALPH WALDO EMERSON

Edited and with an introduction
BY CLIFTON DURRELL, PH. D.

To Jacob Magellan Portman,
and the worlds he has
yet to discover —

ANTHEM BOOKS · NEW YORK

As for life on the island, little has changed. But quiet & orderly is the way we prefer things! I wonder if we would recognize you after so many years, though I'm certain you'd recognize us — those few who remain, that is. It would mean a great deal to have a recent picture of you, if you're one to send. I've included a positively ancient snap of myself.

E misses you terribly. Won't you write to her?

With respect & admiration,
Headmistress Alma Lefay Peregrine

As promised, the writer had enclosed an old snapshot.

I held it under the glow of my desk lamp, trying to read some detail in the woman's silhouetted face, but there was none to find. The image was so strange, and yet it was nothing like my grandfather's pictures. There were no tricks here. It was just a woman — a woman smoking a pipe. It looked like Sherlock Holmes's pipe, curved and drooping from her lips. My eyes kept coming back to it.

Was this what my grandfather had meant for me to find? *Yes,* I thought, *it has to be* — not *the* letters of Emerson, but *a* letter, tucked inside Emerson's book. But who was

this headmistress, this Peregrine woman? I studied the envelope for a return address but found only a fading postmark that read *Cairnholm Is., Cymru, UK.*

UK — that was Britain. I knew from studying atlases as a kid that *Cymru* meant Wales. *Cairnholm Is.* had to be the island Miss Peregrine had mentioned in her letter. Could it have been the same island where my grandfather lived as a boy?

Nine months ago he'd told me to "find the bird." Nine years ago he had sworn that the children's home where he'd lived was protected by one — by "a bird who smoked a pipe." At age seven I'd taken this statement literally, but the headmistress in the picture was smoking a pipe, and her name was Peregrine, a kind of hawk. What if the bird my grandfather wanted me to find was actually the woman who'd rescued him — the headmistress of the children's home? Maybe she was still on the island, after all these years, old as dirt but sustained by a few of her wards, children who'd grown up but never left.

For the first time, my grandfather's last words began to make a strange kind of sense. He wanted me to go to the island and find this woman, his old headmistress. If anyone knew the secrets of his childhood, it would be her. But the envelope's postmark was fifteen years old. Was it possible she was still alive? I did some quick calculations in my head: If she'd been running a children's home in 1939 and was, say, twenty-five at the time, then she'd be in her late nineties today. So it was possible — there were people older than that in Englewood who still lived by themselves and drove — and even if Miss Peregrine *had* passed away in the time since she'd sent the letter, there might still be people on Cairnholm who could help me, people who had known Grandpa Portman as a kid. People who knew his secrets.

We, she had written. *Those few who remain.*

As you can imagine, convincing my parents to let me spend part of my summer on a tiny island off the coast of Wales was no easy task. They — particularly my mother — had many compelling reasons why this was a wretched idea, including the cost, the fact that I was supposed to spend the summer with Uncle Bobby learning how to run a drug empire, and that I had no one to accompany me, since neither of my parents had any interest in going and I certainly couldn't go alone. I had no effective rebuttals, and my reason for wanting to make the trip — *I think I'm supposed to* — wasn't something I could explain without sounding even crazier than they already feared I was. I certainly wasn't going to tell my parents about Grandpa Portman's last words or the letter or the photo — they would've had me committed. The only sane-sounding arguments I could come up with were things like, "I want to learn more about our family history" and the never-persuasive "Chad Kramer and Josh Bell are going to Europe this summer. Why can't I?" I brought these up as frequently as possible without seeming desperate (even once resorting to "it's not like you don't have the money," a tactic I instantly regretted), but it looked like it wasn't going to happen.

Then several things happened that helped my case enormously. First, Uncle Bobby got cold feet about my spending the summer with him — because who wants a nutcase living in their house? So my schedule was suddenly wide open. Next, my dad learned that Cairnholm Island is a superimportant bird habitat, and, like, half the world's population of some bird that gives him a total ornithology boner lives there. He started talking a lot about his hypothetical new bird book, and whenever the subject came up I did my best to encourage him and sound interested. But the most important factor was Dr. Golan. After a surprisingly minimal amount of coaxing by me, he shocked us all by not only signing off on the idea but also encouraging my parents to let me go.

"It could be important for him," he told my mother after a session one afternoon. "It's a place that's been so mythologized by his grandfather that visiting could only serve to demystify it. He'll see that it's just as normal and unmagical as anyplace else, and, by extension, his grandfather's fantasies will lose their power. It could be a highly effective way of combating fantasy with reality."

"But I thought he already didn't believe that stuff," my mother said, turning to me. "Do you, Jake?"

"I don't," I assured her.

"Not consciously he doesn't," Dr. Golan said. "But it's his *un*conscious that's causing him problems right now. The dreams, the anxiety."

"And you really think going there could help?" my mother said, narrowing her eyes at him as if readying herself to hear the unvarnished truth. When it came to things I should or should not be doing, Dr. Golan's word was law.

"I do," he replied.

And that was all it took.

After that, things fell into place with astonishing speed. Plane tickets were bought, schedules scheduled, plans laid. My dad and I would go for three weeks in June. I wondered if that was too long, but he claimed he needed at least that much time to make a thorough study of the island's bird colonies. I thought mom would object — three whole weeks! — but the closer our trip got, the more excited for us she seemed. "My two men," she would say, beaming, "off on a big adventure!"

I found her enthusiasm kind of touching, actually — until the afternoon I overheard her talking on the phone to a friend, venting about how relieved she'd be to "have her life back" for three weeks and not have "two needy children to worry about."

I love you too, I wanted to say with as much hurtful sarcasm as I could muster, but she hadn't seen me, and I kept quiet. I did love her, of course, but mostly just because loving your mom is mandatory, not because she was someone I think I'd like very much if I met her walking down the street. Which she wouldn't be, anyway;

walking is for poor people.

During the three-week window between the end of school and the start of our trip, I did my best to verify that Ms. Alma LeFay Peregrine still resided among the living, but Internet searches turned up nothing. Assuming she was still alive, I had hoped to get her on the phone and at least warn her that I was coming, but I soon discovered that almost no one on Cairnholm even *had* a phone. I found only one number for the entire island, so that's the one I dialed.

It took nearly a minute to connect, the line hissing and clicking, going quiet, then hissing again, so that I could feel every mile of the vast distance my call was spanning. Finally I heard that strange European ring — *waaap-waaap . . . waaap-waaap* —and a man whom I could only assume was profoundly intoxicated answered the phone.

"Piss hole!" he bellowed. There was an unholy amount of noise in the background, the kind of dull roar you'd expect at the height of a raging frat party. I tried to identify myself, but I don't think he could hear me.

"Piss hole!" he bellowed again. "Who's this now?" But before I could say anything he'd pulled the receiver away from his head to shout at someone. "I said shaddap, ya

82

dozy bastards, I'm on the —"

And then the line went dead. I sat with the receiver to my ear for a long, puzzled moment, then hung up. I didn't bother calling back. If Cairnholm's only phone connected to some den of iniquity called the "piss hole," how did that bode for the rest of the island? Would my first trip to Europe be spent evading drunken maniacs and watching birds evacuate their bowels on rocky beaches? Maybe so. But if it meant that I'd finally be able to put my grandfather's mystery to rest and get on with my unextraordinary life, anything I had to endure would be worth it.

CHAPTER THREE

Fog closed around us like a blindfold. When the captain announced that we were nearly there, at first I thought he was kidding; all I could see from the ferry's rolling deck was an endless curtain of gray. I clutched the rail and stared into the green waves, contemplating the fish who might soon be enjoying my breakfast, while my father stood shivering beside me in shirtsleeves. It was colder and wetter than I'd ever known June could be. I hoped, for his sake and mine, that the grueling thirty-six hours we'd braved to get this far — three airplanes, two layovers, shift-napping in grubby train stations, and now this interminable gut-churning ferry ride — would pay off. Then my father shouted, "Look!" and I raised my head to see a towering mountain of rock emerge from the blank canvas before us.

It was my grandfather's island. Looming and bleak, folded in mist, guarded by a mil-

84

lion screeching birds, it looked like some ancient fortress constructed by giants. As I gazed up at its sheer cliffs, tops disappearing in a reef of ghostly clouds, the idea that this was a magical place didn't seem so ridiculous.

My nausea seemed to vanish. Dad ran around like a kid on Christmas, his eyes glued to the birds wheeling above us. "Jacob, look at that!" he cried, pointing to a cluster of airborne specks. "Manx Shearwaters!"

As we drew nearer the cliffs, I began to notice odd shapes lurking underwater. A passing crewman caught me leaning over the rail to stare at them and said, "Never seen a shipwreck before, eh?"

I turned to him. "Really?"

"This whole area's a nautical graveyard. It's like the old captains used to say — 'Twixt Hartland Point and Cairnholm Bay is a sailor's grave by night or day!' "

Just then we passed a wreck that was so near the surface, the outline of its greening carcass so clear, that it looked like it was about to rise out of the water like a zombie from a shallow grave. "See that one?" he said, pointing at it. "Sunk by a U-boat, she was."

"There were U-boats around here?"

"Loads. Whole Irish Sea was rotten with

German subs. Wager you'd have half a navy on your hands if you could unsink all the ships they torpedoed." He arched one eyebrow dramatically, then walked off laughing.

I jogged along the deck to the stern, tracking the shipwreck as it disappeared beneath our wake. Then, just as I was starting to wonder if we'd need climbing gear to get onto the island, its steep cliffs sloped down to meet us. We rounded a headland to enter a rocky half-moon bay. In the distance I saw a little harbor bobbing with colorful fishing boats, and beyond it a town set into a green bowl of land. A patchwork of sheep-speckled fields spread across hills that rose away to meet a high ridge, where a wall of clouds stood like a cotton parapet. It was dramatic and beautiful, unlike any place I'd seen. I felt a little thrill of adventure as we chugged into the bay, as if I were sighting land where maps had noted only a sweep of undistinguished blue.

The ferry docked and we humped our bags into the little town. Upon closer inspection I decided it was, like a lot of things, not as pretty up close as it seemed from a distance. Whitewashed cottages, quaint except for the satellite dishes sprouting from their roofs, lined a small grid of muddy gravel streets. Because Cairnholm was too distant and too inconsequential to justify the cost of running power lines from the mainland, foul-smelling diesel generators buzzed on every corner like angry wasps, harmonizing with the growl of tractors, the island's only vehicular traffic. At the edges of town, ancient-looking cottages stood abandoned and roofless, evidence of a shrinking population, children lured away from centuries-old fishing and farming traditions by more glamorous opportunities elsewhere.

We dragged our stuff through town looking for something called the Priest Home, where my dad had booked a room. I pictured an old church converted into a bed and breakfast — nothing fancy, just somewhere to sleep when we weren't watching birds or chasing down leads. We asked a few locals for directions but got only confused looks in return. "They speak English, right?" my dad wondered aloud. Just as my hand was beginning to ache from the unreasonable weight of my suitcase, we came upon a church. We thought we'd found our accommodations, until we went inside and saw that it had indeed been converted, but into a dingy little museum, not a B&B.

We found the part-time curator in a room

hung with old fishing nets and sheep shears. His face lit up when he saw us, then fell when he realized we were only lost.

"I reckon you're after the Priest *Hole,*" he said. "It's got the only rooms to let on the island."

He proceeded to give us directions in a lilting accent, which I found enormously entertaining. I loved hearing Welsh people talk, even if half of what they said was incomprehensible to me. My dad thanked the man and turned to go, but he'd been so helpful, I hung back to ask him another question.

"Where can we find the old children's home?"

"The old what?" he said, squinting at me.

For an awful moment I was afraid we'd come to the wrong island or, worse yet, that the home was just another thing my grandfather had invented.

"It was a home for refugee kids?" I said. "During the war? A big house?"

The man chewed his lip and regarded me doubtfully, as if deciding whether to help or to wash his hands of the whole thing. But he took pity on me. "I don't know about any refugees," he said, "but I think I know the place you mean. It's way up the other side of the island, past the bog and through

88

the woods. Though I wouldn't go mucking about up there alone, if I was you. Stray too far from the path and that's the last anyone'll hear of you — nothing but wet grass and sheep patties to keep you from going straight over a cliff."

"That's good to know," my dad said, eyeing me. "Promise me you won't go by yourself."

"All right, all right."

"What's your interest in it, anyhow?" the man said. "It's not exactly on the tourist maps."

"Just a little genealogy project," my father replied, lingering near the door. "My dad spent a few years there as a kid." I could tell he was eager to avoid any mention of psychiatrists or dead grandfathers. He thanked the man again and quickly ushered me out the door.

Following the curator's directions, we retraced our steps until we came to a grim-looking statue carved from black stone, a memorial called the Waiting Woman dedicated to islanders lost at sea. She wore a pitiful expression and stood with arms outstretched in the direction of the harbor, many blocks away, but also toward the Priest Hole, which was directly across the street. Now, I'm no hotel connoisseur, but one glance at the weathered sign told me that our stay was unlikely to be a four-star mints-on-your-pillow-type experience. Printed in giant script at the top was *WINES, ALES, SPIRITS.* Below that, in more modest lettering, *Fine Food.* Handwritten along the bottom, clearly an afterthought, was *Rooms to Let,* though the *s* had been struck out, leaving just the singular *Room.* As we lugged our bags toward the door, my father grumbling about con men and false advertising, I glanced back at the Waiting Woman and wondered if she wasn't just waiting for someone to bring her a drink.

We squeezed our bags through the doorway and stood blinking in the sudden gloom of a low-ceilinged pub. When my eyes had adjusted, I realized that *hole* was a pretty accurate description of the place: tiny leaded windows admitted just enough light to find the beer tap without tripping over tables and chairs on the way. The tables, worn and wobbling, looked like they might be more useful as firewood. The bar was half-filled, at whatever hour of the morning it was, with men in various states of hushed intoxication, heads bowed prayerfully over tumblers of amber liquid.

"You must be after the room," said the man behind the bar, coming out to shake our hands. "I'm Kev and these are the fellas. Say hullo, fellas."

"Hullo," they muttered, nodding at their drinks.

We followed Kev up a narrow staircase to a suite of rooms (plural!) that could charitably be described as basic. There were two bedrooms, the larger of which Dad claimed, and a room that tripled as a kitchen, dining room, and living room, meaning that it contained one table, one moth-eaten sofa, and one hotplate. The bathroom worked "most of the time," according to Kev, "but if it ever gets dicey, there's always Old Reliable." He directed our attention to a portable toilet in the alley out back, conveniently visible from my bedroom window.

"Oh, and you'll need these," he said, fetching a pair of oil lamps from a cabinet. "The generators stop running at ten since petrol's so bloody expensive to ship out, so either you get to bed early or you learn to love candles and kerosene." He grinned. "Hope it ain't too medieval for ya!"

We assured Kev that outhouses and kerosene would be just fine, sounded like fun, in fact — a little adventure, yessir — and then he led us downstairs for the final leg of our tour. "You're welcome to take your meals here," he said, "and I expect you will, on

91

account of there's nowhere else to eat. If you need to make a call, we got a phone box in the corner there. Sometimes there's a bit of a queue for it, though, since we get doodly for mobile reception out here and you're looking at the only land-line on the island. That's right, we got it all — only food, only bed, only phone!" And he leaned back and laughed, long and loud.

The only phone on the island. I looked over at it — it was the kind that had a door you could pull shut for privacy, like the ones you see in old movies — and realized with dawning horror that *this* was the Grecian orgy, *this* was the raging frat party I had been connected to when I called the island a few weeks ago. *This was the piss hole.*

Kev handed my dad the keys to our rooms. "Any questions," he said, "you know where to find me."

"I have a question," I said. "What's a piss — I mean, a priest hole?"

The men at the bar burst into laughter. "Why, it's a hole for priests, of course!" one said, which made the rest of them laugh even harder.

Kev walked over to an uneven patch of floorboards next to the fireplace, where a mangy dog lay sleeping. "Right here," he said, tapping what appeared to be a door in the floor with his shoe. "Ages ago, when just being a Catholic could get you hung from a tree, clergyfolk came here seeking refuge. If Queen Elizabeth's crew of thugs come chasing after, we hid whoever needed hiding in snug little spots like this — priest holes." It struck me the way he said *we,* as if he'd known those long-dead islanders personally.

"Snug indeed!" one of the drinkers said. "Bet they were warm as toast and tight as drums down there!"

"I'd take warm and snug to strung up by priest killers any day," said another.

"Here, here!" the first man said. "To Cairnholm — may she always be our rock of refuge!"

"To Cairnholm!" they chorused, and raised their glasses together.

Jet-lagged and exhausted, we went to sleep early — or rather we went to our beds and lay in them with pillows covering our heads to block out the thumping cacophony that issued through the floorboards, which grew so loud that at one point I thought surely the revelers had invaded my room. Then the clock must've struck ten because all at once the buzzing generators outside sputtered and died, as did the music from downstairs and the streetlight that had been shining through my window. Suddenly I was cocooned in silent, blissful darkness, with only the whisper of distant waves to remind me where I was.

For the first time in months, I fell into a deep, nightmare-free slumber. I dreamed instead about my grandfather as a boy, about his first night here, a stranger in a strange land, under a strange roof, owing his life to people who spoke a strange tongue. When I awoke, sun streaming through my window, I realized it wasn't just my grandfather's life that Miss Peregrine had saved, but mine, too, and my father's. Today, with any luck, I would finally get to thank her.

I went downstairs to find my dad already bellied up to a table, slurping coffee and polishing his fancy binoculars. Just as I sat down, Kev appeared bearing two plates loaded with mystery meat and fried toast. "I didn't know you could fry toast," I remarked, to which Kev replied that there wasn't a food he was aware of that couldn't be improved by frying.

Over breakfast, Dad and I discussed our plan for the day. It was to be a kind of scout, to familiarize ourselves with the island. We'd scope out my dad's bird-watching spots first and then find the children's home. I scarfed my food, anxious to get started.

Well fortified with grease, we left the pub and walked through town, dodging tractors and shouting to each other over the din of generators until the streets gave way to fields and the noise faded behind us. It was a crisp and blustery day — the sun hiding behind giant cloudbanks only to burst out moments later and dapple the hills with spectacular rays of light — and I felt energized and hopeful. We were heading for a rocky beach where my dad had spotted a bunch of birds from the ferry. I wasn't sure how we would reach it, though — the island was slightly bowl shaped, with hills that climbed toward its edges only to drop off at precarious seaside cliffs — but at this particular spot the edge had been rounded off and a path led down to a minor spit of sand along the water.

We picked our way down to the beach, where what seemed to be an entire civilization of birds were flapping and screeching and fishing in tide pools. I watched my father's eyes widen. "Fascinating," he muttered, scraping at some petrified guano with the stubby end of his pen. "I'm going to need some time here. Is that all right?"

I'd seen this look on his face before, and I knew exactly what "some time" meant:

hours and hours. "Then I'll go find the house by myself," I said.

"Not alone, you aren't. You promised."

"Then I'll find a person who can take me."

"Who?"

"Kev will know someone."

My dad looked out to sea, where a big rusted lighthouse jutted up from a pile of rocks. "You know what the answer would be if your mom were here," he said.

My parents had differing theories about how much parenting I required. Mom was the enforcer, always hovering, but Dad hung back a little. He thought it was important that I make my own mistakes now and then. Also, letting me go would free him to play with guano all day.

"Okay," he said, "but make sure you leave me the number of whoever you go with."

"Dad, nobody here has phones."

He sighed. "Right. Well, as long as they're reliable."

Kev was out running an errand, and because asking one of his drunken regulars to chaperone me seemed like a bad idea, I went into the nearest shop to ask someone who was at least gainfully employed. The door read *FISHMONGER*. I pushed it open to find myself cowering before a bearded giant in a blood-soaked apron. He left off decapitating fish to glare at me, dripping cleaver in hand, and I vowed never again to discriminate against the intoxicated.

"What the hell for?" he growled when I told him where I wanted to go. "Nothing over there but bogland and barmy weather."

I explained about my grandfather and the children's home. He frowned at me, then leaned over the counter to cast a doubtful glance at my shoes.

"I s'pose Dylan ain't too busy to take you," he said, pointing his cleaver at a kid about my age who was arranging fish in a freezer case, "but you'll be wantin' proper footwear. Wouldn't do to let you go in them trainers — mud'll suck 'em right off!"

"Really?" I said. "Are you sure?"

"Dylan! Fetch our man here a pair of Wellingtons!"

The kid groaned and made a big show of slowly closing the freezer case and cleaning his hands before slouching over to a wall of shelves packed with dry goods.

"Just so happens we've got some good sturdy boots on offer," the fishmonger said. "Buy one get none free!" He burst out laughing and slammed his cleaver on a salmon, its head shooting across the blood-slicked counter to land perfectly in a little

97

guillotine bucket.

I fished the emergency money Dad had given me from my pocket, figuring that a little extortion was a small price to pay to find the woman I'd crossed the Atlantic to meet.

I left the shop wearing a pair of rubber boots so large my sneakers fit inside and so heavy it was difficult to keep up with my begrudging guide.

"So, do you go to school on the island?" I asked Dylan, scurrying to catch up. I was genuinely curious — what was living here like for someone my age?

He muttered the name of a town on the mainland.

"What is that, an hour each way by ferry?"

"Yup."

And that was it. He responded to further attempts at conversation with even fewer syllables — which is to say, none — so finally I just gave up and followed him. On the way out of town we ran into one of his friends, an older boy wearing a blinding yellow track suit and fake gold chains. He couldn't have looked more out of place on Cairnholm if he'd been dressed like an astronaut. He gave Dylan a fist-bump and introduced himself as Worm.

"Worm?"

"It's his stage name," Dylan explained.

"We're the sickest rapping duo in Wales," Worm said. "I'm MC Worm, and this is the Sturgeon Surgeon, aka Emcee Dirty Dylan, aka Emcee Dirty Bizniss, Cairnholm's number one beat-boxer. Wanna show this Yank how we do, Dirty D?"

Dylan looked annoyed. "Now?"

"Drop some next-level beats, son!"

Dylan rolled his eyes but did as he was asked. At first I thought he was choking on his tongue, except there was a rhythm to his sputtering coughs, — *puhh, puh-CHAH, puh-puhhh, puh-CHAH* — over which Worm began to rap.

"I likes to get wrecked up down at the Priest Hole / Your dad's always there 'cause he's on the dole / My rhymes is tight, yeah I make it look easy / Dylan's beats are hot like chicken jalfrezi!"

Dylan stopped. "That don't even make sense," he said. "And it's *your* dad who's on the dole."

"Oh shit, Dirty D let the beat drop!" Worm started beat-boxing while doing a passable robot, his sneakers twisting holes in the gravel. "Take the mic, D!"

Dylan seemed embarrassed but let the rhymes fly anyway. "I met a tight bird and her name was Sharon / She was keen on my tracksuit and the trainers I was wearin' / I showed her the time, like Doctor Who / I thunk up this rhyme while I was in the loo!"

Worm shook his head. "The *loo?*"

"I wasn't ready!"

They turned to me and asked what I thought. Considering that they didn't even like each other's rapping, I wasn't sure what to say.

"I guess I'm more into music with, like, singing and guitars and stuff."

Worm dismissed me with a wave of his hand. "He wouldn't know a dope rhyme if it bit him in the bollocks," he muttered.

Dylan laughed and they exchanged a series of complex, multistage handshake-fist-bump-high-fives.

"Can we go now?" I said.

They grumbled and dawdled a while longer, but pretty soon we were on our way, this time with Worm tagging along.

I took up the rear, trying to figure out what I would say to Miss Peregrine when I met her. I was expecting to be introduced to a proper Welsh lady and sip tea in the parlor and make polite small talk until the time seemed right to break the bad news. *I'm Abraham Portman's grandson,* I would say. *I'm sorry to be the one to tell you this, but he's been taken from us.* Then, once she'd finished quietly dabbing away tears, I would ply her with questions.

I followed Dylan and Worm along a path that wound through pastures of grazing sheep before a lung-busting ascent up a ridge. At the top hovered an embankment of rolling, snaking fog so dense it was like stepping into another world. It was truly biblical; a fog I could imagine God, in one of his lesser wraths, cursing the Egyptians with. As we descended the other side it only seemed to thicken. The sun faded to a pale white bloom. Moisture clung to everything, beading on my skin and dampening my clothes. The temperature dropped. I lost Worm and Dylan for a moment and then the path flattened and I came upon them just standing, waiting for me.

"Yank boy!" Dylan called. "This way!"

I followed obediently. We abandoned the path to plow through a field of marshy grass. Sheep stared at us with big leaky eyes, their wool soggy and tails drooping. A small house appeared out of the mist. It was all boarded up.

"You sure this is it?" I said. "It looks empty."

"Empty? No way, there's *loads* of shit in there," Worm replied.

"Go on," said Dylan. "Have a look."

I had a feeling it was a trick but stepped up to the door and knocked anyway. It was unlatched and opened a little at my touch. It was too dark to see inside, so I took a step through — and, to my surprise, *down* — into what looked like a dirt floor but, I quickly realized, was in fact a shin-deep ocean of excrement. This tenantless hovel, so innocent looking from the outside, was really a makeshift sheep stable. Quite literally a shithole.

"Oh my God!" I squealed in disgust.

Peals of laughter exploded from outside. I stumbled backward through the door before the smell could knock me unconscious and found the boys doubled over, holding their stomachs.

"You guys are assholes," I said, stomping the muck off my boots.

"Why?" said Worm. "We *told* you it was full of shit!"

I got in Dylan's face. "Are you gonna show me the house or not?"

"He's serious," said Worm, wiping tears from his eyes.

"Of course I'm serious!"

Dylan's smile faded. "I thought you were taking a piss, mate."

"Taking a what?"

"Joking, like."

"Well, I wasn't."

The boys exchanged an uneasy look. Dylan whispered something to Worm. Worm whispered something back. Finally Dylan turned and pointed up the path. "If you really want to see it," he said, "keep going past the bog and through the woods. It's a big old place. You can't miss it."

"What the hell. You're supposed to go with me!"

Worm looked away and said, "This is as far as we go."

"Why?"

"It just is." And they turned and began to trudge back the way we'd come, receding into the fog.

I weighed my options. I could tuck tail and follow my tormenters back to town, or I could go ahead alone and lie to Dad about it.

After four seconds of intense deliberation, I was on my way.

A vast, lunar bog stretched away into the mist from either side of the path, just brown grass and tea-colored water as far as I could see, featureless but for the occasional mound of piled-up stones. It ended abruptly at a forest of skeletal trees, branches spindling up like the tips of wet paintbrushes, and for a while the path became so lost beneath fallen trunks and carpets of ivy that navigating it was a matter of faith. I wondered how an elderly person like Miss Peregrine would ever be able to negotiate such an obstacle course. *She must get deliveries,* I thought, though the path looked like it hadn't seen a footprint in months, if not years.

I scrambled over a giant trunk slick with moss, and the path took a sharp turn. The trees parted like a curtain and suddenly there it was, cloaked in fog, looming atop a weed-choked hill. The house. I understood at once why the boys had refused to come.

My grandfather had described it a hundred times, but in his stories the house was always a bright, happy place — big and rambling, yes, but full of light and laughter. What stood before me now was no refuge from monsters but a monster itself, staring down from its perch on the hill with vacant hunger. Trees burst forth from broken windows and skins of scabrous vine gnawed at the walls like antibodies attacking a virus — as if nature itself had waged war against it — but the house seemed unkillable, resolutely upright despite the wrongness of its angles and the jagged teeth of sky visible through sections of collapsed roof.

I tried to convince myself that it was possible someone could still live there, rundown as it was. Such things weren't unheard of where I came from — a falling-down wreck on the edge of town, curtains permanently drawn, that would turn out to have been home to some ancient recluse who'd been surviving on ramen and toenail clippings since time immemorial, though no one realizes it until a property appraiser or an overly ambitious census taker barges in to find the poor soul returning to dust in a La-Z-Boy. People get too old to care for a place, their family writes them off for one reason or another — it's sad, but it happens. Which meant, like it or not, that I was going to have to knock.

I gathered what scrawny courage I had and waded through waist-high weeds to the porch, all broken tile and rotting wood, to peek through a cracked window. All I could make out through the smeared glass were the outlines of furniture, so I knocked on the door and stood back to wait in the eerie silence, tracing the shape of Miss Peregrine's letter in my pocket. I'd taken it along in case I needed to prove who I was, but as a minute ticked by, then two, it seemed less and less likely that I would need it.

Climbing down into the yard, I circled the house looking for another way in, taking the measure of the place, but it seemed almost without measure, as though with every corner I turned the house sprouted new balconies and turrets and chimneys. Then I came around back and saw my opportunity: a doorless doorway, bearded with vines, gaping and black; an open mouth just waiting to swallow me. Just looking at it made my skin crawl, but I hadn't come halfway around the world just to run away screaming at the sight of a scary house. I thought of all the horrors Grandpa Portman had faced in his life, and felt my resolve harden. If there was anyone to find inside, I would find them. I mounted the crumbling steps and crossed the threshold.

Standing in a tomb-dark hallway just inside the door, I stared frozenly at what looked for all the world like skins hanging from hooks. After a queasy moment in which I imagined some twisted cannibal leaping from the shadows with knife in hand, I realized they were only coats rotted to rags and green with age. I shuddered involuntarily and took a deep breath. I'd only explored ten feet of the house and was already about to foul my underwear. *Keep it together,* I told myself, and then slowly moved forward, heart hammering in my chest.

Each room was a disaster more incredible than the last. Newspapers gathered in drifts. Scattered toys, evidence of children long gone, lay skinned in dust. Creeping mold had turned window-adjacent walls black and furry. Fireplaces were throttled with vines that had descended from the roof and begun to spread across the floors like alien tentacles. The kitchen was a science experiment gone terribly wrong — entire shelves of jarred food had exploded from sixty seasons of freezing and thawing, splattering the wall with evil-looking stains — and fallen plaster lay so thickly over the dining room floor that for a moment I thought it had snowed indoors. At the end of a light-starved corridor I tested my weight on a rickety staircase, my boots leaving fresh tracks in layers of dust. The steps groaned as if woken from a long sleep. If anyone was upstairs, they'd been there a very long time.

Finally I came upon a pair of rooms missing entire walls, into which a little forest of underbrush and stunted trees had grown. I stood in the sudden breeze wondering what could possibly have done that kind of damage, and began to get the feeling that something terrible had happened here. I couldn't square my grandfather's idyllic stories with this nightmare house, nor the idea that he'd found refuge here with the sense of disaster that pervaded it. There was more left to explore, but suddenly it seemed like a waste of time; it was impossible that anyone could still be living here, even the most misanthropic recluse. I left the house feeling like I was further than ever from the truth.

CHAPTER FOUR

Once I'd hopped and tripped and felt my way like a blind man through the woods and fog and reemerged into the world of sun and light, I was surprised to find the sun sinking and the light going red. Somehow the whole day had slipped away. At the pub my dad was waiting for me, a black-as-night beer and his open laptop on the table in front of him. I sat down and swiped his beer before he'd had a chance to even look up from typing.

"Oh, my sweet lord," I sputtered, choking down a mouthful, "what is this? Fermented motor oil?"

"Just about," he said, laughing, and then snatched it back. "It's not like American beer. Not that you'd know what that tastes like, right?"

"Absolutely not," I said with a wink, even though it was true. My dad liked to believe I was as popular and adventuresome as he was at my age — a myth it had always seemed easiest to perpetuate.

I underwent a brief interrogation about how I'd gotten to the house and who had taken me there, and because the easiest kind of lying is when you leave things out of a story rather than make them up, I passed with flying colors. I conveniently forgot to mention that Worm and Dylan had tricked me into wading through sheep excrement and then bailed out a half-mile from our destination. Dad seemed pleased that I'd already managed to meet a couple kids my own age; I guess I also forgot to mention the part about them hating me.

"So how was the house?"

"Trashed."

He winced. "Guess it's been a long time since your Grandpa lived there, huh?"

"Yeah. Or anyone."

He closed the laptop, a sure sign I was about to receive his full attention. "I can see you're disappointed."

"Well, I didn't come thousands of miles looking for a house full of creepy garbage."

"So what're you going to do?"

"Find people to talk to. Someone will know what happened to the kids who used to live there. I figure a few of them must still be alive, on the mainland if not around here. In a nursing home or something."

"Sure. That's an idea." He didn't sound convinced, though. There was an odd pause, and then he said, "So do you feel like you're starting to get a better handle on who your grandpa was, being here?"

I thought about it. "I don't know. I guess so. It's just an island, you know?"

He nodded. "Exactly."

"What about you?"

"Me?" He shrugged. "I gave up trying to understand my father a long time ago."

"That's sad. Weren't you interested?"

"Sure I was. Then, after a while, I wasn't anymore."

I could feel the conversation going in a direction I wasn't entirely comfortable with, but I persisted anyway. "Why not?"

"When someone won't let you in, eventually you stop knocking. Know what I mean?"

He hardly ever talked like this. Maybe it was the beer, or that we were so far from home, or maybe he'd decided I was finally old enough to hear this stuff. Whatever the reason, I didn't want him to stop.

"But he was your dad. How could you just give up?"

"It wasn't me who gave up!" he said a little too loudly, then looked down, embarrassed and swirled the beer in his glass. "It's just that — the truth is, I think your grandpa didn't know how to be a dad, but he felt like he had to be one anyway, because none of his brothers or sisters survived the war. So he dealt with it by being gone all the time — on hunting trips, business trips, you name it. And even when he *was* around, it was like he wasn't."

"Is this about that one Halloween?"

"What are you talking about?"

"You know — from the picture."

It was an old story, and it went like this: It was Halloween. My dad was four or five years old and had never been trick-or-treating, and Grandpa Portman had promised to take him when he got off work. My grandmother had bought my dad this ridiculous pink bunny costume, and he put it on and sat by the driveway waiting for Grandpa Portman to come home from five o'clock until nightfall, but he never did. Grandma was so mad that she took a picture of my dad crying in the street just so she could show my grandfather what a huge asshole he was. Needless to say, that picture has long been an object of legend among members of my family, and a great embarrassment to my father.

"It was a lot more than just one Halloween," he grumbled. "Really, Jake, you

JUN   56

113

were closer to him than I ever was. I don't know — there was just something unspoken between the two of you."

I didn't know how to respond. Was he jealous of me?

"Why are you telling me this?"

"Because you're my son, and I don't want you to get hurt."

"Hurt how?"

He paused. Outside the clouds shifted, the last rays of daylight throwing our shadows against the wall. I got a sick feeling in my stomach, like when your parents are about to tell you they're splitting up, but you know it before they even open their mouths.

"I never dug too deep with your grandpa because I was afraid of what I'd find," he said finally.

"You mean about the war?"

"No. Your grandpa kept those secrets because they were painful. I understood that. I mean about the traveling, him being gone all the time. What he was really doing. I think — your aunt and I both thought — that there was another woman. Maybe more than one."

I let it hang between us for a moment. My face tingled strangely. "That's crazy, Dad."

"We found a letter once. It was from a woman whose name we didn't know, addressed to your grandfather. *I love you, I miss you, when are you coming back,* that kind of thing. Seedy, lipstick-on-the-collar type stuff. I'll never forget it."

I felt a hot stab of shame, like somehow it was my own crime he was describing. And yet I couldn't quite believe it.

"We tore up the letter and flushed it down the toilet. Never found another one, either. Guess he was more careful after that."

I didn't know what to say. I couldn't look at my father.

"I'm sorry, Jake. This must be hard to hear. I know how much you worshipped him." He reached out to squeeze my shoulder but I shrugged him off, then scraped back my chair and stood up.

"I don't *worship* anyone."

"Okay. I just . . . I didn't want you to be surprised, that's all."

I grabbed my jacket and slung it over my shoulder.

"What are you doing? Dinner's on the way."

"You're wrong about him," I said. "And I'm going to prove it."

He sighed. It was a letting-go kind of sigh. "Okay. I hope you do."

I slammed out of the Priest Hole and started walking, heading nowhere in particular. Sometimes you just need to go through a door.

It was true, of course, what my dad had said: I did worship my grandfather. There were things about him that I needed to be true, and his being an adulterer was not one of them. When I was a kid, Grandpa Portman's fantastic stories meant it was possible to live a magical life. Even after I stopped believing them, there was still something magical about my grandfather. To have endured all the horrors he did, to have seen the worst of humanity and have your life made unrecognizable by it, to come out of all that the honorable and good and brave person I knew him to be — *that* was magical. So I couldn't believe he was a liar and a cheater and a bad father. Because if Grandpa Portman wasn't honorable and good, I wasn't sure anyone could be.

The museum's doors were open and its lights were on, but no one seemed to be inside. I'd gone there to find the curator, hoping he knew a thing or two about the island's history and people, and could shed some light on the empty house and the whereabouts of its former inhabitants.

Figuring he'd just stepped out for a minute — the crowds weren't exactly kicking down his door — I wandered into the sanctuary to kill time checking out museum displays.

The exhibits, such as they were, were arranged in big open-fronted cabinets that lined the walls and stood where pews had once been. For the most part they were unspeakably boring, all about life in a traditional fishing village and the enduring mysteries of animal husbandry, but one exhibit stood out from the rest. It was in a place of honor at the front of the room, in a fancy case that rested atop what had been the altar. It lived behind a rope I stepped over and a little warning sign I didn't bother to read, and its case had polished wooden sides and a Plexiglas top so that you could only see into it from above.

When I looked inside, I think I actually gasped — and for one panicky second thought *monster!* — because I had suddenly and unexpectedly come face-to-face with a blackened corpse. Its shrunken body bore an uncanny resemblance to the creatures that had haunted my dreams, as did the color of its flesh, which was like something that had been spit-roasted over a flame. But when the body failed to come alive and scar my mind forever by breaking the glass and going for my jugular, my initial panic subsided. It was just a museum display, albeit an excessively morbid one.

"I see you've met the old man!" called a voice from behind me, and I turned to see the curator striding in my direction. "You handled it pretty well. I've seen grown men faint dead away!" He grinned and reached out to shake my hand. "Martin Pagett. Don't believe I caught your name the other day."

"Jacob Portman," I said. "Who's this, Wales's most famous murder victim?"

"Ha! Well, he might be that, too, though I never thought of him that way. He's our island's senior-most resident, better known in archaeological circles as Cairnholm Man — though to us he's just the Old Man. More than twenty-seven hundred years old, to be exact, though he was only sixteen when he died. So he's rather a young old man, really."

"Twenty-seven *hundred?*" I said, glancing at the dead boy's face, his delicate features somehow perfectly preserved. "But he looks so . . ."

"That's what happens when you spend your golden years in a place where oxygen and bacteria can't exist, like the underside of our bog. It's a regular fountain of youth down there — provided you're already dead, that is."

"That's where you found him? The bog?"

He laughed. "Not me! Turf cutters did, digging for peat by the big stone cairn out there, back in the seventies. He looked so fresh they thought there might be a killer loose on Cairnholm — till the cops had a look at the Stone Age bow in his hand and the noose of human hair round his neck. They don't make 'em like that anymore."

I shuddered. "Sounds like a human sacrifice or something."

"Exactly. He was done in by a combination of strangulation, drowning, disembowelment, and a blow to the head. Seems rather like overkill, don't you think?"

"I guess so."

Martin roared with laughter. "He guesses so!"

"Okay, yeah, it does."

"Sure it does. But the really fascinating thing, to us modern folk, anyway, is that in all likelihood the boy went to his death willingly. Eagerly, even. His people believed that bogs — and our bog in particular — were entrances to the world of the gods, and so the perfect place to offer up their most precious gift: themselves."

"That's insane."

"I suppose. Though I imagine we're killing ourselves right now in all manner of ways that'll seem insane to people in the future. And as doors to the next world go, a bog ain't a bad choice. It's not quite water and it's not quite land — it's an in-between place." He bent over the case, studying the figure inside. "Ain't he beautiful?"

I looked at the body again, throttled and flayed and drowned and somehow made immortal in the process.

"I don't think so," I said.

Martin straightened, then began to speak in a grandiose tone. "Come, you, and gaze upon the tar man! Blackly he reposes, tender face the color of soot, withered limbs like veins of coal, feet lumps of driftwood hung with shriveled grapes!" He threw his arms out like a hammy stage actor and began to strut around the case. "Come, you, and bear witness to the cruel art of his wounds! Purled and meandering lines drawn by knives; brain and bone exposed by stones; the rope still digging at his throat. First fruit slashed and dumped–seeker of Heaven–old man arrested in youth–I almost love you!"

He took a theatrical bow as I applauded. "Wow," I said, "did you write that?"

"Guilty!" he replied with a sheepish smile.

"I twiddle about with lines of verse now and then, but it's only a hobby. In any case, thank you for indulging me."

I wondered what this odd, well-spoken man was doing on Cairnholm, with his pleated slacks and half-baked poems, looking more like a bank manager than someone who lived on a windswept island with one phone and no paved roads.

"Now, I'd be happy to show you the rest of my collection," he said, escorting me toward the door, "but I'm afraid it's shutting-up time. If you'd like to come back tomorrow, however —"

"Actually, I was hoping you might know something," I said, stopping him before he could shoo me out. "It's about the house I mentioned this morning. I went to see it."

"Well!" he exclaimed. "I thought I'd scared you off it. How's our haunted mansion faring these days? Still standing?"

I assured him that it was, then got right to the point. "The people that lived there — do you have any idea what happened to them?"

"They're dead," he replied. "Happened a long time ago."

I was surprised — though I probably shouldn't have been. Miss Peregrine was old. Old people die. But that didn't mean my search was over. "I'm looking for anyone else who might have lived there, too, not just the headmistress."

"All dead," he repeated. "No one's lived there since the war."

That took me a moment to process. "What do you mean? What war?"

"When we say 'the war' around here, my boy, there's only one that we mean — the second. It was a German air raid that got 'em, if I'm not mistaken."

"No, that can't be right."

He nodded. "In those days, there was an anti-aircraft gun battery at the far tip of the island, past the wood where the house is. It made Cairnholm a legitimate military target. Not that 'legitimate' mattered much to the Germans one way or another, mind you. Anyway, one of the bombs went off track, and, well . . ." He shook his head. "Nasty luck."

"That can't be right," I said again, though I was starting to wonder.

"Why don't you sit down and let me fix you some tea?" he said. "You look a bit off the mark."

"Just feeling a little light-headed . . ."

He led me to a chair in his office and went to make the tea. I tried to collect my thoughts. *Bombed in the war* — that would

122

certainly explain those rooms with blown-out walls. But what about the letter from Miss Peregrine — postmarked Cairnholm — sent just fifteen years ago?

Martin returned, handing me a mug. "There's a nip of Penderyn in it," he said. "Secret recipe, you know. Should get you sorted in no time."

I thanked him and took a sip, realizing too late that the secret ingredient was high-test whiskey. It felt like napalm flushing down my esophagus. "It does have a certain kick," I admitted, my face going red.

He frowned. "Reckon I ought to fetch your father."

"No, no, I'll be fine. But if there's anything else you can tell me about the attack, I'd be grateful."

Martin settled into a chair opposite me. "About that, I'm curious. You say your grandfather lived here. He never mentioned it?"

"I'm curious about that, too," I said. "I guess it must've been after his time. Did it happen late in the war or early?"

"I'm ashamed to admit I don't know. But if you're keen, I can introduce you to someone who does — my Uncle Oggie. He's eighty-three, lived here his whole life. Still sharp as a tack." Martin glanced at his watch. "If we catch him before *Father Ted* comes on the telly, I'm sure he'd be more than happy to tell you anything you like."

Ten minutes later Martin and I were wedged deep in an overstuffed sofa in Oggie's living room, which was piled high with books and boxes of worn-out shoes and enough lamps to light up Carlsbad Caverns, all but one of them unplugged. Living on a remote island, I was starting to realize, turned people into pack rats. Oggie sat facing us in a threadbare blazer and pajama bottoms, as if he'd been expecting company — just not pants-worthy company — and rocked endlessly in a plastic-covered easy chair as he talked. He seemed happy just to have an audience, and after he'd gone on at length about the weather and Welsh politics and the sorry state of today's youth, Martin was finally able to steer him around to the attack and the children from the home.

"Sure, I remember them," he said. "Odd collection of people. We'd see them in town now and again — the children, sometimes their minder-woman, too — buying milk and medicine and what-have-you. You'd say 'good morning' and they'd look the other way. Kept to themselves, they did, off in that big house. Lot of talk about what might've been going on over there, though no one knew for sure."

"What kind of talk?"

"Lot of rot. Like I said, no one knew. All I can say is they weren't your regular sort of orphan children — not like them Barnardo Home kids they got in other places, who you'll see come into town for parades and things and always have time for a chat. This lot was different. Some of 'em couldn't even speak the King's English. Or any English, for that matter."

"Because they weren't really orphans," I said. "They were refugees from other countries. Poland, Austria, Czechoslovakia . . ."

"Is that what they were, now?" Oggie said, cocking an eyebrow at me. "Funny, I hadn't heard that." He seemed offended, like I'd insulted him by pretending to know more about his island than he did. His chair-rocking got faster, more aggressive. If this was the kind of reception my grandpa and the other kids got on Cairnholm, I thought, no wonder they kept to themselves.

Martin cleared his throat. "So, Uncle, the bombing?"

"Oh, keep your hair on. Yes, yes, the goddamned Jerries. Who could forget them?" He launched into a long-winded description of what life on the island was like under threat of German air raids: the blaring sirens; the panicked scrambles for shelter; the volunteer air-raid warden who ran from house to house at night making sure shades had been drawn and streetlights were put out to rob enemy pilots of easy targets. They prepared as best they could but never really thought they'd get hit, given all the ports and factories on the mainland, all much more important targets than Cairnholm's little gun emplacement. But one night, the bombs began to fall.

"The noise was dreadful," Oggie said. "It was like giants stamping across the island, and it seemed to go on for ages. They gave us a hell of a pounding, though no one in town was killed, thank heaven. Can't say the same for our gunner boys — though they gave as good as they got — nor the poor souls at the orphan home. One bomb was all it took. Gave up their lives for Britain, they did. So wherever they was from, God bless 'em for that."

"Do you remember when it happened?" I asked. "Early in the war or late?"

"I can tell you the exact day," he said. "It was the third of September, 1940."

The air seemed to go out of the room. I flashed to my grandfather's ashen face, his lips just barely moving, uttering those very words. *September third, 1940.*

"Are you — you sure about that? That it was *that day?*"

"I never got to fight," he said. "Too young by a year. That one night was my whole war. So, yes, I'm sure."

I felt numb, disconnected. It was too strange. Was someone playing a joke on me, I wondered — a weird, unfunny joke?

"And there weren't any survivors at all?" Martin asked.

The old man thought for a moment, his gaze drifting up to the ceiling. "Now that you mention it," he said, "I reckon there were. Just one. A young man, not much older than this boy here." His rocking stopped as he remembered it. "Walked into town the morning after with not a scratch upon him. Hardly seemed perturbed at all, considering he'd just seen all his mates go to their reward. It was the queerest thing."

"He was probably in shock," Martin said.

"I shouldn't wonder," replied Oggie. "He spoke only once, to ask my father when the next boat was leaving for the mainland. Said he wanted to take up arms directly and kill the damned monsters who murdered his people."

Oggie's story was nearly as far-fetched as the ones Grandpa Portman used to tell, and yet I had no reason to doubt him.

"I knew him," I said. "He was my grand-father."

They looked at me, astonished. "Well," Billy said. "I'll be blessed."

I excused myself and stood up. Martin, remarking that I seemed out of sorts, offered to walk me back to the pub, but I declined. I needed to be alone with my thoughts. "Come and see me soon, then," he said, and I promised I would.

I took the long way back, past the swaying lights of the harbor, the air heavy with brine and with chimney smoke from a hundred hearth fires. I walked to the end of a dock and watched the moon rise over the water, imagining my grandfather standing there on that awful morning after, numb with shock, waiting for a boat that would take him away from all the death he'd endured, to war, and more death. There was no escaping the monsters, not even on this island, no bigger on a map than a grain of sand, protected by mountains of fog and sharp rocks and seething tides. Not anywhere. That was the awful truth my grandfather had tried to protect me from.

In the distance, I heard the generators sputter and spin down, and all the lights along the harbor and in house windows behind me surged for a moment before going dark. I imagined how such a thing might look from an airplane's height — the whole island suddenly winking out, as if it had never been there at all. A supernova in miniature.

I walked back by moonlight, feeling small. I found my dad in the pub at the same table where he'd been, a half-eaten plate of beef and gravy congealing into grease before him. "Look who's back," he said as I sat down. "I saved your dinner for you."

"I'm not hungry," I said, and told him what I'd learned about Grandpa Portman.

He seemed more angry than surprised. "I can't believe he never brought this up," he said. "Not one time." I could understand his anger: it was one thing for a grandparent to withhold something like that from a grandchild, quite another for a father to keep it from his son — and for so long.

I tried to steer the conversation in a more positive direction. "It's amazing, isn't it? Everything he went through."

My father nodded. "I don't think we'll ever know the full extent of it."

"Grandpa Portman really knew how to keep a secret, didn't he?"

"Are you kidding? The man was an emotional Fort Knox."

"I wonder if it doesn't explain something, though. Why he acted so distant when you were little." Dad gave me a sharp look, and I knew I needed to make my point quickly or risk overstepping. "He'd already lost his family twice before. Once in Poland and then again here — his adopted family. So when you and Aunt Susie came along . . ."

"Once bombed, twice shy?"

"I'm serious. Don't you think this could mean that maybe he wasn't cheating on Grandma, after all?"

"I don't know, Jake. I guess I don't believe things are ever that simple." He let out a sigh, breath fogging the inside of his beer glass. "I think I know what all this really explains, though. Why you and Grandpa were so close."

"Okay . . ."

"It took him fifty years to get over his fear of having a family. You came along at just the right time."

I didn't know how to respond. How do you say *I'm sorry your father didn't love you enough* to your own dad? I couldn't, so instead I just said goodnight and headed upstairs to bed.

I tossed and turned most of the night. I

couldn't stop thinking about the letters — the one my dad and Aunt Susie had found as kids, from this "other woman," and the one I'd found a month ago, from Miss Peregrine. The thought that kept me awake was this: *what if they were the same woman?*

The postmark on Miss Peregrine's letter was fifteen years old, but by all accounts she'd been blown into the stratosphere back in 1940. To my mind, that left two possible explanations: either my grandfather had been corresponding with a dead person — admittedly unlikely — or the person who wrote the letter was not, in fact, Miss Peregrine, but someone who was using her identity to disguise her own.

Why would you disguise your identity in a letter? Because you have something to hide. Because you are the other woman.

What if the only thing I had discovered on this trip was that my grandfather was an adulterous liar? In his last breaths, was he trying to tell me about the death of his adopted family — or admit to some tawdry, decades-long affair? Maybe it was both, and the truth was that by the time he was a young man he'd had his family torn apart so many times he no longer knew how to have one, or to be faithful to one.

It was all just guesswork, though. I didn't

131

know, and there was no one to ask. Anyone who might have had the answer was long dead. In less than twenty-four hours, the whole trip had become pointless.

I fell into an uneasy sleep. At dawn, I woke to the sound of something in my room. Rolling over to see what it was, I bolted upright in bed. A large bird was perched on my dresser, staring me down. It had a sleek head feathered in gray and talons that clacked on the wooden dresser as it sidled back and forth along the edge, as if to get a better look at me. I stared back rigidly, wondering if this could be a dream.

I called out for my dad, and at the sound of my voice the bird launched itself off the dresser. I threw my arm across my face and rolled away, and when I peeked again it was gone, flown out the open window.

My dad stumbled in, bleary-eyed. "What's going on?"

I showed him the talon marks on the dresser and a feather that had landed on the floor. "God, that's weird," he said, turning it over in his hands. "Peregrines almost never come this close to humans."

I thought maybe I'd heard him wrong. "Did you say *peregrines?*"

He held up the feather. "A peregrine falcon," he said. "They're amazing creatures

132

— the fastest birds on earth. They're like shape-shifters, the way they streamline their bodies in the air." The name was just a weird coincidence, but it left me with an uncanny feeling I couldn't shake.

Over breakfast, I began to wonder if I'd given up too easily. Though it was true there was no one left alive whom I could talk to about my grandfather, there was still the house, a lot of it unexplored. If it had ever held answers about my grandfather — in the form of letters, maybe, or a photo album or a diary — they'd probably burned up or rotted away decades ago. But if I left the island without making sure, I knew I'd regret it.

And that is how someone who is unusually susceptible to nightmares, night terrors, the Creeps, the Willies, and Seeing Things That Aren't Really There talks himself into making one last trip to the abandoned, almost-certainly-haunted house where a dozen or more children met their untimely end.

CHAPTER FIVE

It was an almost-too-perfect morning. Leaving the pub felt like stepping into one of those heavily retouched photos that come loaded as wallpaper on new computers: streets of artfully decrepit cottages stretched into the distance, giving way to green fields sewn together by meandering rock walls, the whole scene topped by scudding white clouds. But beyond all that, above the houses and fields and sheep doddering around like little puffs of cotton candy, I could see tongues of dense fog licking over the ridge in the distance, where this world ended and the next one began, cold, damp, and sunless.

I walked over the ridge and straight into a rain shower. True to form, I had forgotten my rubber boots, and the path was a rapidly deepening ribbon of mud. But getting a little wet seemed vastly preferable to climbing that hill twice in one morning, so I bent my head against the spitting rain and trudged onward. Soon I passed the shack, dim outlines of sheep huddled inside against the chill, and then the mist-shrouded bog, silent and ghostly. I thought about the twenty-seven-hundred-year-old resident of Cairnholm's museum and wondered how many more like him these fields held, undiscovered, arrested in death; how many more had given up their lives here, looking for heaven.

By the time I reached the children's home, what had begun as a drizzle was a full-on downpour. There was no time to dally in the house's feral yard and reflect upon its malevolent shape — the way the doorless doorway seemed to swallow me as I dove through it, the way the hall's rain-bloated floorboards gave a little beneath my shoes. I stood wringing water from my shirt and shaking out my hair, and when I was as dry as I was going to get — which was not very — I began to search. For what, I wasn't sure. A box of letters? My grandfather's name scribbled on a wall? It all seemed so unlikely.

I roved around peeling up mats of old newspaper and looking under chairs and tables. I imagined uncovering some horrible scene — a tangle of skeletons dressed in fire-blackened rags — but all I found were rooms that had become more outside than inside, character stripped away by moisture and wind and layers of dirt. The ground floor was hopeless. I went back to the staircase, knowing this time I would have to climb it. The only question was, up or down? One strike against going upstairs was its limited options for quick escape (from squatters or ghouls or whatever else my anxious mind could invent) other than hurling myself from an upper-story window. Downstairs had the same problem, and with the added detractor of being dark, and me without a flashlight. So upstairs it was.

The steps protested my weight with a symphony of shudders and creaks, but they held, and what I discovered upstairs — compared to the bombed-out ground floor, at least — was like a time capsule. Arranged along a hallway striped with peeling wallpaper, the rooms were in surprisingly good shape. Though one or two had been invaded by mold where a broken window had let in the rain, the rest were packed with things that seemed only a layer or two of dust away from new: a mildewed shirt tossed casually over the back of a chair, loose change skimming a nightstand. It was easy to believe that everything was just as the children had left it, as if time had stopped the night they died.

I went from room to room, examining their contents like an archaeologist. There were wooden toys moldering in a box; crayons on a windowsill, their colors dulled by the light of ten thousand afternoons; a dollhouse with dolls inside, lifers in an ornate prison. In a modest library, the creep of moisture had bowed the shelves into crooked smiles. I ran my finger along the balding spines, as if considering pulling one out to read. There were classics like *Peter Pan* and *The Secret Garden,* histories written by authors forgotten by history, textbooks of Latin and Greek. In the corner were corralled a few old desks. This had been their classroom, I realized, and Miss Peregrine, their teacher.

I tried to open a pair of heavy doors, twisting the handle, but they were swelled shut — so I took a running start and rammed them with my shoulder. They flew open with a rasping shriek and I fell face-first into the next room. As I picked myself up and looked around, I realized that it could only have belonged to Miss Peregrine. It was like a room in Sleeping Beauty's castle, with cobwebbed candles mounted in wall sconces, a mirrored vanity table topped with crystal bottles, and a giant oak bed. I pictured the last time she'd been here, scrambling out from under the sheets in the middle of the night to the whine of an air-raid siren, rounding up the children, all groggy and grasping for coats on their way downstairs.

Were you scared? I wondered. *Did you hear the planes coming?*

I began to feel unusual. I imagined I was being watched; that the children were still here, preserved like the bog boy, inside the walls. I could feel them peering at me through cracks and knotholes.

I drifted into the next room. Weak light shone through a window. Petals of powder-blue wallpaper drooped toward a couple of small beds, still clad in dusty sheets. I knew, somehow, that this had been my grand-father's room.

Why did you send me here? What was it you needed me to see?

Then I noticed something beneath one of the beds and knelt down to look. It was an old suitcase.

Was this yours? Is it what you carried onto the train the last time you saw your mother and father, as your first life was slipping away?

I pulled it out and fumbled with its tat-tered leather straps. It opened easily — but except for a family of dead beetles, it was empty.

I felt empty, too, and strangely heavy, like the planet was spinning too fast, heating up gravity, pulling me toward the floor. Suddenly exhausted, I sat on the bed — *his bed, maybe* — and for reasons I can't quite explain, I stretched out on those filthy sheets and stared at the ceiling.

What did you think about, lying here at night? Did you have nightmares, too?

I began to cry.

When your parents died, did you know it? Could you feel them go?

I cried harder. I didn't want to, but I couldn't stop myself.

I couldn't stop myself, so I thought about all the bad things and I fed it and fed it until I was crying so hard I had to gasp for breath between sobs. I thought about how my great-grandparents had starved to death. I thought about their wasted bodies being fed to incinerators because people they didn't know hated them. I thought about how the children who lived in this house had been burned up and blown apart because a pilot who didn't care pushed a button. I thought about how my grandfather's family had been taken from him, and how because of that my dad grew up feeling like he didn't have a dad, and now I had acute stress and nightmares and was sitting alone in a falling-down house and crying hot, stupid tears all over my shirt. All because of a seventy-year-old hurt that had somehow been passed down to me like some poisonous heirloom, and monsters I couldn't fight because they were all dead, beyond killing or punishing or any kind of reckoning. At least my grand-father had been able to join the army and go fight them. What could I do?

When it was over, my head was pounding. I closed my eyes and pushed my knuckles in to stop them from hurting, if only for a moment, and when I finally released the pressure and opened them again, a miracu-lous change had come over the room: There was a single ray of sun shining through the window. I got up, went to the cracked glass, and saw that it was both raining and shin-ing outside — a bit of meteorological weird-ness whose name no one can seem to agree on. My mom, I kid you not, refers to it as "orphans' tears." Then I remembered what Ricky says about it — "the Devil's beatin' his wife!" — and I laughed and felt a little better.

Then, in the patch of quickly fading sun that fell across the room, I noticed some-thing I hadn't before. It was a trunk — or the edge of one, at least — poking out from under the second bed. I went over and peeled back the bed sheet that hid most of it from view.

It was a big old steamer trunk latched with a giant rusting padlock. It couldn't possibly be empty, I thought. You don't lock an empty trunk. *Open me!* it fairly seemed to cry out. *I am full of secrets!*

I grabbed it by the sides and pulled. It didn't move. I pulled again, harder, but it wouldn't give an inch. I wasn't sure if it was just that heavy, or if generations of accumulated moisture and dust had somehow fused it to the floor. I stood up and kicked it a few times, which seemed to jar things loose, and then I managed to move it by pulling on one side at a time, shimmying it forward the way you might move a stove or a fridge, until it had come out all the way from under the bed, leaving a trail of parenthetical scars in the floor. I yanked on the padlock, but despite a thick encrustation of rust it seemed rock solid. I briefly considered searching for a key — it had to be here somewhere — but I could've wasted hours looking, and the lock was so decayed that I wondered if the key would even work anymore. My only option was to break it.

Looking around for something that might

do the job, I found a busted chair in one of the other rooms. I pried off a leg and went to town on the lock, raising the leg over my head like an executioner and bringing it down as hard as I could, over and over, until the leg itself finally broke and I was left holding a splintered stump. I scanned the room for something stronger and quickly spotted a loose railing on the bed frame. After a few stomping kicks, it clattered to the floor. I wedged one end through the lock and pulled the other end backward. Nothing happened.

I hung on it with all my weight, lifting my feet off the floor like I was doing a pull-up with the rail. The trunk creaked a little, but that was it.

I started to get mad. I kicked the trunk and pulled on that rail with every bit of my strength, the veins bulging out of my neck, yelling, *Open god damn you, open you stupid trunk!* Finally my frustration and anger had an object: If I couldn't make my dead grandfather give up his secrets, I would damn well pry the secrets out of this old trunk. And then the rail slipped and I crashed to the floor and got the wind knocked out of me.

I lay there and stared at the ceiling, catching my breath. The orphans' tears had ended and now it was just plain old raining outside, harder than ever. I thought about going back to town for a sledgehammer or a hacksaw — but that would only raise questions I didn't feel like answering.

Then I had a brilliant idea. If I could find a way to break the *trunk,* I wouldn't have to worry about the lock at all. And what force would be stronger than me and my admittedly underdeveloped upper-body muscles wailing on the trunk with random tools? *Gravity.* I was, after all, on the second floor of the house, and while I didn't think there was any way I could lift the trunk high enough to get it through a window, the rail along the top of the staircase landing had long ago collapsed. All I had to do was drag the trunk down the hall and push it over. Whether its contents would survive the impact was another issue — but at least I'd find out what was inside.

I hunkered down behind the trunk and began pushing it toward the hall. After a few inches its metal feet dug into the soft floor and it ground stubbornly to a halt. Undeterred, I moved around to the other side, gripped the padlock with both hands and pulled backward. To my great surprise it moved two or three feet in one go. It wasn't a particularly dignified way of working — this squatting, butt-scooting motion I had to repeat over and over, each slide of the trunk accompanied by an ear-splitting metal-on-wood shriek — but before long I'd gotten it out of the room and was dragging it, foot by foot, doorway by doorway, toward the landing. I lost myself in the echoing rhythm of it, working up a manly lather of sweat in the process.

I finally made it to the landing and, with one final indelicate grunt, pulled the trunk onto it after me. It slid easily now, and after a few more shoves I had it teetering precariously on the edge; one last nudge would be enough to send it over. But I wanted to see it shatter — my reward for all this work — so I got up and carefully shuffled toward the edge until I could glimpse the floor of the gloomy chamber below. Then, holding my breath, I gave the trunk a little tap with my foot.

It hesitated for a moment, wobbling there on the edge of oblivion, and then pitched decisively forward and fell, tumbling end over end in beautiful balletic slow-motion. There came a tremendous echoing crash that seemed to rattle the whole house as a plume of dust shot up at me from below and I had to cover my face and retreat down the hall until it cleared. A minute later I came back and peeked again over the landing and saw not the pile of smashed wood that I had so fondly hoped for, but a jagged trunk-shaped hole in the floorboards. It had fallen straight through into the basement.

I raced downstairs and wriggled up to the edge of the buckled floor on my belly like you would a hole in thin ice. Fifteen feet below, through a haze of dust and darkness, I saw what remained of the trunk. It had shattered like a giant egg, its pieces all mixed up in a heap of debris and smashed floorboards. Scattered throughout were little pieces of paper. It looked like I'd found a box of letters, after all! But then, squinting, I could make out shapes on them — faces, bodies — and that's when I realized they weren't letters at all, but photographs. Dozens of them. I got excited — and then just as quickly went cold, because something dreadful occurred to me.

I have to go down there.

The basement was a meandering complex of rooms so lightless I may as well have explored them blindfolded. I descended the creaking stairs and stood at the bottom for a while, hoping my eyes would eventually adjust, but it was the kind of dark there was no adjusting to. I was also hoping I'd get used to the smell — a strange, acrid stink like the supply closet in a chemistry class-room — but no such luck. So I shuffled in, with my shirt collar pulled up over my nose and my hands held out in front of me, and hoped for the best.

I tripped and nearly fell. Something made of glass went skidding away across the floor. The smell only seemed to get worse. I began to imagine things lurking in the dark ahead of me. Forget monsters and ghosts — what if there was another hole in the floor? They'd never find my body.

Then I realized, in a minor stroke of genius, that by dialing up a menu screen on the cellphone I kept in my pocket (despite being ten miles from the nearest bar of reception), I could make a weak flashlight. I held it out, aiming the screen away from me. It barely penetrated the darkness, so I pointed it at the floor. Cracked flagstone and mouse turds. I aimed it to the side; a faint gleam reflected back.

I took a step closer and swept my phone around. Out of the darkness emerged a wall of shelves lined with glass jars. They were all shapes and sizes, mottled with dust and filled with gelatinous-looking things sus-pended in cloudy fluid. I thought of the kitchen and the exploded jars of fruits and vegetables I'd found there. Maybe the temperature was more stable down here, and that's why these had survived.

But then I got closer still, and looked a little harder, and realized they weren't fruits and vegetables at all, but organs. Brains. Hearts. Lungs. Eyes. All pickled in some kind of home-brewed formaldehyde, which explained the terrific stench. I gagged and stumbled away from them into the dark, simultaneously grossed out and baffled. What kind of place *was* this? Those jars were something you might expect to find in the basement of a fly-by-night medical school, not a house full of children. If not for all the wonderful things Grandpa Portman had said about this place, I might've wondered if Miss Peregrine had rescued the children just to harvest their organs.

When I'd recovered a little, I looked up to see another gleam ahead of me — not a reflection of my phone, but a weak glimmer of daylight. It had to be coming from the hole I'd made. I soldiered on, breathing through my pulled-up shirt and keeping away from the walls and any other ghastly surprises they might've harbored.

The gleam led me around a corner and into a small room with part of the ceiling caved in. Daylight streamed through the hole onto a mound of splintered floorboards and broken glass from which rose coils of silty dust, pieces of torn carpet plastered here and there like scraps of desiccated meat. Beneath the debris I could hear the scrabble of tiny feet, some rodentine dark-dweller that had survived the implosion of its world. In the midst of it all lay the demolished trunk, photographs scattered around it like confetti.

I picked my way through the wreckage, high-stepping javelins of wood and planks studded with rusting nails. Kneeling, I began to salvage what I could from the pile. I felt like a rescue worker, plucking faces from the debris, brushing away glass and wood rot. And though part of me wanted to hurry — there was no telling if or when the rest of the floor might collapse on my head — I couldn't stop myself from studying them.

At first glance, they looked like the kind of pictures you'd find in any old family album. There were shots of people cavorting on beaches and smiling on back porches, vistas from around the island, and lots of kids, posing in singles and pairs, informal snapshots and formal portraits taken in front of backdrops, their subjects clutching dead-eyed dolls, like they'd gone to Glamour Shots in some creepy turn-of-the-century shopping mall. But what I found really creepy wasn't the zombie dolls or the children's weird haircuts or how they never, ever seemed to smile, but that the more I studied the pictures, the more familiar they began to seem. They shared a certain nightmarish quality with my grandfather's old photos, especially the ones he'd kept hidden in the bottom of his cigar box, as if somehow they'd all come from the same batch.

There was, for instance, a photo of two young women posed before a not-terribly-convincing painted backdrop of the ocean. Not so strange in and of itself; the unsettling thing was *how* they were posed. Both had their backs to the camera. Why would you go to all the trouble and expense of having your picture taken — portraits were pricey back then — and then turn your back on the camera? I half-expected to find another photo in the debris of the same girls facing forward, revealing grinning skulls for faces.

Other pictures seemed manipulated in much the same way as some of my grandfather's had been. One was of a lone girl in a cemetery staring into a reflecting pool — but *two* girls were reflected back. It reminded me of Grandpa Portman's photo of

149

the girl "trapped" in a bottle, only whatever darkroom technique had been used wasn't nearly as fake-looking. Another was of a disconcertingly calm young man whose upper body appeared to be swarming with bees. That would be easy enough to fake, right? Like my grandfather's picture of the boy lifting what was certainly a boulder made from plaster. Fake rock — fake bees.

The hairs on the back of my neck stood up as I remembered something Grandpa Portman had said about a boy he'd known here in the children's home — a boy with bees living inside him. *Some would fly out every time he opened his mouth,* he had said, *but they never stung unless Hugh wanted them to.*

I could think of only one explanation. My grandfather's pictures had come from the trunk that lay smashed before me. I wasn't certain, though, until I found a picture of the freaks: two masked ruffle-collared kids who seemed to be feeding each other a coil of ribbon. I didn't know what they were supposed to be, exactly — besides fuel for nightmares; what were they, sadomasochistic ballerinas? — but there was no doubt in my mind that Grandpa Portman had a picture of these same two boys. I'd seen it in his cigar box just a few months ago.

154

It couldn't have been a coincidence, which meant that the photos my grandfather had shown me — that he'd sworn were of children he'd known in this house — *had really come from this house.* But could that mean, despite the doubts I'd harbored even as an eight-year-old, that the pictures were genuine? What about the fantastic stories that went along with them? That any of them could be true — *literally* true — seemed unthinkable. And yet, standing there in dusty half-light in that dead house that seemed so alive with ghosts, I thought, *maybe . . .*

Suddenly there came a loud crash from somewhere in the house above me, and I startled so badly that all the pictures slipped from my hands.

It's just the house settling, I told myself — *or caving in!* But as I bent down to gather the photos, the crash came again, and in an instant what meager light had shone through the hole in the floor faded away, and I found myself squatting in inky darkness.

I heard footsteps, and then voices. I strained to make out what they were saying, but I couldn't. I didn't dare move, afraid that the slightest motion would set off a noisy avalanche of debris all around me. I knew that my fear was irrational — it was probably just those dumb rapper kids pulling another prank — but my heart was beating a hundred miles an hour, and some deep animal instinct commanded me to be silent.

My legs began to go numb. As quietly as I could, I shifted my weight from one leg to the other to get the blood flowing again. A tiny piece of something came loose from the pile and rolled away, making a sound that seemed huge in the silence. The voices went quiet. Then a floorboard creaked right over my head and a little shower of plaster dust sprinkled down. Whoever was up there, they knew exactly where I was.

I held my breath.

Then, I heard a girl's voice say softly, "Abe? Is that you?"

I thought I'd dreamed it. I waited for the girl to speak again, but for a long moment there was only the sound of rain banking off the roof, like a thousand fingers tapping way off somewhere. Then a lantern glowed to life above me, and I craned my neck to see a half dozen kids kneeling around the craggy jaws of broken floor, peering down.

I recognized them somehow, though I didn't know where from. They seemed like faces from a half-remembered dream. Where had I seen them before — and how did they know my grandfather's name?

156

Then it clicked. Their clothes, strange even for Wales. Their pale unsmiling faces. The pictures strewn before me, staring up at me just as the children stared down. Suddenly I understood.

I'd seen them in the photographs.

The girl who'd spoken stood up to get a better look at me. In her hands she held a flickering light, which wasn't a lantern or a candle but seemed to be a ball of raw flame, attended by nothing more than her bare skin. I'd seen her picture not five minutes earlier, and in it she looked much the same as she did now, even cradling the same strange light between her hands.

I'm Jacob, I wanted to say. *I've been looking for you.* But my jaw had come unhinged, and all I could do was stare.

The girl's expression soured. I was wretched looking, damp from rain and dust-covered and squatting in a mound of debris. Whatever she and the other children had been expecting to find inside this hole in the floor, I was not it.

A murmur passed among them, and they stood up and quickly scattered. Their sudden movement knocked something loose in me and I found my voice again and shouted for them to wait, but they were already pounding the floorboards toward the door.

I tripped through the wreckage and stumbled blindly across the stinking basement to the stairs. But by the time I made it back to the ground floor, where the daylight they'd stolen had somehow returned, they had vanished from the house.

I bolted outside and down the crumbling brick steps into the grass, screaming, "Wait! Stop!" But they were gone. I scanned the yard, the woods, breathing hard, cursing myself.

Something snapped beyond the trees. I wheeled around to look and, through a screen of branches, caught a flash of blurred movement — the hem of a white dress. It was her. I crashed into the woods, sprinting after. She took off running down the path.

I hurdled fallen logs and ducked low branches, chasing her until my lungs burned. She kept trying to lose me, cutting from the path into the trackless forest and back. Finally the woods fell away and we broke into open bogland. I saw my chance. Now she had nowhere to hide — to catch her I had only to pour on the speed — and with me in sneakers and jeans and her in a dress it would be no contest. Just as I started to catch up, though, she made a sudden turn and plunged straight into the bog. I had no choice but to follow.

Running became impossible. The ground couldn't be trusted: It kept giving way, tripping me into knee-deep bog holes that soaked my pants and sucked at my legs. The girl, though, seemed to know just where to step, and she pulled farther and farther away, finally disappearing into the mist so that I had only her footprints to follow.

After she'd lost me, I kept expecting her prints to veer back toward the path, but they plowed ever-deeper into the bog. Then the mist closed behind me and I couldn't see the path anymore, and I began to wonder if I'd ever find my way out. I tried calling to her — *My name is Jacob Portman! I'm Abe's grandson! I won't hurt you!* — but the fog and the mud seemed to swallow my voice.

Her footprints led to a mound of stones. It looked like a big gray igloo, but it was a cairn — one of the Neolithic tombs after which Cairnholm was named.

The cairn was a little taller than me, long and narrow with a rectangular opening in one end, like a door, and it rose from the mud on a tussock of grass. Climbing out of the mire onto the relatively solid ground that ringed it, I saw that the opening was the entrance to a tunnel that burrowed deep inside. Intricate loops and spirals had been carved on either side, ancient hieroglyphs the meaning of which had been lost to the ages. *Here lies bog boy,* I thought. Or, more likely, *Abandon hope, all ye who enter here.*

But enter I did, because that's where the girl's footprints led. Inside, the cairn tunnel was damp and narrow and profoundly dark, so cramped that I could only move forward in a kind of hunchbacked crab-walk. Luckily, enclosed spaces were not one of the many things that scared the hell out of me.

Imagining the girl frightened and trembling somewhere up ahead, I talked to her as I went along, doing my best to reassure her that I meant no harm. My words came slapping back at me in a disorienting echo. Just as my thighs were starting to ache from the bizarre posture I'd been forced to adopt, the tunnel widened into a chamber, pitch black but big enough that I could stand and stretch my arms to either side without touching a wall.

I pulled out my phone and once more pressed it into service as a makeshift flashlight. It didn't take long to size up the place. It was a simple stone-walled chamber about as large as my bedroom — and it was completely empty. There was no girl to be found.

I was standing there trying to figure out how the hell she'd managed to slip by when something occurred to me — something so obvious that I felt like a fool for having taken this long to realize it. There never *was* any girl. I'd imagined her, and the rest of them, too. My brain had conjured them up at the very moment I was looking at their pictures. And the sudden, strange darkness that had preceded their arrival? A blackout.

It was impossible, anyway; those kids had all died a lifetime ago. Even if they hadn't, it was ridiculous to believe they would still look exactly as they had when the photos were taken. Everything had happened so quickly, though, I never had a chance to stop and wonder if I might be chasing a hallucination.

I could already predict Dr. Golan's explanation: *That house is such an emotionally loaded place for you, just being inside was enough to trigger a stress reaction.* Yeah, he was a psychobabble-spewing prick. But that didn't make him wrong.

I turned back, humiliated. Rather than crab-walking, I let go of the last of my dignity and just crawled on my hands and knees toward the gauzy light coming from the mouth of the tunnel. Looking up, I realized I'd seen this view before: in a photograph in Martin's museum of the place where they'd discovered the bog boy. It was baffling to think that people had once believed this foul-smelling wasteland was a gateway to heaven — and believed it with such conviction that a kid my age was willing to give up his life to get there. What a sad, stupid waste.

I decided then that I wanted to go home. I didn't care about the photos in the basement, and I was sick of riddles and mysteries and last words. Indulging my grandfather's obsession with them had made me worse, not better. It was time to let go.

I unfolded myself from the cramped cairn tunnel and stepped outside only to be blinded by light. Shielding my eyes, I squinted through split fingers at a world I hardly recognized. It was the same bog and the same path and the same everything as before, but for the first time since my arrival it was bathed in cheery yellow sunlight, the sky a candy blue, no trace of the twisting fog that, for me, had come to define this part of the island. It was warm, too, more like the dog days of summer than the breezy beginnings of it. *God, the weather changes fast around here,* I thought.

I slogged back to the path, trying to ignore the skin-crawly feeling of bog-mud gooshing into my socks, and headed for town. Strangely, the path wasn't muddy at all —

as if it had dried out in just a few minutes — but it had been carpet-bombed with so many grapefruit-size animal turds that I couldn't walk in a straight line. How had I not noticed this earlier? Had I been in some kind of psychotic haze all morning? Was I in one now?

I didn't look up from the turdy checkerboard that stretched out before me until I'd crossed the ridge and was coming back into town, which is when I realized where all the mess had come from. Where this morning a battalion of tractors had plied the gravel paths, hauling carts loaded with fish and peat-bricks up and down from the harbor, now those carts were being pulled by horses and mules. The clip-clop of hooves had replaced the growl of engines.

Missing, too, was the ever-present buzz of diesel generators. Had the island run out of gas in the few hours I'd been gone? And where had the townspeople been hiding all these big animals?

Also, why was everyone *looking* at me? Every person I passed stared at me goggle-eyed, stopping whatever they were doing to rubberneck as I walked by. *I must look as crazy as I feel,* I thought, glancing down to see that I was covered in mud from the waist down and plaster from the waist up, so I ducked my head and walked as fast as I could toward the pub, where at least I could hide in the anonymous gloom until Dad came back for lunch. I decided that when he did, I would tell him straight out that I wanted to go home as soon as possible. If he hesitated, I would admit that I'd been hallucinating, and we'd be on the next ferry, guaranteed.

Inside the Hole were the usual collection of inebriated men bent over foamy pint glasses and the battered tables and dingy decor I'd come to know as my home away from home. But as I headed for the staircase I heard an unfamiliar voice bark, "Where d'ya think yer going?"

I turned, one foot on the bottom step, to see the bartender looking me up and down. Only it wasn't Kev, but a scowling bullet-headed man I didn't recognize. He wore a bartender's apron and had a bushy unibrow and a caterpillar mustache that made his face look striped.

I might've said, *I'm going upstairs to pack my suitcase, and if my dad still won't take me home I'm going to fake a seizure,* but instead I answered, "Just up to my room," which came out sounding more like a question than a statement of fact.

"That so?" he said, clapping down the

glass he'd been filling. "This look like a hotel to you?"

Wooden creaks as patrons swiveled around in their stools to get a look at me. I quickly scanned their faces. Not one of them was familiar.

I'm having a psychotic episode, I thought. *Right now. This is what a psychotic episode feels like.* Only it didn't feel like anything. I wasn't seeing lightning bolts or having palm sweats. It was more like the world was going crazy, not me.

I told the bartender that there had obviously been some mistake. "My dad and I have the upstairs rooms," I said. "Look, I've got the key," and I produced it from my pocket as evidence.

"Lemme see that," he said, leaning over the counter to snatch it out of my hand. He held it up to the dingy light, eyeing it like a jeweler. "This ain't our key," he growled, then slipped it into his own pocket. "Now tell me what you really want up there — and this time, don't lie!"

I felt my face go hot. I'd never been called a liar by a nonrelative adult before. "I told you already. We rented those rooms! Just ask Kev if you don't believe me!"

"I don't know no Kev, and I don't fancy bein' fed stories," he said coolly. "There

167

ain't any rooms to let around here, and the only one lives upstairs is me!"

I looked around, expecting someone to crack a smile, to let me in on the joke. But the men's faces were like stone.

"He's American," observed a man sporting a prodigious beard. "Army, could be."

"Bollocks," another one growled. "Look at 'im. He's practically a fetus!"

"His mack, though," the bearded one said, reaching out to pinch the sleeve of my jacket. "You'd have a helluva time finding that in a shop. Army — gotta be."

"Look," I said, "I'm not in the army, and I'm not trying to pull anything on you, I swear! I just want to find my dad, get my stuff, and —"

"American, my arse!" bellowed a fat man. He peeled his considerable girth off a stool to stand between me and the door, toward which I'd been slowly backing. "His accent sounds rubbish to me. I'll wager he's a Jerry spy!"

"I'm not a spy," I said weakly. "Just lost."

"Got that right," he said with a laugh. "I say we get the truth out of 'im the old-fashioned way. With a rope!"

Drunken shouts of assent. I couldn't tell if they were being serious or just "taking a piss," but I didn't much care to stick around and find out. One undiluted instinct coursed through the anxious muddle in my brain: *Run.* It would be a lot easier to figure out what the hell was going on without a roomful of drunks threatening to lynch me. Of course, running away would only convince them of my guilt, but I didn't care.

I tried to step around the fat man.

He made a grab for me, but slow and drunk is no match for fast and scared shitless. I faked left and then dodged around him to the right. He howled with rage as the rest unglued themselves from barstools to lunge at me, but I slipped through their fingers and ran out the door and into the bright afternoon.

I charged down the street, my feet pounding divots into the gravel, the angry voices gradually fading behind me. At the first corner I made a skidding turn to escape their line of sight, cutting through a muddy yard, where squawking chickens dove out of my way, and then an open lot, where a line of women stood waiting to pump water from an old well, their heads turning as I flew past. A thought I had no time to entertain flitted through my head — *Hey, where'd the Waiting Woman go?* — but then I came to a low wall and had to concentrate on vaulting it — *plant the hand, lift the feet, swing over.* I landed in a busy path where I was nearly run down by a speeding cart. The driver yelled something derogatory about my mother as his horse's flank brushed my chest, leaving hoof prints and a wheel track just inches from my toes.

I had no idea what was happening. I understood only two things: that I was quite possibly in the midst of losing my mind, and that I needed to get away from people until I could figure out whether or not I actually was. To that end, I dashed into an alley behind two rows of cottages, where it seemed there would be lots of hiding places, and made for the edge of town. I slowed to a fast walk, hoping that a muddy and bedraggled American boy who was not running would attract somewhat less attention than one who was.

My attempt to act normal was not helped by the fact that every little noise or fleeting movement made me jump. I nodded and waved to a woman hanging laundry, but like everyone else she just stared at me. I walked faster.

I heard a strange noise behind me and ducked into an outhouse. As I waited there, hunkering behind the half-closed door, my eyes scanned the graffitied walls.

Dooleys a buggerloving arsehumper.
Wot, no sugar?

Finally, a dog slinked by, trailed by a litter of yapping puppies. I let out my breath and began to relax a little. Collecting my nerves, I stepped back into the alley.

Something grabbed me by the hair. Before I'd even had a chance to cry out, a hand whipped around from behind and pressed something sharp to my throat.

"Scream and I'll cut you," came a voice.

Keeping the blade to my neck, my assailant pushed me against the outhouse wall and stepped around to face me. To my great surprise, it wasn't one of the men from the pub. It was the girl. She wore a simple white dress and a hard expression, her face strikingly pretty even though she appeared to be giving serious thought to gouging out my windpipe.

"What are you?" she hissed.

"An — uh — I'm an American," I stammered, not quite sure what she was asking. "I'm Jacob."

She pressed the knife harder against my throat, her hand shaking. She was scared — which meant she was dangerous. "What were you doing in the house?" she demanded. "Why are you chasing me?"

"I just wanted to talk to you! Don't kill me!"

She fixed me with a scowl. "Talk to me about what?"

"About the house — about the people who lived there."

"Who sent you here?"

"My grandfather. His name was Abraham Portman."

Her mouth fell open. "That's a lie!" she cried, her eyes flashing. "You think I don't know what you are? I wasn't born yesterday! Open your eyes — let me see your eyes!"

"I am! They are!" I opened my eyes as wide as I could. She stood on tiptoes and stared into them, then stamped her foot and shouted, "No, your *real* eyes! Those fakes don't fool me any more than your ridiculous lie about Abe!"

"It's not a lie — and these *are* my eyes!" She was pushing so hard against my windpipe that it was difficult to breathe. I was glad the knife was dull or she surely would've cut me. "Look, I'm not whatever it is you think I am," I croaked. "I can prove it!"

Her hand relaxed a little. "Then prove it, or I'll water the grass with your blood!"

"I have something right here." I reached into my jacket.

She leapt back and shouted at me to stop, raising her blade so that it hung quivering in the air just between my eyes.

"It's only a letter! Calm down!"

She lowered the blade back to my throat, and I slowly drew Miss Peregrine's letter and photo from my jacket, holding it for her to see. "The letter's part of the reason I came here. My grandfather gave it to me. It's from the Bird. That's what you call your headmistress, isn't it?"

"This doesn't prove anything!" she said, though she'd hardly glanced at it. "And how do you know so bloody much about us?"

"I told you, my grandfather —"

She slapped the letter out of my hands. "I don't want to hear another word of that rubbish!" Apparently, I'd touched a nerve. She went quiet for a moment, face pinched with frustration, as if she were deciding how best to dispose of my body once she'd followed through on her threats. Before she could decide, though, shouts erupted from the other end of the alley. We turned to see the men from the pub running toward us, armed with wooden clubs and farm implements.

"What this? What've you done?"

"You're not the only person who wants to kill me!"

She took the knife from my throat and held it at my side instead, then grabbed me by the collar. "You are now my prisoner. Do exactly as I say or you'll regret it!"

I made no argument. I didn't know if my chances were any better in the hands of this unbalanced girl than with that slavering mob of club-wielding drunks, but at least with her I figured I had a shot at getting some answers.

She shoved me and we were off and running down a connecting alley. Halfway to the end she darted to one side and pulled me after her, both of us ducking under a line of sheets and hopping a chicken-wire fence into the yard of a little cottage.

"In here," she whispered and, looking around to make sure we hadn't been seen, pushed me through a door into a cramped hovel that reeked of peat smoke.

There was no one inside save an old dog asleep on a sofa. He opened one eye to look at us, didn't think much of what he saw, and went back to sleep. We darted to a window that looked out on the street and flattened ourselves against the wall next to it. We stood there listening, the girl careful to keep a hand on my arm and her knife at my side.

A minute passed. The men's voices

seemed to fade and then return; it was hard to tell where they were. My eyes drifted around the little room. It seemed excessively rustic, even for Cairnholm. Tilting in a corner was a stack of hand-woven baskets. A chair upholstered in burlap stood before a giant coal-fired cooking range cast from iron. Hung on the wall opposite us was a calendar, and though it was too dim to read from where we stood, just looking at it sparked a bizarre thought.

"What year is it?"

The girl told me to shut up.

"I'm serious," I whispered.

She regarded me strangely for a moment. "I don't know what you're playing at, but go have a look for yourself," she said, pushing me toward the calendar.

The top half was a black-and-white photo of a tropical scene, full-bodied girls with enormous bangs and vintage-looking swimsuits smiling on a beach. Printed above the seam was "September 1940." The first and second days of the month had been crossed out.

A detached numbness spread over me. I considered all the strange things I'd seen that morning: the bizarre and sudden change in the weather; the island I thought I'd known, now populated by strangers; how the style of everything around me looked old but the things themselves were new. It could all be explained by the calendar on the wall.

September 3, 1940. But *how?*

And then one of the last things my grandfather said came to me. *On the other side of the old man's grave.* It was something I'd never been able to figure out. There was a time I'd wondered if he'd meant ghosts — that since all the children he'd known here were dead, I'd have to go to the other side of the grave to find them — but that was too poetic. My grandfather was literal minded, not a man who traded in metaphor or suggestion. He'd given me straight-forward directions that he simply hadn't had time to explain: "The Old Man," I realized, was what the locals called the bog boy, and his grave was the cairn. And earlier today I had gone inside it and come out someplace else: September third, 1940.

All this occurred to me in the time it took for the room to turn upside down and my knees to go out from under me, and for everything to fade into pulsing, velvety black.

I awoke on the floor with my hands tied to the cooking range. The girl was pacing

176

nervously and appeared to be having an animated conversation with herself. I kept my eyes most of the way shut and listened.

"He *must* be a wight," she was saying. "Why else would he have been snooping around the old house like a burglar?"

"I haven't the slightest idea," someone else said, "but neither, it seems, does he." So she wasn't talking to herself, after all — though from where I was lying, I couldn't see the young man who'd spoken. "You say he didn't even realize he was in a loop?"

"See for yourself," she said, gesturing toward me. "Can you imagine any relative of Abe's being so perfectly clueless?"

"Can you imagine a wight?" said the young man. I turned my head slightly, scanning the room, but still I didn't see him.

"I can imagine a wight *faking* it," the girl replied.

The dog, awake now, trotted over and began to lick my face. I squeezed my eyes shut and tried to ignore it, but the tongue bath he gave me was so slobbery and gross that I finally had to sit up just to rescue myself.

"Well, look who's up!" the girl said. She clapped her hands, giving me a sarcastic round of applause. "That was quite the performance you gave earlier. I particularly enjoyed the fainting. I'm sure the theater lost a fine actor when you chose to devote yourself instead to murder and cannibalism."

I opened my mouth to protest my innocence — and stopped when I noticed a cup floating toward me.

"Have some water," the young man said. "Can't have you dying before we get you back to the headmistress, now can we?"

His voice seemed to come from the empty air. I reached for the cup, and as my pinky brushed an unseen hand, I nearly dropped it.

"He's clumsy," the young man said.

"You're invisible," I replied dumbly.

"Indeed. Millard Nullings, at your service."

"Don't tell him your name!" the girl cried.

"And this is Emma," he continued. "She's a bit paranoid, as I'm sure you've gathered."

Emma glared at him — or at the space I imagined him to occupy — but said nothing. The cup shook in my hand. I began another fumbling attempt to explain myself but was interrupted by angry voices from outside the window.

"Quiet!" Emma hissed. Millard's footsteps moved to the window, and the blinds parted an inch.

"What's happening?" asked Emma.

"They're searching the houses," he replied. "We can't stay here much longer."

"Well, we can't very well go out there!"

"I think perhaps we can," he said. "Just to be certain, though, let me consult my book." The blinds fell closed again and I saw a small leather-bound notebook rise from a table and crack open in midair. Millard hummed as he flipped the pages. A minute later he snapped the book shut.

"As I suspected!" he said. "We have only to wait a minute or so and then we can walk straight out the front door."

"Are you mad?" Emma said. "We'll have every one of those knuckle-draggers on us with brick bats!"

"Not if we're less interesting than what's about to happen," he replied. "I assure you, this is the best opportunity we'll have for hours."

I was untied from the range and led to the door, where we crouched, waiting. Then came a noise from outside even louder than the men's shouting: engines. Dozens, by the sound of it.

"Oh! Millard, that's brilliant!" cried Emma.

He sniffed. "And you said my studies were a waste of time."

Emma put her hand on the doorknob and then turned to me. "Take my arm. Don't run. Act like nothing's the matter." She put away her knife but assured me that if I tried to escape I'd see it again — just before she killed me with it.

"How do I know you won't anyway?"

She thought for a moment. "You don't." And then she pushed open the door.

The street outside was thronged with people, not only the men from the pub, whom I spotted immediately just down the block, but grimfaced shopkeepers and women and cart drivers who'd stopped what they were doing to stand in the middle of the road and crane their heads toward the sky. There, not far overhead, a squadron of Nazi fighter planes was roaring by in perfect formation. I'd seen photos of planes like these at Martin's museum, in a display titled "Cairnholm under Siege." How strange it must be, I thought, to find yourself, in the midst of an otherwise unremarkable afternoon, suddenly in the shadow of enemy death machines that could rain fire down upon you at a moment's notice.

We crossed the street as casually as possible, Emma clutching my arm in a death grip. We nearly made it to the alley on the

other side before someone finally noticed us. I heard a shout and we turned to see the men start after us.

We ran. The alley was narrow and lined with stables. We'd covered half its length when I heard Millard say, "I'll hang back and trip them up! Meet me behind the pub in precisely five and a half minutes!"

His footsteps fell away behind us, and when we'd reached the end of the alley Emma stopped me. We looked back to see a length of rope uncoil itself and float across the gravel at ankle height. It pulled taut just as the mob reached it, and they went sprawling over it and into the mud, a tangled heap of flailing limbs. Emma let out a cheer, and I was almost certain I could hear Millard laughing.

We ran on. I didn't know why Emma had agreed to meet Millard at the Priest Hole, since it was in the direction of the harbor, not the house. But since I also couldn't explain how Millard had known exactly when those planes were going to fly over, I didn't bother asking. I was even more baffled when, instead of sneaking around the back, any hope of our passing undetected was dashed by Emma pushing me right through the front door.

There was no one inside but the bartender. I turned and hid my face.

"Barman!" Emma said. "When's the tap open round here? I'm thirsty as a bloody mermaid!"

He laughed. "I ain't in the custom of servin' little girls."

"Never mind that!" she cried, slapping her hand on the bar. "Pour me a quadruple dram of your finest cask-strength whiskey. And none of that frightful watered-down piss you generally serve!"

I began to get the feeling she was just messing around — taking the piss, I should say — trying to one-up Millard and his rope-across-the-alley trick.

The bartender leaned across the bar. "So it's the hard stuff yer wantin', is it?" he said, grinning lecherously. "Just don't let your mum and dad hear, or I'll have the priest and constable after me both." He fetched a bottle of something dark and evil looking and began pouring her a tumbler full. "What about your friend, here? Drunk as a deacon already, I suppose?"

I pretended to study the fireplace.

"Shy one, ain't he?" said the barman. "Where's he from?"

"Says he's from the future," Emma replied. "I say he's mad as a box of weasels."

A strange look came over the bartender's

face. "Says he's what?" he asked. And then he must've recognized me because he gave a shout, slammed down the whiskey bottle, and began to scramble toward me.

I was poised to run, but before the bartender could even get out from behind the bar Emma had upended the drink he'd poured her, spilling brown liquor everywhere. Then she did something amazing. She held her hand palm-side down just above the alcohol-soaked bar, and a moment later a wall of foot-high flames erupted.

The bartender howled and began beating at the wall of fire with his towel.

"This way, prisoner!" Emma announced, and, hooking my arm, she pulled me toward the fireplace. "Now give me a hand! Pry and lift!"

She knelt and wedged her fingers into a crack that ran along the floor. I jammed my fingers in beside hers, and together we lifted a small section, revealing a hole about the width of my shoulders: the priest hole. As smoke filled the room and the bartender struggled to put out the flames, we lowered ourselves down one after another and disappeared.

The priest hole was little more than a shaft that dropped about four feet to a crawl space. It was pure black down there, but the next thing I knew it was filled with soft orange light. Emma had made a torch of her hand, a tiny ball of flame that seemed to hover just above her palm. I gaped at it, all else forgotten.

"Move it!" she barked, giving me a shove. "There's a door up ahead."

I shuffled forward until the crawl space came to a dead end. Then Emma pushed past me, sat down on her butt, and kicked the wall with both heels. It fell open into daylight.

"*There* you are," I heard Millard say as we crawled into an alley. "Can't resist a spectacle, can you?"

"I don't know what you're talking about," replied Emma, though I could tell she was pleased with herself.

Millard led us to a horse-drawn wagon that seemed to be waiting just for us. We crawled into the back, stowing away beneath a tarpaulin. In what seemed like no time, a man walked up and climbed onto the horse, flicked its reins, and we lurched into juddering motion.

We rode in silence for a while. I could tell from the changing noises around us that we were headed out of town.

I worked up the courage to ask a ques-

185

tion. "How'd you know about the wagon? And the planes? Are you psychic or something?"

Emma snickered. "Hardly."

"Because it all happened yesterday," Millard answered, "and the day before that. Isn't that how things go in your loop?"

"My what?"

"He isn't *from* any loop," Emma said, keeping her voice low. "I keep telling you — he's a damned wight."

"I think not. A wight never would've let you take him alive."

"See," I whispered. "I'm not a whatever-you-said. I'm Jacob."

"We'll just see about that. Now keep quiet." And she reached up and peeled back the tarpaulin a little, revealing a blue stripe of shifting sky.

Chapter Six

When the last cottages had disappeared behind us, we slipped quietly from the wagon and then crossed the ridge on foot in the direction of the forest. Emma walked on one side of me, silent and brooding, never letting go of my arm, while on the other Millard hummed to himself and kicked at stones. I was nervous and baffled and queasily excited all at the same time. Part of me felt like something momentous was about to happen. The other part of me expected to wake up at any moment, to come out of this fever dream or stress episode or whatever it was and wake up with my face in a puddle of drool on the Smart Aid break room table and think, *Well, that was strange,* and then return to the boring old business of being me.

But I didn't wake up. We just kept walking, the girl who could make fire with her hands and the invisible boy and me. We walked through the woods, where the path was as wide and clear as any trail in a national park, then emerged onto a broad expanse of lawn blooming with flowers and striped with neat gardens. We'd reached the house.

I gazed at it in wonder — not because it was awful, but because it was beautiful. There wasn't a shingle out of place or a broken window. Turrets and chimneys that had slumped lazily on the house I remembered now pointed confidently toward the sky. The forest that had seemed to devour its walls stood at a respectful distance.

I was led down a flagstone path and up a set of freshly painted steps to the porch. Emma no longer seemed to regard me as the threat she once did, but before going inside she tied my hands behind me — I think just for the sake of appearances. She was playing the returning hunter, and I was the captured prey. She was about to take me inside when Millard stopped her.

"His shoes are caked with filth," he said. "Can't have him tracking in mud. The Bird'll have an attack." So, as my captors waited, I removed my shoes and socks, also stained with mud. Then Millard suggested I roll up the cuffs of my jeans so they wouldn't drag on the carpet, and I did, and

Emma grabbed me impatiently and yanked me through the door.

We proceeded down a hall I remembered being almost impassably clogged with broken furniture, past the staircase, now gleaming with varnish, curious faces peeking at me through the banisters, through the dining room. The snowfall of plaster was gone; in its place was a long wooden table ringed by chairs. It was the same house I'd explored, but everything had been restored to order. Where I remembered patinas of green mold there was wallpaper and wainscoting and cheerful shades of paint. Flowers were arranged in vases. Sagging piles of rotted wood and fabric had rebuilt themselves into fainting couches and armchairs, and sunlight streamed through high windows once so grimy I'd thought they were blacked out.

Finally we came to a small room that looked out onto the back. "Keep hold of him while I inform the headmistress," Emma said to Millard, and I felt his hand grasp my elbow. When she left, it fell away.

"You're not afraid I'll eat your brain or something?" I asked him.

"Not particularly."

I turned to the window and gazed out in wonder. The yard was full of children, almost all of whom I recognized from yellowed photographs. Some lazed under shade trees; others tossed a ball and chased one another past flowerbeds exploding with color. It was exactly the paradise my grandfather had described. This was the enchanted island; these were the magical children. If I was dreaming, I no longer wanted to wake up. Or at least not anytime soon.

Out on the grassy pitch, someone kicked a ball too hard, and it flew up into a giant topiary animal and got stuck. Arranged all in a row were several of these animal bushes — fantastic creatures as tall as the house, standing guard against the woods — including a winged griffin, a rearing centaur, and a mermaid. Chasing after their lost ball, a pair of teenage boys ran to the base of the centaur, followed by a young girl. I instantly recognized her as the "levitating girl" from my grandfather's pictures, only now she wasn't levitating. She walked slowly, every plodding step a chore, anchored to the ground as if by some surplus of gravity.

When she reached the boys she raised her arms and they looped a rope around her waist. She slipped carefully out of her shoes and then bobbed up in the air like a balloon. It was astonishing. She rose until the rope around her waist went taut, then hovered ten feet off the ground, held by the two boys.

The girl said something and the boys nodded and began letting out the rope. She rose slowly up the side of the centaur; when she was level with its chest she reached into the branches for the ball, but it was stuck deep inside. She looked down and shook her head, and the boys reeled her down to the ground, where she stepped back into her weighted shoes and untied the rope.

"Enjoying the show?" asked Millard. I nodded silently. "There are far easier ways to retrieve that ball," he said, "but they know they have an audience."

Outside, a second girl was approaching the centaur. She was in her late teens and wild looking, her hair a nest well on its way to becoming dreadlocks. She bent down, took hold of the topiary's long leafy tail and wrapped it around her arm, then closed her eyes as if concentrating. A moment later I saw the centaur's hand move. I stared through the glass, fixed on that patch of green, thinking it must've been the breeze, but then each of its fingers flexed as if sensation were slowly returning to them. I watched, astonished, as the centaur's huge arm bent at the elbow and reached into its own chest, plucked out the ball, and tossed

191

it back to the cheering kids. As the game resumed, the wild-haired girl dropped the centaur's tail, and it went still once more.

Millard's breath fogged the window by me. I turned to him in amazement. "I don't mean to be rude," I said, "but what *are* you people?"

"We're peculiar," he replied, sounding a bit puzzled. "Aren't you?"

"I don't know. I don't think so."

"That's a shame."

"Why have you let go of him?" a voice behind us demanded, and I turned to see Emma standing in the doorway. "Oh, never mind," she said, coming over to grab the rope. "Come on. The headmistress will see you now."

We walked through the house, past more curious eyes peeping through door cracks and from behind sofas, and into a sunny sitting room, where on an elaborate Persian rug, in a high-backed chair, a distinguished-looking lady sat knitting. She was dressed head to toe in black, her hair pinned in a perfectly round knot atop her head, with lace gloves and a high-collared blouse fastened tightly at her throat — as fastidiously neat as the house itself. I could've guessed who she was even if I hadn't remembered her picture from those I'd found in the smashed trunk. This was Miss Peregrine.

Emma guided me onto the rug and cleared her throat, and the steady rhythm of Miss Peregrine's needles came to a halt.

"Good afternoon," the lady said, looking up. "You must be Jacob."

Emma gaped at her. "How do you know his —"

"My name is Headmistress Peregrine," she said, holding up a finger to silence Emma, "or if you prefer, since you are not currently under my care, Miss Peregrine. Pleased to finally meet you."

Miss Peregrine dangled a gloved hand in my direction and, when I failed to take it, noticed the rope that bound my wrists.

"Miss Bloom!" she cried. "What is the meaning of this? Is that any way to treat a guest? Free him at once!"

"But Headmistress! He's a snoop and a liar and I don't know what else!" Casting a mistrustful glance at me, Emma whispered something in Miss Peregrine's ear.

"Why, Miss Bloom," said Miss Peregrine, letting out a booming laugh. "What undiluted balderdash! If this boy were a wight you'd already be stewing in his soup kettle. Of course he's Abraham Portman's grand-

194

son. Just look at him!"

I felt a flush of relief; maybe I wouldn't have to explain myself after all. She'd been expecting me!

Emma began to protest, but Miss Peregrine shut her down with a withering glare. "Oh, all right," Emma sighed, "but don't say I didn't warn you." And with a few tugs at the knot, the rope fell away.

"You'll have to pardon Miss Bloom," said Miss Peregrine as I rubbed at my chafed wrists. "She has a certain flair for the dramatic."

"So I've noticed."

Emma scowled. "If he's who he says he is, then why don't he know the first thing about loops — or even what year he's in? Go on, ask him!"

"Why *doesn't* he know," Miss Peregrine corrected. "And the only person whom I'll be subjecting to questioning is you, tomorrow afternoon, regarding the proper use of grammatical tenses!"

Emma groaned.

"Now, if you don't mind," Miss Peregrine said, "I need to have a word with Mr. Portman in private."

The girl knew it was useless to argue. She sighed and went to the door, but before leaving turned to give me one last look over her shoulder. On her face was an expression I hadn't seen from her before: concern.

"You, too, Mr. Nullings!" Miss Peregrine called out. "Polite persons do not eavesdrop on the conversations of others!"

"I was only lingering to inquire if you should like some tea," said Millard, who I got the feeling was a bit of a suck-up.

"We should not, thank you," Miss Peregrine answered curtly. I heard Millard's bare feet slap away across the floorboards, and the door swung shut behind him.

"I would ask you to sit," said Miss Peregrine, gesturing at a cushy chair behind me, "but you appear to be encrusted with filth." Instead I knelt on the floor, feeling like a pilgrim begging advice from an all-knowing oracle.

"You've been on the island for several days now," Miss Peregrine said. "Why have you dawdled so long before paying us a visit?"

"I didn't know you were here," I said. "How'd you know *I* was?"

"I've been watching you. You've seen me as well, though perhaps you didn't realize it. I had assumed my alternate form." She reached up and pulled a long gray feather from her hair. "It's vastly preferable to assume the shape of a bird when observing humans," she explained.

My jaw dropped. "That was *you* in my room this morning?" I said. "The hawk?"

"The falcon," she corrected. "A peregrine, naturally."

"Then it's true!" I said. "You *are* the Bird!"

"It's a moniker I tolerate but do not encourage," she replied. "Now, to my question," continued Miss Peregrine. "What on earth were you searching for in that depressing old wreck of a house?"

"You," I replied, and her eyes widened a bit. "I didn't know how to find you. I only figured out yesterday that you were all —"

And then I paused, realizing how strange my next words would sound. "I didn't realize you were dead."

She flashed me a tight smile. "My goodness. Hasn't your grandfather told you *anything* about his old friends?"

"Some things. But for a long time I thought they were fairy tales."

"I see," she replied.

"I hope that doesn't offend you."

"It's a little surprising, that's all. But in general that is how we prefer to be thought of, for it tends to keep away unwanted visitors. These days fewer and fewer people believe in those things — fairies and goblins and all such nonsense — and thus common folk no longer make much of an effort to seek us out. That makes our lives a good bit easier. Ghost stories and scary old houses have served us well, too — though not, apparently, in your case." She smiled. "Lionheartedness must run in your family."

"Yeah, I guess so," I said with a nervous laugh, though in truth I felt as if I might pass out at any moment.

"In any case, as regards *this* place," she said, gesturing grandly. "As a child you believed your grandfather was 'making it all up,' as they say? Feeding you a great walloping pack of lies. Is that right?"

"Not *lies* exactly, but —"

"Fictions, whoppers, paradiddles — whatever terminology you like. When did you realize Abraham was telling you the truth?"

"Well," I said, staring at the labyrinth of interlocking patterns woven into the carpet, "I guess I'm just realizing it now."

Miss Peregrine, who had been so animated, seemed to fade a little. "Oh my, I see." And then her expression turned grim, as if, in the brief silence between us, she had intuited the terrible thing I'd come to tell her. And yet I still had to find a way to say it aloud.

"I think he wanted to explain everything," I said, "but he waited too long. So he sent me here to find you instead." I pulled the crumpled letter out of my jacket. "This is yours. It's what brought me here."

She smoothed it carefully over the arm of her chair and held it up, moving her lips as she read. "How ungraceful! the way I practically beg him for a reply." She shook her head, wistful for a moment. "We were always so desperate for news of Abe. I asked him once if he should like to worry me to death, the way he insisted on living out in the open like that. He could be so deucedly stubborn!"

She refolded the letter into its envelope, and a dark cloud seemed to pass over her. "He's gone, isn't he?"

I nodded. Haltingly, I told her what had happened — that is, I told her the story the cops had settled on and that, after a great deal of counseling, I, too, had come to believe. To keep from crying, I gave her only the broad strokes: He lived on the rural outskirts of town; we'd just been through a drought and the woods were full of starving, desperate animals; he was in the wrong place at the wrong time. "He shouldn't have been living alone," I explained, "but like you said, he was stubborn."

"I was afraid of this," she said. "I warned him not to leave." She made tight fists around the knitting needles in her lap, as if considering who to stab with them. "And then to make his poor grandson bear the awful news back to us."

I could understand her anger. I'd been through it myself. I tried to comfort her, reciting all the reassuring half-truths my parents and Dr. Golan had spun during my blackest moments last fall: "It was time for him to go. He was lonely. My grandma had been dead a lot of years already, and his mind wasn't sharp anymore. He was always forgetting things, getting mixed up. That's why he was out in the woods in the first place."

Miss Peregrine nodded sadly. "He let himself grow old."

"He was lucky in a way. It wasn't long and drawn-out. No months in a hospital hooked up to machines." That was ridiculous, of course — his death had been needless, obscene — but I think it made us both feel a little better to say it.

Setting aside her needlework, Miss Peregrine rose and hobbled to the window. Her gait was rigid and awkward, as if one of her legs were shorter than the other.

She looked out at the yard, at the kids playing. "The children mustn't hear of this," she said. "Not yet, at least. It would only

200

upset them."

"Okay. Whatever you think."

She stood quietly at the glass for a while, her shoulders trembling. When she finally turned to face me again, she was composed and businesslike. "Well, Mr. Portman," she said briskly, "I think you've been adequately interrogated. You must have questions of your own."

"Only about a thousand."

She pulled a watch from her pocket and consulted it. "We have some time before supper-hour. I hope that will prove sufficient to enlighten you."

Miss Peregrine paused and cocked her head. Abruptly, she strode to the sitting room door and threw it open to find Emma crouched on the other side, her face red and streaked with tears. She'd heard everything.

"Miss Bloom! Have you been eavesdropping?"

Emma struggled to her feet, letting out a sob.

"Polite persons do not listen to conversations that were not meant for —" but Emma was already running from the room, and Miss Peregrine cut herself short with a frustrated sigh. "That was most unfortunate. I'm afraid she's quite sensitive as regards your grandfather."

"I noticed," I said. "Why? Were they . . . ?"

"When Abraham left to fight in the war, he took all our hearts with him, but Miss Bloom's especially. Yes, they were admirers, paramours, sweethearts."

I began to understand why Emma had been so reluctant to believe me; it would mean, in all likelihood, that I was here to deliver bad news about my grandfather.

Miss Peregrine clapped her hands as if breaking a spell. "Ah, well," she said, "it can't be helped."

I followed her out of the room to the staircase. Miss Peregrine climbed it with grim resolve, holding the banister with both hands to pull herself up one step at a time, refusing any help. When we reached the landing, she led me down the hall to the library. It looked like a real classroom now, with desks arranged in a row and a chalkboard in one corner and books dusted and organized on the shelves. Miss Peregrine pointed to a desk and said, "Sit," so I squeezed into it. She took her place at the front of the room and faced me.

"Allow me to give you a brief primer. I think you'll find the answers to most of your questions contained herein."

"Okay."

"The composition of the human species is

infinitely more diverse than most humans suspect," she began. "The real taxonomy of Homo sapiens is a secret known to only a few, of whom you will now be one. At base, it is a simple dichotomy: there are the *coerlfolc,* the teeming mass of common people who make up humanity's great bulk, and there is the hidden branch — the cryptosapiens, if you will — who are called *syndrigast,* or "peculiar spirit" in the venerable language of my ancestors. As you have no doubt surmised, we here are of the latter type."

I bobbed my head as if I understood, though she'd already lost me. Hoping to slow her down a little, I asked a question.

"But why don't people know about you? Are you the only ones?"

"There are peculiars all over the world," she said, "though our numbers are much diminished from what they once were. Those who remain live in hiding, as we do." She lapsed into a soft regretful voice. "There was a time when we could mix openly with common folk. In some corners of the world we were regarded as shamans and mystics, consulted in times of trouble. A few cultures have retained this harmonious relationship with our people, though only in places where both modernity and the major religions have failed to gain a foothold, such as the black-magic island of Ambrym in the New Hebrides. But the larger world turned against us long ago. The Muslims drove us out. The Christians burned us as witches. Even the pagans of Wales and Ireland eventually decided that we were all malevolent faeries and shape-shifting ghosts."

"So why didn't you just — I don't know — make your own country somewhere? Go and live by yourselves?"

"If only it had been that simple," she said. "Peculiar traits often skip a generation, or ten. Peculiar children are not always, or even usually, born to peculiar parents, and peculiar parents do not always, or even usually, bear peculiar children. Can you imagine, in a world so afraid of otherness, why this would be a danger to all peculiar-kind?"

"Because normal parents would be freaked out if their kids started to, like, throw fire?"

"Exactly, Mr. Portman. The peculiar offspring of common parents are often abused and neglected in the most horrific ways. It wasn't so many centuries ago that the parents of peculiar children simply assumed that their 'real' sons or daughters had been made off with and replaced with changelings — that is, enchanted and malevolent, not to mention entirely fictitious, lookalikes — which in darker times was considered a license to abandon the poor children, if not kill them outright."

"That's awful."

"Extremely. Something had to be done, so people like myself created places where young peculiars could live apart from common folk — physically and temporally isolated enclaves like this one, of which I am enormously proud."

"People like yourself?"

"We peculiars are blessed with skills that common people lack, as infinite in combination and variety as others are in the pigmentation of their skin or the appearance of their facial features. That said, some skills are common, like reading thoughts, and others are rare, such as the way I can manipulate time."

"Time? I thought you turned into a bird."

"To be sure, and therein lies the key to my skill. Only birds can manipulate time. Therefore, all time manipulators must be able to take the form of a bird."

She said this so seriously, so matter-of-factly, that it took me a moment to process. "Birds . . . are time travelers?" I felt a goofy smile spread across my face.

Miss Peregrine nodded soberly. "Most, however, slip back and forth only occasionally, by accident. We who can manipulate time fields consciously — and not only for ourselves, but for others — are known as *ymbrynes.* We create temporal loops in which peculiar folk can live indefinitely."

"A loop," I repeated, remembering my grandfather's command: *find the bird, in the loop.* "Is that what this place is?"

"Yes. Though you may better know it as the third of September, 1940."

I leaned toward her over the little desk. "What do you mean? It's only the one day? It repeats?"

"Over and over, though our experience of it is continuous. Otherwise we would have no memory of the last, oh, seventy years that we've resided here."

"That's amazing," I said.

"Of course, we were here on Cairnholm a decade or more *before* the third of September, 1940 — physically isolated, thanks to the island's unique geography — but it wasn't until that date that we also needed temporal isolation."

"Why's that?"

"Because otherwise we all would've been killed."

"By the bomb."

"Assuredly so."

I gazed at the surface of the desk. It was all starting to make sense — though just barely. "Are there other loops besides this one?"

"Many," she said, "and nearly all the ymbrynes who mother over them are friends of mine. Let me see: There's Miss Gannett in Ireland, in June of 1770; Miss Nightjar in Swansea on April 3, 1901; Miss Avocet and Miss Bunting together in Derbyshire on Saint Swithin's Day of 1867; Miss Treecreeper I don't remember where exactly — oh, and dear Miss Finch. Somewhere I have a lovely photograph of her."

Miss Peregrine wrestled a massive photo album down from a shelf and set it before me on the desk. She leaned over my shoulder as she turned the stiff pages, looking for a certain picture but pausing to linger over others, her voice tinged with dreamy nostalgia. As they flicked by I recognized photos from the smashed trunk in the basement and from my grandfather's cigar box. Miss Peregrine had collected them all. It was strange to think that she'd shown these same pictures to my grandfather all those years ago, when he was my age — maybe right here in this room, at this desk — and now she was showing them to me, as if somehow I'd stepped into his past.

Finally she came to a photo of an ethereal-looking woman with a plump little bird perched on her hand, and said, "This is Miss Finch and her auntie, Miss Finch." The woman and the bird seemed to be communicating.

"How could you tell them apart?" I asked.

"The elder Miss Finch preferred to stay a finch most all of the time. Which was just as well, really. She never was much of a conversationalist."

Miss Peregrine turned a few more pages, this time landing on a group portrait of women and children gathered humorlessly around a paper moon.

"Ah, yes! I'd nearly forgotten about this one." She slipped the photo out of its album sleeve and held it up reverently. "The lady in front there, that's Miss Avocet. She's as close to royalty as we peculiars have. They tried for fifty years to elect her leader of the Council of Ymbrynes, but she would never give up teaching at the academy she and Miss Bunting founded. Today there's not an ymbryne worth her wings who didn't pass under Miss Avocet's tutelage at one time, myself included! In fact, if you look closely you might recognize that little girl in the glasses."

I squinted. The face she pointed to was dark and slightly blurred. "Is that you?"

"I was one of the youngest Miss Avocet ever took on," she said proudly.

"What about the boys in the picture?" I said. "They look even younger than you."

Miss Peregrine's expression darkened. "You're referring to my misguided brothers. Rather than split us up, they came along to the academy with me. Mollycoddled like a pair of little princes, they were. I dare say it's what turned them rotten."

"They weren't ymbrynes?"

"Oh, *no,*" she huffed. "Only *women* are born ymbrynes, and thank heaven for that! Males lack the seriousness of temperament required of persons with such grave responsibilities. We ymbrynes must scour the countryside for young peculiars in need, steer clear of those who would do us harm, and keep our wards fed, clothed, hidden, and steeped in the lore of our people. And as if that weren't enough, we must also ensure that our loops reset each day like clockwork."

"What happens if they don't?"

She raised a fluttering hand to her brow and staggered back, pantomiming horror. "Catastrophe, cataclysm, disaster! I dare not even think of it. Fortunately, the mechanism

by which loops are reset is a simple one: One of us must cross through the entryway every so often. This keeps it pliable, you see. The ingress point is a bit like a hole in fresh dough; if you don't poke a finger into it now and then the thing may just close up on its own. And if there's no ingress or egress — no valve through which may be vented the various pressures that accrue naturally in a closed temporal system —" She made a little *poof!* gesture with her hands, as if miming the explosion of a firecracker. "Well, the whole thing becomes unstable."

She bent over the album again and riffled through its pages. "Speaking of which, I may have a picture of — yes, here it is. An ingress point if ever there was one!" She pulled another picture from its sleeve. "This is Miss Finch and one of her wards in the magnificent entryway to Miss Finch's loop, in a rarely used portion of the London Underground. When it resets, the tunnel fills with the most terrific glow. I've always thought our own rather modest by comparison," she said with a hint of envy.

"Just to make sure I understand," I said. "If today is September third, 1940, then tomorrow is . . . *also* September third?"

"Well, for a few of the loop's twenty-four

hours it's September second, but, yes, it's the third."

"So tomorrow never comes."

"In a manner of speaking."

Outside, a distant clap of what sounded like thunder echoed, and the darkening window rattled in its frame. Miss Peregrine looked up and again drew out her watch.

"I'm afraid that's all the time I have at the moment. I do hope you'll stay for supper."

I said that I would; that my father might be wondering where I was hardly crossed my mind. I squeezed out from behind the desk and began following her to the door, but then another question occurred to me, one that had been nagging at me for a long time.

"Was my grandfather really running from the Nazis when he came here?"

"He was," she said. "A number of children came to us during those awful years leading up to the war. There was so much upheaval." She looked pained, as if the memory was still fresh. "I found Abraham at a camp for displaced persons on the mainland. He was a poor, tortured boy, but so strong. I knew at once that he belonged with us."

I felt relieved; at least that part of his life was as I had understood it to be. There was one more thing I wanted to ask, though, and I didn't quite know how to put it.

"Was he — my grandfather — was he like . . ."

"Like us?"

I nodded.

She smiled strangely. "He was like you, Jacob." And she turned and hobbled toward the stairs.

Miss Peregrine insisted that I wash off the bog mud before sitting down to dinner, and asked Emma to run me a bath. I think she hoped that by talking to me a little, Emma would start to feel better. But she wouldn't even look at me. I watched as she ran cold water into the tub and then warmed it with her bare hands, swirling them around until steam rose.

"That is awesome," I said. But she left without saying a word in response.

Once I'd turned the water thoroughly brown, I toweled off and found a change of clothes hanging from the back of the door — baggy tweed pants, a button-up shirt, and a pair of suspenders that were far too short but that I couldn't figure out how to adjust. I was left with the choice of wearing the pants either around my ankles or hitched up to my bellybutton. I decided the latter was the lesser of evils, so I went downstairs to have what would likely be the strangest meal of my life while dressed like a clown without makeup.

Dinner was a dizzying blur of names and faces, many of them half-remembered from photographs and my grandfather's long-ago descriptions. When I came into the dining room, the kids, who'd been clamoring noisily for seats around the long table, froze and stared at me. I got the feeling they didn't get a lot of dinner guests. Miss Peregrine, already seated at the head of the table, stood up and used the sudden quiet as an opportunity to introduce me.

"For those of you who haven't already had the pleasure of meeting him," she announced, "this is Abraham's grandson, Jacob. He is our honored guest and has come a very long way to be here. I hope you will treat him accordingly." Then she pointed to each person in the room and recited their names, most of which I immediately forgot, as happens when I'm nervous. The introductions were followed by a barrage of questions, which Miss Peregrine batted away with rapid-fire efficiency.

"Is Jacob going to stay with us?"

"Not to my knowledge."

"Where's Abe?"

"Abe is busy in America."

"Why does Jacob got Victor's trousers on?"

"Victor doesn't need them anymore, and Mr. Portman's are being washed."

"What's Abe doing in America?"

At this question I saw Emma, who had been glowering in a corner, rise from her chair and stalk out of the room. The others, apparently used to her volatile moods, paid no attention.

"Never mind what Abe's doing," Miss Peregrine snapped.

"When's he coming back?"

"Never mind that, too. Now let's eat!"

Everyone stampeded to their seats. Thinking I'd found an empty chair, I went to sit and felt a fork jab my thigh. "Excuse me!" cried Millard. But Miss Peregrine made him give it up anyway, sending him out to put on clothes.

"How many times must I tell you," she called after him, "polite persons do not take their supper in the nude!"

Kids with kitchen duty appeared bearing trays of food, all covered with gleaming silver tops so that you couldn't see what was inside, sparking wild speculation about what might be for dinner.

"Otters Wellington!" one boy cried.

"Salted kitten and shrew's liver!" another

said, to which the younger children responded with gagging sounds. But when the covers were finally lifted, a feast of kingly proportions was revealed: a roasted goose, its flesh a perfect golden brown; a whole salmon and a whole cod, each outfitted with lemons and fresh dill and pats of melting butter; a bowl of steamed mussels; platters of roasted vegetables; loaves of bread still cooling from the oven; and all manner of jellies and sauces I didn't recognize but that looked delicious. It all glowed invitingly in the flicker of gaslight lamps, a world away from the oily stews of indeterminate origin I'd been choking down at the Priest Hole. I hadn't eaten since breakfast and proceeded to stuff myself silly.

It shouldn't have surprised me that peculiar children have peculiar eating habits, but between forkfuls of food I found myself sneaking glances around the room. Olive the levitating girl had to be belted into a chair screwed to the floor so that she wouldn't float up to the ceiling. So the rest of us wouldn't be plagued by insects, Hugh, the boy who had bees living in his stomach, ate under a large mosquito net at a table for one in the corner. Claire, a doll-like girl with immaculate golden curls, sat next to Miss Peregrine but ate not a morsel.

"Aren't you hungry?" I asked her.

"Claire don't eat with the rest of us," Hugh volunteered, a bee escaping from his mouth. "She's embarrassed."

"I am not!" she said, glaring at him.

"Yeah? Then eat something!"

"No one here is *embarrassed* of their gift," Miss Peregrine said. "Miss Densmore simply prefers to dine alone. Isn't that right, Miss Densmore?"

The girl stared at the empty place before her, clearly wishing that all the attention would vanish.

"Claire has a backmouth," explained Millard, who sat beside me now in a smoking jacket (and nothing else).

"A what?"

"Go on, show him!" someone said. Soon everyone at the table was pressuring Claire to eat something. And finally, just to shut them up, she did.

A leg of goose was set before her. She turned around in her chair, and gripping its arms she bent over backward, dipping the back of her head to the plate. I heard a distinct smacking sound, and when she lifted her head again a giant bite had disappeared from the goose leg. Beneath her golden hair was a set of sharp-toothed jaws. Suddenly, I understood the strange picture of Claire that I'd seen in Miss Peregrine's album, to which the photographer had devoted two panels: one for her daintily pretty face and another for the curls that so thoroughly masked the back of her head.

Claire turned forward and crossed her arms, annoyed that she'd let herself be talked into such a humiliating demonstration. She sat in silence while the others peppered me with questions. After Miss Peregrine had dismissed a few more about my grandfather, the children turned to other subjects. They seemed especially interested in what life in the twenty-first century was like.

"What sort of flying motorcars do you have?" asked a pubescent boy named Horace, who wore a dark suit that made him look like an apprentice undertaker.

"None," I said. "Not yet, anyway."

"Have they built cities on the moon?" another boy asked hopefully.

"We left some garbage and a flag there in the sixties, but that's about it."

"Does Britain still rule the world?"

"Uh . . . not exactly."

They seemed disappointed. Sensing an opportunity, Miss Peregrine said, "You see, children? The future isn't so grand after all. Nothing wrong with the good old here and

now!" I got the feeling this was something she often tried to impress upon them, with little success. But it got me wondering: Just how long had they been here, in the "good old here and now?"

"Do you mind if I ask how old you all are?" I said.

"I'm eighty-three," said Horace.

Olive raised her hand excitedly. "I'll be seventy-five and a half next week!" I wondered how they kept track of the months and years if the days never changed.

"I'm either one hundred seventeen or one hundred eighteen," said a heavy-lidded boy named Enoch. He looked no more than thirteen. "I lived in another loop before this one," he explained.

"I'm nearly eighty-seven," said Millard with his mouth full of goose drippings, and as he spoke a half-chewed mass quavered in his invisible jaw for all to see. There were groans as people covered their eyes and looked away.

Then it was my turn. I was sixteen, I told them. I saw a few kids' eyes widen. Olive laughed in surprise. It was strange to them that I should be so young, but what was strange to me was how young *they* seemed. I knew plenty of eighty-year-olds in Florida, and these kids acted nothing like them. It was as if the constance of their lives here, the unvarying days — this perpetual death-less summer — had arrested their emotions as well as their bodies, sealing them in their youth like Peter Pan and his Lost Boys.

A sudden boom sounded from outside, the second one this evening, but louder and closer than the first, rattling silverware and plates.

"Hurry up and finish, everyone!" Miss Peregrine sang out, and no sooner had she said it than another concussion jolted the house, throwing a framed picture off the wall behind me.

"What *is* that?" I said.

"It's those damned Jerries again!" growled Olive, thumping her little fist on the table, clearly in imitation of some ill-tempered adult. Then I heard what sounded like a buzzer going off somewhere far away, and suddenly it occurred to me what was hap-pening. This was the night of September third, 1940, and in a little while a bomb was going to fall from the sky and blow a giant hole in the house. The buzzer was an air-raid siren, sounding from the ridge.

"We have to get out of here," I said, panic rising in my throat. "We have to go before the bomb hits!"

"He doesn't know!" giggled Olive. "He

thinks we're going to die!"

"It's only the changeover," said Millard with a shrug of his smoking jacket. "No reason to get your knickers in a twist."

"This happens every night?"

Miss Peregrine nodded. "Every single evening," she said. Somehow, though, I was not reassured.

"May we go outside and show Jacob?" said Hugh.

"Yes, may we?" Claire begged, suddenly enthused after twenty minutes of sulking. "The changeover is ever so beautiful!"

Miss Peregrine demurred, pointing out that they hadn't yet finished their dinners, but the children pleaded with her until she relented. "All right, so long as you all wear your masks," she said.

The children burst out of their seats and ran from the room, leaving poor Olive behind until someone took pity and came to unbelt her from her chair. I ran after them through the house into the wood-paneled foyer, where they each grabbed something from a cabinet before bounding out the door. Miss Peregrine gave me one, too, and I stood turning it over in my hands. It looked like a sagging face of black rubber, with wide glass portholes like eyes that were frozen in shock, and a droopy snout that ended in a perforated canister.

"Go ahead," said Miss Peregrine. "Put it on." Then I realized what it was: a gas mask.

I strapped it over my face and followed her out onto the lawn, where the children stood scattered like chess pieces on an unmarked board, anonymous behind their upturned masks, watching billows of black smoke roll across the sky. Treetops burned in the hazy distance. The drone of unseen airplanes seemed to come from everywhere.

Now and then came a muffled blast I could feel in my chest like the thump of a second heart, followed by waves of broiling heat, like someone opening and closing an oven right in front of me. I ducked at each concussion, but the kids never so much as flinched. Instead they sang, their lyrics timed perfectly to the rhythm of the bombs.

Run, rabbit, run, rabbit, run, run, RUN!
Bang, bang, BANG goes the farmer's gun
He'll get by without his rabbit pie, so
Run, rabbit, run, rabbit, RUN!

Bright tracer bullets scored the heavens just as the song ended. The kids applauded like onlookers at a fireworks display, violent slashes of color reflected in their masks. This nightly assault had become such a regular

225

part of their lives that they'd ceased to think of it as something terrifying — in fact, the photograph I'd seen of it in Miss Peregrine's album had been labeled *Our beautiful display.* And in its own morbid way, I suppose it was.

It began to drizzle, as if all that flying metal had riven holes in the clouds. The concussions came less frequently. The attack seemed to be ending.

The children started to leave. I thought we were going back inside, but they passed the front door and headed for another part of the yard.

"Where are we going?" I asked two masked kids.

They said nothing, but seeming to sense my anxiety, they took me gently by the hands and led me along with the others. We rounded the house to the back corner, where everyone was gathering around a giant topiary. This one wasn't a mythical creature, though, but a man reposing in the grass, one arm supporting him, the other pointing to the sky. It took a moment before I realized that it was a leafy replica of Michelangelo's fresco of Adam from the Sistine Chapel. Considering that it was made from bushes, it was really impressive. You could almost make out the placid

our beautiful display

expression on Adam's face, which had two blooming gardenias for eyes.

I saw the wild-haired girl standing nearby. She wore a flower-print dress that had been patched so many times it almost looked like a quilt. I went over to her and, pointing to Adam, said, "Did you make this?"

The girl nodded.

"How?"

She bent down and held one of her palms above the grass. A few seconds later, a hand-shaped section of blades wriggled and stretched and grew until they were brushing the bottom of her palm.

"That," I said, "is crazy." Clearly, I was not at my most articulate.

Someone shushed me. The children were all standing silently with their necks craned, pointing at a section of sky. I looked up but could see only clouds of smoke, the flickering orange of fires reflected against them.

Then I heard a single airplane engine cut through the rest. It was close, and getting closer. Panic flooded me. *This is the night they were killed. Not just the night, but the moment.* Could it be, I wondered, that these children died every evening only to be resurrected by the loop, like some Sisyphean suicide cult, condemned to be blown up and stitched back together for eternity?

Something small and gray parted the clouds and came hurtling toward us. *A rock,* I thought, but rocks don't whistle as they fall.

Run, rabbit, run, rabbit, run. I would've but now there was no time; all I could do was scream and dive to the ground for cover. But there was no cover, so I hit the grass and threw my arms over my head as if somehow that would keep it attached to my body.

I clenched my jaw and shut my eyes and held my breath, but instead of the deafening blast I was bracing for, everything went completely, profoundly quiet. Suddenly there were no growling engines, no whistling bombs, no pops of distant guns. It was as if someone had muted the world.

Was I dead?

I uncovered my head and slowly looked behind me. The windbent boughs of trees were frozen in place. The sky was a photograph of arrested flames licking a cloud bank. Drops of rain hung suspended before my eyes. And in the middle of the circle of children, like the object of some arcane ritual, there hovered a bomb, its downward-facing tip seemingly balanced on Adam's outstretched finger.

Then, like a movie that burns in the

projector while you're watching it, a bloom of hot and perfect whiteness spread out before me and swallowed everything.

The first thing I heard when I could hear again was laughter. Then the white faded away and I saw that we were all arranged around Adam just as we had been before, but now the bomb was gone and the night was quiet and the only light in the cloudless sky was a full moon. Miss Peregrine appeared above me and held out her hand. I took it, stumbling to my feet in a daze.

"Please accept my apologies," she said. "I should have better prepared you." She couldn't hide her smile, though, and neither could the other kids as they stripped off their masks. I was pretty sure I'd just been hazed.

I felt lightheaded and out-of-sorts. "I should probably head home for the night," I said to Miss Peregrine. "My dad'll worry." Then I added quickly, "I *can* go home, right?"

"Of course you can," she replied, and in a loud voice asked for a volunteer to escort me back to the cairn. To my surprise, Emma stepped forward. Miss Peregrine seemed pleased.

"Are you sure about her?" I whispered to

the headmistress. "A few hours ago she was ready to slit my throat."

"Miss Bloom may be hot-tempered, but she is one of my most trusted wards," she replied. "And I think you and she may have a few things to discuss away from curious ears."

Five minutes later the two of us were on our way, only this time my hands weren't tied and she wasn't poking a knife in my spine. A few of the younger kids trailed us as far as the edge of the yard. They wanted to know whether I'd be back again tomorrow. I made vague assurances, but I could hardly wrap my mind around what was happening at this moment, much less in the future.

We passed into the dark woods alone. When the house had disappeared behind us, Emma held out an upturned palm, flicked her wrist, and a petite ball of fire flared to life just above her fingers. She held it before her like a waiter carrying a tray, lighting the path and casting our twin shadows across the trees.

"Have I told you how cool that is?" I said, trying to break a silence that grew more awkward by the second.

"It isn't cool at all," she replied, swinging the flame close enough that I could feel its radiating heat. I dodged it and fell back a few paces.

"I didn't mean — I meant it's cool that you can *do* that."

"Well, if you'd speak properly I might understand you," she snapped, then stopped walking.

We stood facing each other from a careful distance. "You don't have to be afraid of me," she said.

"Oh yeah? How do I know you don't think I'm some evil creature and this is just a plot to get me alone so you can finally kill me?"

"Don't be stupid," she said. "You came unannounced, a stranger I didn't recognize, and chased after me like a madman. What was I meant to think?"

"Fine, I get it," I said, though I didn't really mean it.

She dropped her eyes and began digging a little hole in the dirt with the tip of her boot. The flame in her hand changed color, fading from orange to a cool indigo. "It's not true, what I said. I did recognize you." She looked up at me. "You look so much like him."

"People tell me that sometimes."

"I'm sorry I said all those terrible things earlier. I didn't want to believe you — that you were who you said. I knew what it would mean."

"It's okay," I replied. "When I was growing up, I wanted so much to meet all of you. Now that it's finally happening . . ." I shook my head. "I'm just sorry it has to be because of this."

And then she rushed at me and threw her arms around my neck, the flame in her hand snuffing out just before she touched me, her skin hot where she'd held it. We stood like that in the darkness for a while, me and this teenaged old woman, this rather beautiful girl who had loved my grandfather when he was the age I am now. There was nothing I could do but put my arms around her, too, so I did, and after a while I guess we were both crying.

I heard her take a deep breath in the dark, and then she broke away. The fire flared back to life in her hand.

"Sorry about that," she said. "I'm not usually so . . ."

"Don't worry about it."

"We should be getting on."

"Lead the way," I said.

We walked through the woods in a comfortable silence. When we came to the bog she said, "Step only where I step," and I did, planting my feet in her prints. Bog gases flared up in green pyres in the distance, as if in sympathy with Emma's light.

We reached the cairn and ducked inside, shuffling in single-file to the rear chamber and then out again to a world shrouded in mist. She guided me back to the path, and when we reached it she laced her fingers through mine and squeezed. We were quiet for a moment. Then she turned and went back, the fog swallowing her so quickly that for a moment I wondered if she'd been there at all.

Returning to town, I half-expected to find horse-drawn wagons roaming the streets. Instead I was welcomed by the hum of generators and the glow of TV screens behind cottage windows. I was home, such as it was.

Kev was manning the bar again and raised a glass in my direction as I came in. None of the men in the pub offered to lynch me. All seemed right with the world.

I went upstairs to find Dad asleep in front of his laptop at our little table. When I shut the door he woke with a start.

"Hi! Hey! You're out late. Or are you? What time is it?"

"I don't know," I said. "Before nine I think. The gennies are still on."

He stretched and rubbed his eyes.

"What'd you do today? I was hoping I'd see you for dinner."

"Just explored the old house some more."

"Find anything good?"

"Uh . . . not really," I said, realizing that I probably should've bothered to concoct a more elaborate cover story.

He looked at me strangely. "Where'd you get those?"

"Get what?"

"Your clothes," he said.

I looked down and realized I'd completely forgotten about the tweed-pants-and-suspenders outfit I was wearing. "I found them in the house," I said, because I didn't have time to think of a less weird answer. "Aren't they cool?"

He grimaced. "You put on clothes that you *found?* Jake, that's unsanitary. And what happened to your jeans and jacket?"

I needed to change the subject. "They got super dirty, so I, uh . . ." I trailed off, making a point of noticing the document on his computer screen. "Whoa, is that your book? How's it coming?"

He slapped the laptop shut. "My book isn't the issue right now. What's important is our time here be therapeutic for you. I'm not sure that spending your days alone in that old house is really what Dr. Golan had in mind. When he green-lighted this trip."

"Wow, I think that was the record," I said.

"What?"

"The longest streak ever of you not mentioning my psychiatrist." I pretended to look at a nonexistent wristwatch. "Four days, five hours, and twenty-six minutes." I sighed. "It was good while it lasted."

"That man has been a great help to you," he said. "God only knows the state you'd be in right now if we hadn't found him."

"You're right, Dad. Dr. Golan did help me. But that doesn't mean he has to control every aspect of my life. I mean, Jesus, you and mom might as well buy me one of those little bracelets that says *What Would Golan Do?* That way I can ask myself before I do anything. Before I take a dump. How would Dr. Golan want me to take this dump? Should I bank it off the side or go straight down the middle? What would be the most psychologically beneficial dump I could take?"

Dad didn't say anything for a few seconds, and when he did his voice was all low and gravelly. He told me I was going birding with him the next day whether I liked it or not. When I replied that he was sadly mistaken, he got up and went downstairs to the pub. I thought he'd be drinking or something, so I went to change out of my clown clothes, but a few minutes later he knocked on my bedroom door and said there was someone on the phone for me.

I figured it was Mom, so I gritted my teeth and followed him downstairs to the phone booth in the far corner of the pub. He handed me the receiver and went to sit at a table. I slid the door closed.

"Hello?"

"I just spoke to your father," a man said. "He sounded a little upset."

It was Dr. Golan.

I wanted to say that he and my dad could both stuff it up their asses, but I knew this situation required some tact. If I pissed Golan off now it would be the end of my trip. I couldn't leave yet, not with so much more to learn about the peculiar children. So I played along and explained what I'd been up to — all except the kids-in-a-time-loop part — and tried to make it sound like I was coming around to the idea that there was nothing special about the island or my grandfather. It was like a mini-session over the phone.

"I hope you're not just telling me what I want to hear," he said. That had become his standard line. "Maybe I should come out there and check on you. I could use a little vacation. How does that sound?"

Please be joking, I prayed.

"I'm okay. Really," I said.

"Relax, Jacob, I'm only kidding, though Lord knows I *could* use some time away from the office. And actually, I believe you. You do sound okay. In fact, just now I told your father that probably the best thing he could do is to give you a little breathing room and let you sort things out on your own."

"Really?"

"You've had your parents and me hovering over you for so long. At a certain point it becomes counterproductive."

"Well, I really appreciate that."

He said something else I couldn't quite hear; there was a lot of noise on his end. "It's hard to hear you," I said. "Are you in a mall or something?"

"The airport," he replied. "Picking up my sister. Anyway, all I said was to enjoy yourself. Explore and don't worry too much. I'll see you soon, all right?"

"Thanks again, Dr. G."

As I hung up the phone, I felt bad for having ragged on him earlier. That was twice now he'd stuck up for me when my own parents wouldn't.

My dad was nursing a beer across the

room. I stopped by his table on my way upstairs. "About tomorrow . . ." I said.

"Do what you want, I guess."

"Are you sure?"

He shrugged sullenly. "Doctor's orders."

"I'll be home for dinner. Promise."

He just nodded. I left him in the bar and went up to bed.

Falling asleep, my thoughts drifted to the peculiar children and the first question they'd asked after Miss Peregrine had introduced me: *Is Jacob going to stay with us?* At the time I'd thought, *Of course not.* But why not? If I never went home, what exactly would I be missing? I pictured my cold cavernous house, my friendless town full of bad memories, the utterly unremarkable life that had been mapped out for me. It had never once occurred to me, I realized, to refuse it.

CHAPTER SEVEN

Morning brought rain and wind and fog, pessimistic weather that made it hard to believe the previous day had been anything more than a strange and wonderful dream. I wolfed down my breakfast and told my dad I was going out. He looked at me like I was nuts.

"In *this?* To do what?"

"To hang out with —" I started, without thinking. Then, to cover my tracks, I pretended to have a piece of food stuck in my throat. But it was too late; he'd heard me.

"Hang out with who? Not those rapper hoodlums, I hope."

The only way out of this hole was to dig deeper. "No. You've probably never seen them, they live on the other side of, um, the island, and —"

"Really? I didn't think anyone lived over there."

"Yeah, well, just a few people. Like, sheep-tenders and whatnot. Anyway, they're cool — they watch my back while I'm at the house." Friends and safety: two things my dad couldn't possibly object to.

"I want to meet them," he said, trying to look stern. He often put on this face, an imitation of the sensible, no-nonsense dad I think he aspired to be.

"Sure thing. We're meeting up over there, though, so another time."

He nodded and took another bite of his breakfast.

"Be back by dinner," he said.

"Roger Wilco, Dad."

I practically raced to the bog. As I picked my way through its shifting muck, trying to remember the route of semi-invisible grass islands Emma had used to cross it, I worried that all I would find on the other side was more rain and a ruined house. So it was with great relief that I emerged from the cairn to find September third, 1940, just as I'd left it: the day warm and sunny and fogless, the sky a dependable blue, clouds forming shapes that seemed comfortingly familiar. Even better, Emma was there waiting for me, sitting on the edge of the mound casting stones into the bog. "About time!" she cried, jumping to her feet. "Come on, everyone's waiting for you."

"They are?"

"*Ye-es,*" she said with an impatient eye roll, taking my hand and pulling me after her. I sparked with excitement — not only at her touch, but at the thought of the day that lay ahead, full of endless possibility. Though in a million superficial ways it would be identical to the day before — the same breeze would blow and the same tree limbs would fall — my experience of it would be new. So would the peculiar children's. They were the gods of this strange little heaven, and I was their guest.

We dashed across the bog and through the forest as if late for an appointment. When we reached the house, Emma led me around to the backyard, where a small wooden stage had been erected. Kids were bustling in and out of the house, carrying props, buttoning up suit jackets, and zipping into sequined dresses. Warming up was a little orchestra, made up of just an accordion, a battered trombone, and a musical saw that Horace played with a bow.

"What's this?" I asked Emma. "Are you guys putting on a play?"

"You'll see," she said.

"Who's in it?"

"You'll see."

"What's it about?"

She pinched me.

A whistle blew and everyone ran to claim seats in a row of folding chairs that faced the stage. Emma and I sat down just as the curtain opened, revealing a straw boater hat floating atop a gaudy red-and-white striped suit. It was only when I heard a voice did I realize that — of course — it was Millard.

"Ladieeees and gentlemen!" he crowed. "It gives me the utmost pleasure to present to you a performance like no other in history! A show of such unrivaled daring, of such accomplished magicianship, that you simply won't believe your eyes! Good citizens, I give you Miss Peregrine and her Peculiar Children!"

The audience burst into uproarious applause. Millard tipped his hat.

"For our first illusion, I will produce Miss Peregrine herself!" He ducked behind the curtain and emerged a moment later, a folded sheet draped over one arm and a peregrine falcon perched on the other. He nodded to the orchestra, which lurched into a kind of wheezing carnival music.

Emma elbowed me. "Watch this," she whispered.

Millard set the falcon down and held the sheet in front, screening the bird from the audience. He began counting backward.

"Three, two, one!"

On "one" I heard the unmistakable flap of wings and then saw Miss Peregrine's head — her *human* head — pop up from behind the sheet to even more uproarious applause. Her hair was mussed and I could only see her from the shoulders up; she seemed to be naked behind the sheet. Apparently, when you change into a bird, your clothes don't go along for the ride. Taking the edges of the sheet, she wrapped it chastely around herself.

"Mr. Portman!" she said, peering down at me from the stage. "I'm so happy you've returned. This is a little exhibition we used to tour around the Continent back in the halcyon days. I thought you might find it instructive." And then she swept offstage in a flourish, heading into the house to retrieve her clothes.

One after another, the peculiar children came out of the audience and took the stage, each with an act of their own. Millard removed his tuxedo so that he was completely invisible and juggled glass bottles. Olive removed her leaden shoes and performed a gravity-defying gymnastics routine on a set of parallel bars. Emma made fire, swallowed it, then blew it out again without burning herself. I applauded until I thought my hands would blister.

When Emma returned to her seat, I turned to her and said, "I don't understand. You performed this for people?"

"Of course," she replied.

"*Normal* people?"

"Of course, normal people. Why would peculiars pay to see things they can do themselves?"

"But wouldn't this, like, blow your cover?"

She chuckled. "Nobody suspected a thing," she said. "People come to sideshows to see stunts and tricks and what-all, and as far as anybody knew that's exactly what we showed them."

"So you were hiding in plain sight."

"Used to be the way most peculiars made a living," she said.

"And no one ever caught on?"

"Once in a while we'd get some knob-head backstage asking nosey questions, which is why there'd always be a strong-arm on hand to toss them out on their bums. Speak of the devil — here she is now!"

Up on stage, a mannish-looking girl was dragging a boulder the size of a small refrigerator out from behind the curtain. "She may not be the sharpest tool in the woodshed," Emma whispered, "but she's got a massive heart and she'd go to the grave for her mates. We're thick as thieves, Bronwyn and me."

Someone had passed around a stack of promotional cards Miss Peregrine had used to advertise their act. It reached me with Bronwyn's card on top. In her picture she stood barefoot, challenging the camera with an icy stare. Emblazoned across the back was *THE AMAZING STRONG-GIRL OF SWANSEA!*

"Why isn't she lifting a boulder, if that's what she does on stage?" I asked.

"She was in a foul mood because the Bird made her 'dress like a lady' for the picture. She refused to lift so much as a hatbox."

"Looks like she drew the line at wearing shoes, too."

"She generally does."

Bronwyn finished dragging the rock to the middle of the stage, and for an awkward moment she just stared into the crowd, as if someone had told her to pause for dramatic effect. Then she bent down and gripped the rock between her big hands and slowly lifted it above her head. Everyone clapped and hooted, the kids' enthusiasm undimmed though they'd probably seen her do this trick a thousand times. It was almost like

246

being at a pep rally for a school I didn't attend.

Bronwyn yawned and walked off with the boulder tucked under one arm. Then the wild-haired girl took the stage. Her name was Fiona, Emma said. She stood facing the crowd behind a planter filled with dirt, her hands raised above it like a conductor. The orchestra began to play "Flight of the Bumblebee" (as well as they could, anyway), and Fiona pawed the air above the planter, her face contorted in effort and concentration. As the song crescendoed, a row of daisies poked up from the dirt and unfurled toward her hands. It was like one of those fast-motion videos of plants blooming, except she seemed to be reeling the flowers up from their loamy bed by invisible strings. The kids ate it up, jumping out of their seats to cheer her on.

Emma flipped through the stack of postcards to Fiona's. "Her card's my favorite," she said. "We worked for days on her costume."

I looked at it. She was dressed like a beggar girl and stood holding a chicken. "What's she supposed to be?" I asked. "A homeless farmer?"

Emma pinched me. "She's meant to look *natural,* like a savage-type person. Jill of the

Jungle, we called her."

"Is she really from the jungle?"

"She's from Ireland."

"Are there a lot of chickens in the jungle?"

She pinched me again. While we'd been whispering, Hugh had joined Fiona on stage. He stood with his mouth open, letting bees fly out to pollinate the flowers that Fiona had grown, like a weird mating ritual.

"What else does Fiona grow besides bushes and flowers?"

"All these vegetables," Emma said, gesturing to the garden beds in the yard. "And trees, sometimes."

"Really? Whole trees?"

She sorted through the postcards again. "Sometimes we'll play Jill and the Beanstalk. Someone will grab hold of one of the saplings at the edge of the woods and we'll see how high Fiona can get it to go while we're riding it." She arrived at the photo she'd been hunting for and tapped it with her finger. "That was the record," she said proudly. "Twenty meters."

"You guys get pretty bored around here, huh?"

She moved to pinch me again but I blocked her hand. I'm no expert on girls, but when one tries to pinch you four times, I'm pretty sure that's flirting.

250

There were a few more acts after Fiona and Hugh left the stage but by then the kids were getting antsy, and soon we dispersed to spend the rest of the day in summery bliss: lazing in the sun sipping limeade; playing croquet; tending to gardens that, thanks to Fiona, hardly needed tending; discussing our options for lunch. I wanted to ask Miss Peregrine more about my grandfather — a subject I avoided with Emma, who turned morose at any mention of his name — but the headmistress had gone to conduct a lesson in the study for the younger kids. It seemed like I had plenty of time, though, and the languid pace and midday heat sapped my will to do anything more taxing than wander the grounds in dreamy amazement.

After a decadent lunch of goose sandwiches and chocolate pudding, Emma began to agitate for the older kids to go swimming. "Out of the question," Millard groaned, the top button of his pants popping open. "I'm stuffed like a Christmas turkey." We were sprawled on velvet chairs around the sitting room, full to bursting. Bronwyn lay curled with her head between two pillows. "I'd sink straight to the bottom," came her muffled reply.

But Emma persisted. After ten minutes of

wheedling she'd roused Hugh, Fiona, and Horace from their naps and challenged Bronwyn, who apparently could not forgo a competition of any kind, to a swimming race. Upon seeing us all trooping out of the house, Millard scolded us for trying to leave him behind.

The best spot for swimming was by the harbor, but getting there meant walking straight through town. "What about those crazy drunks who think I'm a German spy?" I said. "I don't feel like getting chased with clubs today."

"You twit," Emma said. "That was *yesterday*. They won't remember a thing."

"Just hang a towel 'round you so they don't see your, er, future clothes," said Horace. I had on jeans and a T-shirt, my usual outfit, and Horace wore his customary black suit. He seemed to be of the Miss Peregrine school of dress: morbidly ultraformal, no matter the occasion. His photograph was among those I'd found in the smashed trunk, and in an attempt to "dress up" for it he'd gone completely overboard: top hat, cane, monocle — the works.

"You're right," I said, cocking an eyebrow at Horace. "I wouldn't want anyone to think I was dressed weird."

"If it's my waistcoat you're referring to,"

253

he replied haughtily, "yes, I admit I am a follower of fashion." The others snickered. "Go ahead, have a laugh at old Horace's expense! Call me a dandy if you will, but just because the villagers won't remember what you wear doesn't give you license to dress like a vagabond!" And with that he set about straightening his lapels, which only made the kids laugh harder. In a snit, he pointed an accusing finger at my clothes. "As for him, God help us if *that's* all our wardrobes have to look forward to!"

When the laughter had died down, I pulled Emma aside and whispered, "What exactly is it that makes Horace peculiar — aside from his clothes, I mean?"

"He has prophetic dreams. Gets these great nightmares every so often, which have a disturbing tendency to come true."

"How often? A lot?"

"Ask him yourself."

But Horace was in no mood to entertain my questions. So I filed it away for another time.

As we came into town I wrapped a towel around my waist and hung another from my shoulders. Though it wasn't exactly prophecy, Horace was right about one thing: nobody recognized me. Walking down the main path we got a few odd looks, but

no one bothered us. We even passed the fat man who'd made such a stink over me in the bar. He was stuffing a pipe outside the tobacconist's shop and blathering on about politics to a woman who was barely listening. I couldn't help staring at him as we passed. He stared back, without even a flicker of recognition.

It was like someone had hit "reset" on the whole town. I kept noticing things I'd seen the day before: the same wagon rushing wildly down the path, its back wheel fishtailing in the gravel; the same women lining up outside the well; a man tarring the bottom of a rowboat, no further along in his task than he'd been twenty-four hours ago. I almost expected to see my doppelgänger sprinting across town pursued by a mob, but I guess things didn't work that way.

"You guys must know a lot about what goes on around here," I said. "Like yesterday, with the planes and that cart."

"It's Millard who knows everything," said Hugh.

"It's true," said Millard. "In fact, I am in the midst of compiling the world's first complete account of one day in the life of a town, as experienced by everyone in it. Every action, every conversation, every sound made by each of the one hundred fifty-nine human and three hundred thirty-two animal residents of Cairnholm, minute by minute, sunup to sundown."

"That's incredible," I said.

"I can't help but agree," he replied. "In just twenty-seven years I've already observed half the animals and nearly all the humans."

My mouth fell open. "Twenty-seven *years?*"

"He spent three years on pigs alone!" Hugh said. "That's all day every day for three years taking notes on *pigs!* Can you imagine? 'This one dropped a load of arse biscuits!' 'That one said *oink-oink* and then went to sleep in its own filth!' "

"Notes are absolutely essential to the process," Millard explained patiently. "But I can understand your jealousy, Hugh. It promises to be a work unprecedented in the history of academic scholarship."

"Oh, don't cock your nose," Emma said. "It'll also be unprecedented in the history of dull things. It'll be the dullest thing ever written!"

Rather than responding, Millard began pointing things out just before they happened. "Mrs. Higgins is about to have a coughing fit," he'd say, and then a woman in the street would cough and hack until she was red in the face, or "Presently, a fisherman will lament the difficulty of plying his trade during wartime," and then a man leaning on a cart filled with nets would turn to another man and say, "There's so many damned U-boats in the water now it ain't even safe for a bloke to go tickle his own lines!"

I was duly impressed, and told him so. "I'm glad *someone* appreciates my work," he replied.

We walked along the bustling harbor until the docks ran out and then followed the rocky shore toward the headlands to a sandy cove. We boys stripped down to our underwear (all except Horace, who would remove only his shoes and tie) while the girls disappeared to change into modest, old-school bathing suits. Then we all swam. Bronwyn and Emma raced each other while the rest of us paddled around; once we'd exhausted ourselves, we climbed onto the sand and napped. When the sun was too hot we fell back into the water, and when the chilly sea made us shiver we crawled out again, and so it went until our shadows began to lengthen across the cove.

We got to talking. They had a million questions for me, and, far away from Miss Peregrine, I could answer them frankly. What was my world like? What did people eat, drink, wear? When would sickness and death be overcome by science? They lived in splendor but were starving for new faces and new stories. I told them whatever I could, racking my brain for nuggets of twentieth-century history from Mrs. Johnston's class — the moon landing! the Berlin Wall! Vietnam! — but they were hardly comprehensive.

It was my time's technology and standard of living that amazed them most. Our houses were air-conditioned. They'd heard of televisions but had never seen one and were shocked to learn that my family had a talking-picture box in almost every room. Air travel was as common and affordable to us as train travel was to them. Our army fought with remote-controlled drones. We carried telephone-computers that fit in our pockets, and even though mine didn't work here (nothing electronic seemed to), I pulled it out just to show them its sleek, mirrored enclosure.

It was edging toward sunset when we finally started back. Emma stuck to me like glue, the back of her hand brushing mine as we walked. Passing an apple tree on the outskirts of town, she stopped to pick one, but even on tiptoes the lowest fruit was out of reach, so I did what any gentleman would do and gave her a boost, wrapping my arms around her waist and trying not to groan as I lifted, her white arm outstretched, wet hair glinting in the sun. When I let her down she gave me a little kiss on the cheek and handed me the apple.

"Here," she said, "you earned it."

"The apple or the kiss?"

She laughed and ran off to catch up with the others. I didn't know what to call it, what was happening between us, but I liked it. It felt silly and fragile and good. I put the apple in my pocket and ran after her.

When we came to the bog and I said I had to go home, she pretended to pout. "At least let me escort you," she said, so we waved goodbye to the others and crossed over to the cairn, me doing my best to memorize the placement of her feet as we went.

When we got there I said, "Come with me to the other side a minute."

"I shouldn't. I've got to get back or the Bird will suspect us."

"Suspect us of what?"

She smiled coyly. "Of . . . something."

"Something."

"She's always on the lookout for something," she said, laughing.

I changed tactics. "Then why don't you come see me tomorrow instead?"

"See you? Over there?"

"Why not? Miss Peregrine won't be around to watch us. You could even meet my dad. We won't tell him who you are, obviously. And then maybe he'll ease up a little about where I'm going and what I'm doing all the time. Me hanging out with a hot girl? That's like his fondest dad-dream wish."

I thought she might smile at the hot girl thing, but instead she turned serious. "The Bird only allows us to go over for a few minutes at a time, just to keep the loop open, you know."

"So tell her that's what you're doing!"

She sighed. "I want to. I do. But it's a bad idea."

"She's got you on a pretty short leash."

"You don't know what you're talking about," she said with a scowl. "And thanks for comparing me to a dog. That was brilliant."

I wondered how we'd gone from flirting to fighting so quickly. "I didn't mean it like that."

"It's not that I wouldn't like to," she said. "I just can't."

"Okay, I'll make you a deal. Forget coming for the whole day. Just come over for a minute, right now."

"One minute? What can we do in one minute?"

I grinned. "You'd be surprised."

"Tell me!" she said, pushing me.

"Take your picture."

Her smile disappeared. "I'm not exactly at my most fetching," she said doubtfully.

"No, you're great. Really."

"Just one minute? Promise?"

I let her go into the cairn first. When we came out again the world was misty and cold, though thankfully the rain had stopped. I pulled out my phone and was happy to see that my theory was right. On this side of the loop, electronic things worked fine.

"Where's your camera?" she said, shivering. "Let's get this over with!"

I held up the phone and took her picture. She just shook her head, as if nothing about my bizarre world could surprise her anymore. Then she dodged away, and I had to chase her around the cairn, both of us laughing, Emma ducking out of view only to pop up again and vamp for the camera. A minute later I'd taken so many pictures that my phone had nearly run out of memory.

Emma ran to the mouth of the cairn and blew me an air-kiss. "See you tomorrow, future boy!"

I lifted my hand to wave goodbye, and she ducked into the stone tunnel.

I skipped back to town freezing and wet and grinning like an idiot. I was still blocks away from the pub when I heard a strange sound rising above the hum of generators — someone calling my name. Following the voice, I found my father standing in the street in a soggy sweater, breath pluming before him like muffler exhaust on a cold morning.

"Jacob! I've been looking for you!"

"You said be back by dinner, so here I am!"

"Forget dinner. Come with me."

My father never skipped dinner. Something was most definitely amiss.

"What's going on?"

"I'll explain on the way," he said, marching me toward the pub. Then he got a good look at me. "You're all wet!" he exclaimed. "For God's sake, did you lose your *other* jacket, too?"

"I, uh . . ."

"And why is your face red? You look sunburned."

Crap. A whole afternoon at the beach without sunblock. "I'm all hot from running," I said, though the skin on my arms was pimpled from cold. "What's happening? Did someone die, or what?"

"No, no, no," he said. "Well, sort of. Some sheep."

"What's that got to do with us?"

"They think it was kids who did it. Like a vandalism thing."

"They who? The sheep police?"

"The farmers," he said. "They've interrogated everyone under the age of twenty. Naturally, they're pretty interested in where you've been all day."

My stomach sank. I didn't exactly have a watertight cover story, and I raced to think of one as we approached the Priest Hole.

Outside the pub, a small crowd was gathered around a quorum of very pissed-off-looking sheep farmers. One wore muddy coveralls and leaned threateningly on a pitchfork. Another had Worm by the collar. Worm was dressed in neon track pants and a shirt that read *I LOVE IT WHEN THEY CALL ME BIG POPPA.* He'd been crying, snot bubbling on his upper lip.

A third farmer, rail-thin and wearing a knit cap, pointed at me as we approached. "Here he is!" he called out. "Where you been off to, son?"

Dad patted me on the back. "Tell them,"

he said confidently.

I tried to sound like I had nothing to hide. "I was exploring the other side of the island. The big house."

Knit Cap looked confused. "Which big house?"

"That wonky old heap in the forest," said Pitchfork. "Only a certified idiot would set foot in there. Place is witched, and a death-trap to boot."

Knit Cap squinted at me. "In the big house with *who?*"

"Nobody," I said, and saw Dad give me a funny look.

"Bollocks! I think you was with this one," said the man holding Worm.

"I never killed any sheep!" cried Worm.

"Shaddap!" the man roared.

"Jake?" said my dad. "What about your friends?"

"Ahh, crap, Dad."

Knit Cap turned and spat. "Why you little liar. I oughta belt you right here in fronta God and everybody."

"You stay away from him," my father said, doing his best Stern Dad voice. Knit Cap swore and took a step toward him, and he and my dad squared off. Before either could throw a punch, a familiar voice said, "Hang on, Dennis, we'll get this sorted," and Martin stepped out of the crowd to wedge himself between them. "Just start by telling us whatever your boy told you," he said to my father.

Dad glared at me. "He said he was going to see friends on the other side."

"*What* friends?" Pitchfork demanded.

I could see this was only going to get uglier unless I did something drastic. Obviously, I couldn't tell them about the children — not that they'd believe me anyway — so instead I took a calculated risk.

"It wasn't anybody," I said, dropping my eyes in feigned shame. "They're imaginary."

"What'd he say?"

"He said his friends were imaginary," my dad repeated, sounding worried.

The farmers exchanged baffled glances.

"See?" Worm said, a flicker of hope on his face. "Kid's a bloody psycho! It *had* to be him!"

"I never touched them," I said, though no one was really listening.

"It weren't the American," said the farmer who had Worm. He gave Worm's shirt a wrench. "This one here, he's got a history. Few years back I watched him kick a lamb down a cliffside. Wouldn't of believed it if I hadn't seen it wi' me own eyes. After he done it I asked him why. To see if it could fly, he says. He's a sickie, all right."

People muttered in disgust. Worm looked uncomfortable but didn't dispute the story.

"Where's his fishmongerin' mate?" said Pitchfork. "If this one was in on it, you can bet the other one was, too." Someone said they'd seen Dylan by the harbor, and a posse was dispatched to collect him.

"What about a wolf — or a wild dog?" my dad said. "My father was killed by dogs."

"Only dogs on Cairnholm are sheepdogs," replied Knit Cap. "And it ain't exactly in a sheepdog's nature to go about killin' sheep."

I wished my father would give it up and leave while the leaving was good, but he was on the case like Perry Mason. "Just how many sheep are we talking about?" he asked.

"Five," replied the fourth farmer, a short, sour-faced man who hadn't spoken until then. "All mine. Killed right in their pen. Poor devils never even had a chance to run."

"Five sheep. How much blood do you think is in five sheep?"

"A right tubful, I shouldn't wonder," said Pitchfork.

"So wouldn't whoever did this be covered in it?"

The farmers looked at one another. They looked at me, and then at Worm. Then they shrugged and scratched their heads.

"Reckon it coulda been foxes," said Knit Cap.

"A whole pack of foxes, maybe," said Pitchfork doubtfully, "if the island's even got that many."

"I still say the cuts are too clean," said the one holding Worm. "Had to have been done with a knife."

"I just don't believe it," my dad replied.

"Then come see for yourself," said Knit Cap. So as the crowd began to disperse, a small group of us followed the farmers out to the scene of the crime. We trudged over a low rise, through a nearby field, to a little brown shed with a rectangular animal pen beyond it. We approached tentatively and peeked through the fence slats.

The violence inside was almost cartoonish, like the work of some mad impressionist who painted only in red. The tramped grass was bathed in blood, as were the pen's weathered posts and the stiff white bodies of the sheep themselves, flung about in attitudes of sheepish agony. One had tried to climb the fence and got its spindly legs caught between the slats. It hung before me at an odd angle, clam-shelled open from throat to crotch, as if it had been unzipped.

I had to turn away. Others muttered and shook their heads, and someone let out a

268

low whistle. Worm gagged and began to cry, which was seen as a tacit admission of guilt; the criminal who couldn't face his own crime. He was led away to be locked in Martin's museum — in what used to be the sacristy and was now the island's makeshift jail cell — until he could be remanded to police on the mainland.

We left the farmer to ponder his slain sheep and went back to town, plodding across wet hills in the slate-gray dusk. Back in the room, I knew I was in for a Stern Dad talking-to, so I did my best to disarm him before he could start in on me.

"I lied to you, Dad, and I'm sorry."

"Yeah?" he said sarcastically, trading his wet sweater for a dry one. "That's big of you. Now which lie are we talking about? I can hardly keep track."

"The one about meeting friends. There aren't any other kids on the island. I made it up because I didn't want you to worry about me being alone over there."

"Well, I do worry, even if your doctor tells me not to."

"I know you do."

"So what about these imaginary friends? Does Golan know about this?"

I shook my head. "That was a lie, too. I just had to get those guys off my back."

Dad folded his arms, not sure what to believe. "Really."

"Better to have them think I'm a little eccentric than a sheep killer, right?"

I took a seat at the table. Dad looked down at me for a long moment, and I wasn't sure if he trusted me or not. Then he went to the sink and splashed water on his face. When he'd toweled off and turned around again, he seemed to have decided it was a lot less trouble to trust me.

"You sure we don't need to call Dr. Golan again?" he asked. "Have a nice long talk?"

"If you want to. But I'm okay."

"This is exactly why I didn't want you hanging out with those rapper guys," he said, because he needed to close with something sufficiently parental for it to count as a proper talking-to.

"You were right about them, Dad," I said, though secretly I couldn't believe either of them was capable of it. Worm and Dylan talked tough, but that was all.

Dad sat down across from me. He looked tired. "I'd still like to know how someone manages to get a sunburn on a day like this."

Right. The sunburn. "Guess I'm pretty sensitive," I said.

"You can say that again," he said dryly.

He let me go, and I went to take a shower and thought about Emma. Then I brushed my teeth and thought about Emma and washed my face and thought about Emma. After that I went to my room and took the apple she'd given me out of my pocket and set it on the nightstand, and then, as if to reassure myself she still existed, I got out my phone and looked through the pictures of her I'd taken that afternoon. I was still looking when I heard my father go to bed in the next room, and still looking when the gennies kicked off and my lamp went out, and when there was no light anywhere but her face on my little screen, I lay there in the dark, still looking.

CHAPTER EIGHT

Hoping to duck another lecture, I got up early and set out before Dad was awake. I slipped a note under his door and went to grab Emma's apple, but it wasn't on my nightstand where I'd left it. A thorough search of the floor uncovered a lot of dust bunnies and one leathery thing the size of a golf ball. I was starting to wonder if someone had swiped it when I realized that the leathery thing *was* the apple. At some point during the night it had gone profoundly bad, spoiling like I've never seen fruit spoil. It looked as though it had spent a year locked in a food dehydrator. When I tried to pick it up it crumbled in my hand like a clump of soil.

Puzzled, I shrugged it off and went out. It was pissing rain but I soon left gray skies behind for the reliable sun of the loop. This time, however, there were no pretty girls waiting for me on the other side of the cairn

— or anyone, for that matter. I tried not to be too disappointed, but I was, a little.

As soon as I got to the house I started looking for Emma, but Miss Peregrine intercepted me before I'd even made it past the front hall.

"A word, Mr. Portman," she said, and led me into the privacy of the kitchen, still fragrant from the rich breakfast I'd missed. I felt like I'd been summoned to the principal's office.

Miss Peregrine propped herself against the giant cooking range. "Are you enjoying your time with us?" she said.

I told her I was, very much.

"That's good," she replied, and then her smile vanished. "I understand you had a pleasant afternoon with some of my wards yesterday. And a lively discussion as well."

"It was great. They're all really nice." I was trying to keep things light, but I could tell she was winding me up for something.

"Tell me," she said, "how would you describe the nature of your discussion?"

I tried to remember. "I don't know . . . we talked about lots of things. How things are here. How they are where I'm from."

"Where you're from."

"Right."

"And do you think it's wise to discuss

273

events in the future with children from the past?"

"Children? Is that really how you think of them?" I regretted saying this even as the words were passing my lips.

"It is how they regard *themselves* as well," she said testily. "What would you call them?"

Given her mood, it wasn't a subtlety I was prepared to argue. "Children, I guess."

"Indeed. Now, as I was saying," she said, emphasizing her words with little cleaver-chops of her hand on the range, "do you think it's wise to discuss the future with children from the past?"

I decided to go out on a limb. "No?"

"Ah, but apparently you do! I know this because last night at dinner we were treated by Hugh to a fascinating disquisition on the wonders of twenty-first-century telecommunications technology." Her voice dripped with sarcasm. "Did you know that when you send a letter in the twenty-first century, it can be received almost instantaneously?"

"I think you're talking about e-mail."

"Well, Hugh knew *all* about it."

"I don't understand," I said. "Is that a problem?"

She unleaned herself from the range and took a limping step toward me. Even though she was a full foot shorter than I was, she still managed to be intimidating.

"As an ymbryne, it is my sworn duty to keep those children safe and above all that means keeping them *here* — in the loop — on this island."

"Okay."

"Yours is a world they can never be part of, Mr. Portman. So what's the use in filling their heads with grand talk about the exotic wonders of the future? Now you've got half the children begging for a jet-airplane trip to America and the other half dreaming of the day when they can own a telephone-computer like yours."

"I'm sorry. I didn't realize."

"This is their home. I have tried to make it as fine a place as I could. But the plain fact is they cannot leave, and I'd appreciate it if you didn't make them want to."

"But why can't they?"

She narrowed her eyes at me for a moment and then shook her head. "Forgive me. I continue to underestimate the breadth of your ignorance." Miss Peregrine, who seemed to be constitutionally incapable of idleness, took a saucepan from the stove top and began scouring it with a steel brush. I wondered if she was ignoring my question or simply weighing how best to dumb down the answer.

When the pan was clean she clapped it back on the stove and said, "They cannot linger in your world, Mr. Portman, because in a short time they would grow old and die."

"What do you mean, die?"

"I'm not certain how I can be more direct. They'll die, Jacob." She spoke tersely, as if wishing to put the topic behind us as quickly as possible. "It may appear to you that we've found a way to cheat death, but it's an illusion. If the children loiter too long on your side of the loop, all the many years from which they have abstained will descend upon them at once, in a matter of hours."

I pictured a person shriveling up and crumbling to dust like the apple on my nightstand. "That's awful," I said with a shudder.

"The few instances of it that I've had the misfortune to witness are among the worst memories of my life. And let me assure you, I've lived long enough to see some truly dreadful things."

"Then it's happened before."

"To a young girl under my own care, regrettably, a number of years ago. Her name was Charlotte. It was the first and last time I ever took a trip to visit one of my sister ymbrynes. In that brief time Charlotte managed to evade the older children who were minding her and wander out of the loop. It was 1985 or '86 at that time, I believe. Charlotte was roving blithely about the village by herself when she was discovered by a constable. When she couldn't explain who she was or where she'd come from — not to his liking, anyhow — the poor girl was shipped off to a child welfare agency on the mainland. It was two days before I could reach her, and by that time she'd aged thirty-five years."

"I think I've seen her picture," I said. "A grown woman in little girl's clothes."

Miss Peregrine nodded somberly. "She never was the same after that. Not right in the head."

"What happened to her?"

"She lives with Miss Nightjar now. Miss Nightjar and Miss Thrush take all the hard cases."

"But it's not as if they're confined to the island, is it?" I asked. "Couldn't they still leave *now,* from 1940?"

"Yes, and begin aging again, as normal. But to what end? To be caught up in a ferocious war? To encounter people who fear and misunderstand them? And there are other dangers as well. It's best to stay here."

"What other dangers?"

Her face clouded, as if she regretted having brought it up. "Nothing you need concern yourself with. Not yet, at least."

With that she shooed me outside. I asked again what she meant by "other dangers," but she shut the screen door in my face. "Enjoy the morning," she chirped, forcing a smile. "Go find Miss Bloom, I'm sure she's dying to see you." And she disappeared into the house.

I wandered into the yard, wondering how I was supposed to get the image of that withered apple out of my head. Before long, though I did. It's not that I forgot; it just stopped bothering me. It was the strangest thing.

Resuming my mission to find Emma, I learned from Hugh that she was on a supply run to the village, so I settled under a shade tree to wait. Within five minutes I was half-asleep in the grass, smiling like a dope, wondering serenely what might be on the menu for lunch. It was as if just being here had some kind of narcotic effect on me; like the loop itself was a drug — a mood enhancer and a sedative combined — and if I stayed too long, I'd never want to leave.

If that were true, I thought, it would explain a lot of things, like how people could live the same day over and over for decades without losing their minds. Yes, it was beautiful and life was good, but if every day were exactly alike and if the kids really couldn't leave, as Miss Peregrine had said, then this place wasn't just a heaven but a kind of prison, too. It was just so hypnotizingly pleasant that it might take a person years to notice, and by then it would be too late; leaving would be too dangerous.

So it's not even a decision, really. You stay. It's only later — years later — that you begin to wonder what might've happened if you hadn't.

I must've dozed off, because around midmorning I awoke to something nudging my foot. I cracked an eye to discover a little humanoid figure trying to hide inside my shoe, but it had gotten tangled in the laces. It was stiff-limbed and awkward, half a hubcap tall, dressed in army fatigues. I watched it struggle to free itself for a moment and then go rigid, a wind-up toy on its last wind. I untied my shoe to extricate it and then turned it over, looking for the wind-up key, but I couldn't find one. Up close it was a strange, crude-looking thing, its head a stump of rounded clay, its face a smeared thumbprint.

"Bring him here!" someone called from across the yard. A boy sat waving at me from a tree stump at the edge of the woods.

Lacking any pressing engagements, I picked up the clay soldier and walked over. Arranged around the boy was a whole menagerie of wind-up men, staggering around like damaged robots. As I drew near, the one in my hands jerked to life again, squirming as if he were trying to get away. I put it with the others and wiped shed clay on my pants.

"I'm Enoch," the boy said. "You must be him."

"I guess I am," I replied.

"Sorry if he bothered you," he said, herding the one I'd returned back to the others. "They get ideas, see. Ain't properly trained yet. Only made 'em last week." He spoke with a slight cockney accent. Cadaverous black circles ringed his eyes like a raccoon, and his overalls — the same ones he'd worn in pictures I'd seen — were streaked with clay and dirt. Except for his pudgy face, he might've been a chimney sweep out of *Oliver Twist.*

"You made these?" I asked, impressed. "How?"

"They're homunculi," he replied. "Sometimes I put doll heads on 'em, but this time

I was in a hurry and didn't bother."

"What's a homunculi?"

"More than one homunculus." He said it like it was something any idiot would know. "Some people think its homunculuses, but I think that sounds daft, don't you?"

"Definitely."

The clay soldier I'd returned began wandering again. With his foot, Enoch nudged it back toward the group. They seemed to be going haywire, colliding with one another like excited atoms. "Fight, you nancies!" he commanded, which is when I realized they weren't simply bumping into one another, but hitting and kicking. The errant clay man wasn't interested in fighting, however, and when he began to totter away once more, Enoch snatched him up and snapped off his legs.

"That's what happens to deserters in my army!" he cried, and tossed the crippled figure into the grass, where it writhed grotesquely as the others fell upon it.

"Do you treat all your toys that way?"

"Why?" he said. "Do you feel sorry for them?"

"I don't know. Should I?"

"No. They wouldn't be alive at all if it wasn't for me."

I laughed, and Enoch scowled at me.

"What's so funny?"

"You made a joke."

"You are a bit thick, aren't you?" he said. "Look here." He grabbed one of the soldiers and stripped off its clothes. Then with both hands he cracked it down the middle and removed from its sticky chest a tiny, convulsing heart. The soldier instantly went limp. Enoch held the heart between his thumb and forefinger for me to see.

"It's from a mouse," he explained. "That's what I can do — take the life of one thing and give it to another, either clay like this or something that used to be alive but ain't anymore." He tucked the stilled heart into his overalls. "Soon as I figger out how to train 'em up proper, I'll have a whole army like this. Only they'll be *massive*." And he raised an arm up over his head to show me just how massive.

"What can *you* do?" he said.

"Me? Nothing, really. I mean, nothing special like you."

"Pity," he replied. "Are you going to come live with us anyway?" He didn't say it like he wanted me to, exactly; he just seemed curious.

"I don't know," I said. "I hadn't thought about it." That was a lie, of course. I had thought about it, but mostly in a daydreaming sort of way.

He looked at me suspiciously. "But don't you *want* to?"

"I don't know yet."

Narrowing his eyes, he nodded slowly, as if he'd just figured me out.

Then he leaned in and said under his breath, "Emma told you about Raid the Village, didn't she?"

"Raid the what?"

He looked away. "Oh, it's nothing. Just a game some of us play."

I got the distinct feeling I was being set up. "She didn't tell me," I said.

Enoch scooted toward me on the stump. "I *bet* she didn't," he said. "I bet there's a *lot* of things about this place she wouldn't like you to know."

"Oh yeah? Why?"

"Cause then you'll see it's not as great as everybody wants you to think, and you won't stay."

"What kinds of things?" I asked.

"Can't tell," he said, flashing me a devilish smile. "I could get in big trouble."

"Whatever," I said. "You brought it up."

I stood to go. "Wait!" he cried, grabbing my sleeve.

"Why should I if you're not going to tell me anything?"

He rubbed his chin judiciously. "It's true, I ain't allowed to *say* anything . . . but I reckon I couldn't stop you if you was to go upstairs and have a look in the room at the end of the hall."

"Why?" I said. "What's in there?"

"My friend Victor. He wants to meet you. Go up and have a chat."

"Fine," I said. "I will."

I started toward the house and then heard Enoch whistle. He mimed running a hand along the top of a door. *The key,* he mouthed.

"What do I need a key for if someone's in there?"

He turned away, pretending not to hear.

I sauntered into the house and up the stairs like I had business there and didn't care who knew it. Reaching the second floor unobserved, I crept to the room at the end of the hall and tried the door. It was locked. I knocked, but there was no answer. Glancing over my shoulder to make sure no one was watching, I ran my hand along the top of the doorframe. Sure enough, I found a key.

I unlocked the door and slipped inside. It was like any other bedroom in the house — there was a dresser, a wardrobe, a vase of flowers on a nightstand. Late-morning sun shone through drawn curtains the color of mustard, throwing such yellow light everywhere that the whole room seemed encased in amber. Only then did I notice a young man lying in the bed, his eyes closed and mouth slightly open, half-hidden behind a lace curtain.

I froze, afraid I'd wake him. I recognized him from Miss Peregrine's album, though I hadn't seen him at meals or around the house, and we'd never been introduced. In the picture he'd been asleep in bed, just as he was now. Had he been quarantined, infected with some sleeping sickness? Was Enoch trying to get me sick, too?

"Hello?" I whispered. "Are you awake?"

He didn't move. I put a hand on his arm and shook him gently. His head lolled to one side.

Then something terrible occurred to me. To test a theory, I held my hand in front of his mouth. I couldn't feel his breath. My finger brushed his lips, which were cold as ice. Shocked, I pulled my hand away.

Then I heard footsteps and spun around to see Bronwyn in the doorway. "You ain't supposed to be in here!" she hissed.

"He's dead," I said.

Bronwyn's eyes went to the boy and her face puckered. "That's Victor."

Suddenly it came to me, where I'd seen his face. He was the boy lifting the boulder in my grandfather's pictures. Victor was Bronwyn's brother. There was no telling how long he might've been dead; as long as the loop kept looping, it could be fifty years and only look like a day.

"What happened to him?" I asked.

"Maybe I'll wake old Victor up," came a voice from behind us, "and you can ask him yourself." It was Enoch. He came in and shut the door.

Bronwyn beamed at him through welling tears. "Would you wake him? Oh *please,* Enoch."

"I shouldn't," he said. "I'm running low on hearts as it is, and it takes a right lot of 'em to rise up a human being, even for just a minute."

Bronwyn crossed to the dead boy and began to smooth his hair with her fingers. "Please," she begged, "it's been *ages* since we talked to Victor."

"Well, I do have some cow hearts pickling in the basement," he said, pretending to consider it. "But I *hate* to use inferior ingredients. Fresh is always better!"

Bronwyn began to cry in earnest. One of her tears fell onto the boy's jacket, and she hurried to wipe it away with her sleeve.

"Don't get so choked," Enoch said, "you know I can't stand it. Anyway, it's cruel, waking Victor. He likes it where he is."

"And where's that?" I said.

"Who knows? But whenever we rouse him for a chat he seems in a dreadful hurry to get back."

"What's cruel is you toying with Bronwyn like that, and tricking me," I said. "And if Victor's dead, why don't you just bury him?"

Bronwyn flashed me a look of utter derision. "Then we'd never get to *see* him," she said.

"That stings, mate," said Enoch. "I only mentioned coming up here because I wanted you to have all the facts, like. I'm on your side."

"Yeah? What are the facts, then? How did Victor die?"

Bronwyn looked up. "He got killed by an — *owww!*" she squealed as Enoch pinched the back of her arm.

"Hush!" he cried. "It ain't for you to tell!"

"This is ridiculous!" I said. "If neither of you will tell me, I'll just go ask Miss Peregrine."

Enoch took a quick stride toward me, eyes wide. "Oh no, you mustn't do that."

"Yeah? Why mustn't I?"

"The Bird don't like us talking about Victor," he said. "It's why she wears black all the time, you know. Anyway, she can't find out we been in here. She'll hang us by our pinky toes!"

As if on cue, we heard the unmistakable sound of Miss Peregrine limping up the stairs. Bronwyn turned white and dashed past me out the door, but before Enoch could escape I blocked his path. "Out of the way!" he hissed.

"Tell me what happened to Victor!"

"I *can't!*"

"Then tell me about Raid the Village."

"I can't tell you that, neither!" He tried to shove past me again, but when he realized he couldn't, he gave up. "All right, just shut the door and I'll whisper it to you!"

I closed it just as Miss Peregrine was reaching the landing. We stood with our ears pressed to the door for a moment, listening for a sign that we'd been spotted. The headmistress's footsteps came halfway down the hall toward us, then stopped. Another door creaked open, then shut.

"She's gone into her room," Enoch whispered.

"So," I said. "Raid the Village."

Looking like he was sorry he'd brought it up, he motioned me away from the door. I followed, leaning down so he could whisper into my ear. "Like I said, it's a game we play. It works just like the name says."

"You mean you actually *raid* the village?"

"Smash it up, chase people round, take what we like, burn things down. It's all a good laugh."

"But that's terrible!"

"We got to practice our skills somehow, don't we? Case we ever need to defend ourselves. Otherwise we'd get rusty. Plus there's rules. We ain't allowed to kill anybody. Just scare 'em up a bit, like. And if someone does get hurt, well, they're back right as rain the next day and don't remember nothing about it."

"Does Emma play, too?"

"Nah. She's like you. Says it's *evil*."

"Well, it is."

He rolled his eyes. "You two deserve each other."

"What's *that* supposed to mean?"

He rose up to his full five-foot-four-inch height and poked a finger into my chest. "It means you better not get all high an' mighty with *me,* mate. Because if we didn't raid the damned village once in a while, most of this lot woulda gone off their heads ages ago." He went to the door and put his hand on the knob and then turned back to face me.

"And if you think *we're* wicked, wait'll you see *them.*"

"Them *who?* What the hell is everyone talking about?"

He held up one finger to shush me, then went out.

I was alone again. My eyes were drawn to the body on the bed. *What happened to you, Victor?*

Maybe he'd gone crazy and killed himself, I thought — gotten so sick of this cheerful but futureless eternity that he'd guzzled rat poison or taken a dive off a cliff. Or maybe it was *them,* those "other dangers" Miss Peregrine had alluded to.

I stepped into the hall and had just started toward the stairs when I heard Miss Peregrine's voice behind a half-closed door. I dove into the nearest room, and stayed hidden until she'd limped past me and down the stairs. Then I noticed a pair of boots at the front of a crisply made bed — Emma's boots. I was in her bedroom.

Along one wall was a chest of drawers and a mirror, on the other a writing desk with a chair tucked underneath. It was the room of a neat girl with nothing to hide, or so it seemed until I found a hatbox just inside the closet. It was tied up with string, and in grease pencil across the front was written

Private

Correspondence of
Emma Bloom
Do not open

It was like waving red underwear at a bull. I sat down with the box in my lap and untied the string. It was packed with a hundred or more letters, all from my grandfather.

My heart picked up speed. This was exactly the kind of gold mine I'd hoped to find in the old ruined house. Sure, I felt bad about snooping, but if people here insisted on keeping things secret, well, I'd just have to find stuff out for myself.

I wanted to read them all but was afraid someone would walk in on me, so I thumbed through them quickly to get an overview. Many were dated from the early 1940s, during Grandpa Portman's time in the army. A random sampling revealed them to be long and sappy, full of declarations of his love and awkward descriptions of Emma's beauty in my grandfather's then-broken English ("You are pretty like flower, have good smell also, may I pick?"). In one he'd enclosed a picture of himself posing atop a bomb with a cigarette dangling from his lips.

Over time, his letters grew shorter and less frequent. By the 1950s there was maybe one a year. The last was dated April 1963; inside the envelope was no letter, just a few pictures. Two were of Emma, snapshots she'd sent him that he'd sent back. The first was from early on — a jokey pose to answer his — of her peeling potatoes and pretending to smoke one of Miss Peregrine's pipes. The next one was sadder, and I imagined she'd sent it after my grandfather had failed to write for a while. The last photo — the last thing he'd ever sent her, in fact — showed my grandfather at middle age, holding a little girl.

I had to stare at the last picture for a minute before I realized who the little girl was. It was my aunt Susie, maybe four years old then. After that, there were no more letters. I wondered how much longer Emma had continued writing to my grandfather without receiving a reply, and what he'd done with her letters. Thrown them out? Stashed them somewhere? Surely, it had to be one of those letters that my father and aunt had found as kids, that made them think their father was a liar and a cheat. How wrong they were.

I heard a throat clear behind me, and turned to see Emma glaring from the doorway. I scrambled to gather the letters, my face flushing, but it was too late. I was caught.

"I'm sorry. I shouldn't be in here."

"I'm bloody well aware of that," she said,

Peeling spuds & dreaming of you. Come home soon.
Love, your potato.

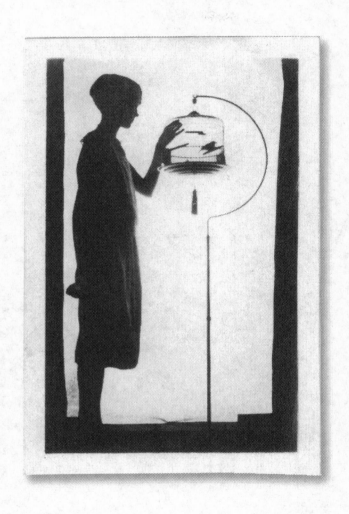

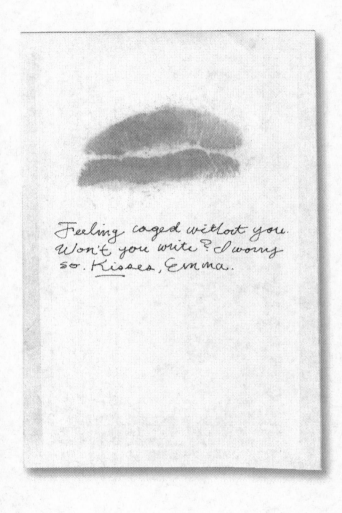

Feeling caged without you.
Won't you write? I worry
so. Kisses, Emma.

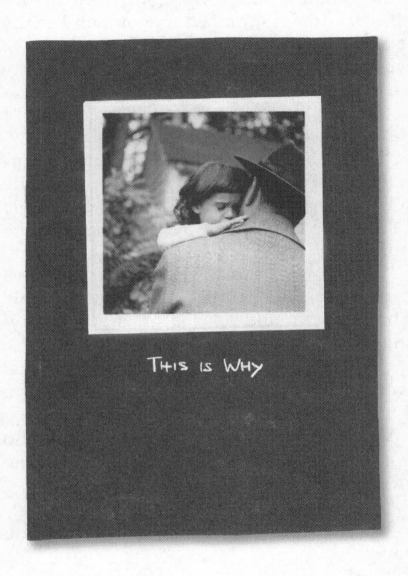

THIS IS WHY

"but by all means, don't let me interrupt your reading." She stamped over to her chest of drawers, yanked one out, and threw it clattering to the floor. "While you're at it, why don't you have a look through my knickers, too!"

"I'm really, really sorry," I repeated. "I *never* do things like this."

"Oh, I shouldn't wonder. Too busy peeping in ladies' windows, I suppose!" She towered over me, shaking with anger, while I struggled to fit all the letters back into the box.

"There's a *system*, you know. Just give them here, you're mucking everything up!" She sat down and pushed me aside, emptying the box onto the floor and sorting the letters into piles with the speed of a postal worker. Thinking it best to shut my mouth, I watched meekly while she worked.

When she'd calmed a little, she said, "So you want to know about Abe and me, is that it? Because you could've just asked."

"I didn't want to pry."

"Rather a moot point now, wouldn't you say?"

"I guess."

"So? What is it you want to know?"

I thought about it. I wasn't really sure where to start. "Just . . . what happened?"

"All right then, we'll skip all the nice bits and go right to the end. It's simple, really. He left. He said he loved me and promised to come back one day. But he never did."

"But he had to go, didn't he? To fight?"

"*Had* to? I don't know. He said he wouldn't be able to live with himself if he sat out the war while his people were being hunted and killed. Said it was his duty. I suppose duty meant more to him than I did. Anyhow, I waited. I waited and worried through that whole bloody war, thinking every letter that came was a death notice. Then, when the war was finally over, he said he couldn't possibly come back. Said he'd go stark raving. Said he'd learned how to defend himself in the army and he damn well didn't need a nanny like the Bird to look after him anymore. He was going to America to make a home for us, and then he'd send for me. So I waited more. I waited so long that if I'd actually gone to be with him I would've been forty years old. By then he'd taken up with some commoner. And that, as they say, was that."

"I'm sorry. I had no idea."

"It's an old story. I don't drag it out much anymore."

"You blame him for being stuck here," I said.

303

She gave me a sharp look. "Who says I'm stuck?" Then she sighed. "No, I don't blame him. Just miss him is all."

"Still?"

"Every day."

She finished sorting the letters. "There you have it," she said, clapping the lid on them. "The entire history of my love life in a dusty box in the closet." She drew a deep breath and then shut her eyes and pinched the bridge of her nose. For a moment I could almost see the old woman hiding behind her smooth features. My grandfather had trampled her poor, pining heart, and the wound was still raw, even these many years later.

I thought of putting my arm around her, but something stopped me. Here was this beautiful, funny, fascinating girl who, miracle of miracles, really seemed to *like* me. But now I understood that it wasn't me she liked. She was heartbroken for someone else, and I was merely a stand-in for my grandfather. That's enough to give anyone pause, I don't care how horny you are. I know guys who are grossed-out by the idea of dating a *friend's* ex. By that standard, dating your grandfather's ex would practically be incest.

The next thing I knew, Emma's hand was

on my arm. Then her head was on my shoulder, and I could feel her chin tracking slowly toward my face. This was kiss-me body language if there ever was such a thing. In a minute our faces would be level and I'd have to choose between locking lips or seriously offending her by pulling away, and I'd already offended her once. It's not that I didn't *want* to — more than anything I did — but the idea of kissing her two feet from a box of obsessively well-preserved love letters from my grandfather made me feel weird and nervous.

Then her cheek was against mine, and I knew it was now or never, so I said the first mood-killing thing that popped into my head.

"Is there something going on between you and Enoch?"

She pulled away instantly, looking at me like I'd suggested we dine on puppies. "What?! No! Where on earth did you get a twisted idea like that?"

"From him. He sounds kind of bitter when he talks about you, and I get the distinct impression he doesn't want me around, like I'm horning in on his game or something."

Her eyes kept getting wider. "First of all, he doesn't have any 'game' to 'horn in' on, I

305

can assure you of that. He's a jealous fool and a liar."

"Is he?"

"Is he which?"

"A liar."

She narrowed her eyes. "Why? What kind of nonsense has he been spouting?"

"Emma, what happened to Victor?"

She looked shocked. Then, shaking her head, she muttered, "Damn that selfish boy."

"There's something no one here is telling me, and I want to know what it is."

"I can't," she said.

"That's all I've been hearing! I can't talk about the future. You can't talk about the past. Miss Peregrine has us all tied up in knots. My grandfather's last wish was for me to come here and find out the truth. Doesn't that mean anything?"

She took my hand and brought it into her lap and looked down at it. She seemed to be searching for the right words. "You're right," she said finally. "There is something."

"Tell me."

"Not here," she whispered. "Tonight."

We arranged to meet late that night, when my dad and Miss Peregrine would be asleep. Emma insisted it was the only way, because the walls had ears and it was impossible to slip off together during the day without arousing suspicion. To complete the illusion that we had nothing to hide, we spent the rest of the afternoon hanging out in the yard in full view of everyone, and when the sun began to set I walked back to the bog alone.

It was another rainy evening in the twenty-first century, and by the time I reached the pub I was thankful just to be somewhere dry. I found my dad alone, nursing a beer at a table, so I pulled up a chair and began fabricating stories about my day while toweling off my face with napkins. (Something I was beginning to discover about lying: The more I did it, the easier it got.)

He was hardly even listening. "Huh," he'd say, "that's interesting," and then his gaze would drift off and he'd take another swig of beer.

"What's up with you?" I said. "Are you still pissed at me?"

"No, no, nothing like that." He was about to explain but waved it away. "Ahh, it's stupid."

"Dad. Come on."

"It's just . . . this guy who showed up a couple days ago. Another birder."

"Someone you know?"

He shook his head. "Never seen him before. At first I thought he was just some part-time enthusiast yahoo, but he keeps coming back to the same sites, the same nesting grounds, taking notes. He definitely knows what he's doing. Then today I saw him with a banding cage and a pair of Predators, so I know he's a pro."

"Predators?"

"Binoculars. Real serious glass." He'd wadded up his paper placemat and re-smoothed it three times now, a nervous habit. "It's just that I thought I had the scoop on this bird population, you know? I really wanted this book to be something special."

"And then this asshole comes along."

"Jacob."

"I mean, this no-good sonofabitch."

He laughed. "Thank you, son, that'll do."

"It *will* be special," I said reassuringly.

He shrugged. "I dunno. Hope so." But he didn't sound too certain.

I knew exactly what was about to happen. It was part of this pathetic cycle my dad was caught in. He'd get really passionate about some project, talk about it nonstop for months. Then, inevitably, some tiny problem would crop up and throw sand in the gears, and instead of dealing with it he'd let it completely overwhelm him. The next thing you knew, the project would be off and he'd be on to the next one, and the cycle would start again. He got discouraged too easily. It was the reason why he had a dozen unfinished manuscripts locked in his desk, and why the bird store he tried to open with Aunt Susie never got off the ground, and why he had a bachelor's degree in Asian languages but had never been to Asia. He was forty-six years old and still trying to find himself, still trying to prove he didn't need my mother's money.

What he really needed was a pep talk that I didn't feel at all qualified to give, so instead I tried to subtly change the subject. "Where's this interloper staying?" I asked. "I thought we had the only rooms in town."

"I assume he's camping," my dad replied.

"In this weather?"

"It's kind of a hardcore ornithology-geek thing. Roughing it gets you closer to your subjects, both physically and psychologically. Achievement through adversity and all that."

I laughed. "Then why aren't *you* out there?" I said, then immediately wished I hadn't.

"Same reason my book probably won't happen. There's always someone more

309

dedicated than I am."

I shifted awkwardly in my chair. "I didn't mean it like that. What I meant was —"

"Ssh!" My dad stiffened, glancing furtively toward the door. "Look quick but don't make it obvious. He just walked in."

I shielded my face with the menu and peeked over the top. A scruffy-looking bearded guy stood in the doorway, stamping water from his boots. He wore a rain hat and dark glasses and what appeared to be several jackets layered on top of one another, which made him look both fat and vaguely transient.

"I love the homeless Santa Claus thing he's got going," I whispered. "Not an easy look to pull off. Very next-season."

He ignored me. The man bellied up to the bar, and conversations around him quieted a notch or two. Kev asked what he'd like and the man said something and Kev disappeared into the kitchen. He stared straight ahead as he waited, and a minute later Kev came back and handed the guy a doggie bag. He took it, dropped some bills on the bar, and went to the door. Before leaving, he turned to slowly scan the room. Then, after a long moment, he left.

"What'd he order?" my dad shouted when the door had swung shut.

"Coupla steaks," Kev replied. "Said he didn't care how they were cooked, so he got 'em ten-seconds-a-side rare. No complaints."

People began to mutter and speculate, the volume of their conversations rising again.

"Raw steak," I said to my father. "You gotta admit, even for an ornithologist that's a little weird."

"Maybe he's a raw foodist," Dad replied.

"Yeah, right. Or maybe he got tired of feasting on the blood of lambs."

Dad rolled his eyes. "The man obviously has a camp stove. He probably just prefers to cook out in the open."

"In the rain? And why are you defending him, anyway? I thought he was your arch-nemesis."

"I don't expect you to understand," he said, "but it would be nice if you didn't make fun of me." And he stood up to go to the bar.

A few hours later my dad stumbled upstairs, reeking of alcohol, and flopped into his bed. He was asleep instantly, ripping out monster snores. I grabbed a coat and set out to meet Emma, no sneaking necessary.

The streets were deserted and so quiet you could almost hear the dew fall. Clouds stretched thinly across the sky, with just enough moonlight glowing through to light my way. As I crested the ridge, a prickly feeling crept over me, and I looked around to see a man watching me from a distant outcropping. He had his hands raised to his face and his elbows splayed out like he was looking through binoculars. The first thing I thought was *damn it, I'm caught,* assuming it was one of the sheep farmers out on watch, playing detective. But if so, why wasn't he coming over to confront me? Instead he just stood and watched, and I watched back.

Finally I figured *if I'm caught, I'm caught,* because whether I went back now or kept going, one way or another word of my late-night excursion would circle back to my dad. So I raised my arm in a one-fingered salute and descended into the chilly fog.

Coming out of the cairn, it looked like the clouds had been peeled back and the moon pumped up like a big, yellow balloon, so bright I almost had to squint. A few minutes later Emma came wading through the bog, apologizing and talking a mile a minute.

"Sorry I'm late. It took ages for everyone to get to bed! Then on my way out I stumbled over Hugh and Fiona snogging each other's faces off in the garden. But don't worry. They promised not to tell if I didn't."

She threw her arms around my neck. "I missed you," she said. "Sorry about before."

"I am, too," I said, patting her back awkwardly. "So, let's talk."

She pulled away. "Not here. There's a better place. A special place."

"I don't know . . ."

She took my hand. "Don't be that way. You'll adore it, I promise. And when we get there, I'll tell you everything."

I was pretty certain it was a plot to get me to make out with her, and had I been any older or wiser, or one of those guys for whom make-out sessions with hot girls were so frequent as to be of no consequence, I might've had the emotional and hormonal fortitude to demand that we have our talk right then and there. But I was none of those things. Besides, there was the way she beamed at me, smiling with her whole self, and how a coy gesture like tucking her hair back could make me want to follow her, help her, do anything she asked. I was hopelessly outmatched.

I'll go, but I'm not going to kiss her, I told myself. I repeated it like a mantra as she led me across the bog. *Do not kiss! Do not kiss!* We headed for town but veered off toward the rocky beach that looked out onto the lighthouse, picking our way down the steep path to the sand.

Reaching the water's edge, she told me to wait and ran off to retrieve something. I stood watching the lighthouse beam wheel around and wash over everything — a million seabirds sleeping in the pitted cliffs; giant rocks exposed by the low tide; a rotted skiff drowning in the sand. When Emma came back I saw that she had changed into her swimsuit and was holding a pair of snorkel masks.

"Oh no," I said. "No way."

"You might want to strip to your skivvies," she said, looking doubtfully at my jeans and coat. "Your outfit's all wrong for swimming."

"That's because I'm not *going* swimming! I agreed to sneak out and meet you in the middle of the night, fine, but just to *talk,* not to —"

"We *will* talk," she insisted.

"Underwater. In my boxers."

She kicked sand at me and started to walk away but then turned and came back. "I'm not going to attack you, if that's what you're in a knit about. Don't flatter yourself."

"I'm not."

"Then quit mucking about and take off

those silly trousers!" And then she did attack me, wrestling me to the ground and struggling to remove my belt with one hand while rubbing sand in my face with the other.

"Blaggh!" I cried, spitting out sand, "dirty fighter, dirty fighter!" I had no choice but to return the favor with a fistful of my own, and pretty soon things devolved into a no-holds-barred sand fight. When it was over we were both laughing and trying in vain to brush it all out of our hair.

"Well, now you need a bath, so you might as well get in the damned water."

"Okay, *fine.*"

The water was shockingly cold at first — not a great situation vis-à-vis wearing only boxer shorts — but I got used to the temperature pretty quickly. We waded out past the rocks where, lashed to a depth marker, was a canoe. We clambered into it and Emma handed me an oar and we both started paddling, headed toward the lighthouse. The night was warm and the sea calm, and for a few minutes I lost myself in the pleasant rhythm of oars slapping water. About a hundred yards from the lighthouse, Emma stopped paddling and stepped overboard. To my amazement, she didn't slip under the waves but stood up, submerged only to her knees.

"Are you on a sandbar or something?" I asked.

"Nope." She reached into the canoe, pulled out a little anchor, and dropped it. It fell about three feet before stopping with a metallic *clang*. A moment later the light-house beam swept past and I saw the hull of a ship stretching beneath us on all sides.

"A shipwreck!"

"Come on," she said, "we're nearly there. And bring your mask." She started walking across the wrecked boat's hull.

I stepped out gingerly and followed. To anyone watching from shore, it would've looked like we were walking on water.

"How big is this thing, anyway?" I said.

"Massive. It's an allied warship. Hit a friendly mine and sank right here."

She stopped. "Look away from the light-house for a minute," she said. "Let your eyes get used to the dark."

So we stood facing the shore and waited as small waves slapped at our thighs. "All right, now follow me and take a giant breath." She walked over to a dark hole in the ship's hull — a door, from the look of it — then sat down on the edge and plunged in.

This is insane, I thought. And then I

strapped on the mask she'd given me and plunged in after her.

I peered into the enveloping blackness between my feet to see Emma pulling herself even farther down by the rungs of a ladder. I grabbed the top of it and followed, descending hand over hand until it stopped at a metal floor, where she was waiting. We seemed to be in some sort of cargo hold, though it was too dark to tell much more than that.

I tapped her elbow and pointed to my mouth. *I need to breathe.* She patted my arm condescendingly and reached for a length of plastic tubing that hung nearby; it was connected to a pipe that ran up the ladder to the surface. She put the tube in her mouth and blew, her cheeks puffing out with the effort, then took a breath from it and passed it to me. I sucked in a welcome lungful of air. We were twenty feet underwater, inside an old shipwreck, and we were breathing.

Emma pointed at a doorway in front of us, little more than a black hole in the murk. I shook my head. *Don't want to.* But she took my hand as though I were a frightened toddler and led me toward it, bringing the tube along.

We drifted through the doorway into total

darkness. For a while we just hung there, passing the breathing tube between us. There was no sound but our breaths bubbling up and obscure thuds from deep inside the ship, pieces of the broken hull knocking in the current. If I had shut my eyes it wouldn't have been any darker. We were like astronauts floating in a starless universe.

But then a baffling and magnificent thing happened — one by one, the stars came out, here and there a green flash in the dark. I thought I was hallucinating. But then more lit up, and still more, until a whole constellation surged around us like a million green twinkling stars, lighting our bodies, reflecting in our masks. Emma held out a hand and flicked her wrist, but rather than producing a ball of fire her hand glowed a scintillating blue. The green stars coalesced around it, flashing and whirling, echoing her movements like a school of fish, which, I realized, is just what they were.

Mesmerized, I lost all track of time. We stayed there for what seemed like hours, though it was probably only a few minutes. Then I felt Emma nudge me, and we retreated through the doorway and up the ladder, and when we broke the surface again the first thing I saw was the great bold stripe of the Milky Way painted across the heavens, and it occurred to me that together the fish and the stars formed a complete system, coincident parts of some ancient and mysterious whole.

We pulled ourselves onto the hull and took off our masks. For a while we just sat like that, half-submerged, thighs touching, speechless.

"What were those?" I said finally.

"We call them flashlight fish."

"I've never seen one before."

"Most people never do," she said. "They hide."

"They're beautiful."

"Yes."

"And peculiar."

Emma smiled. "They are that, too." And then her hand crept onto my knee, and I let it stay there because it felt warm and good in the cool water. I listened for the voice in my head telling me not to kiss her, but it had gone silent.

And then we were kissing. The profoundness of our lips touching and our tongues pressing and my hand cupping her perfect white cheek barred any thoughts of right or wrong or any memory of why I had followed her there in the first place. We were kissing and kissing and then suddenly it was over.

As she pulled away I followed her face with mine. She put a hand on my chest, at once gentle and firm. "I need to breathe, dummy."

I laughed. "Okay."

She took my hands and looked at me, and I looked back. It was almost more intense than kissing, the just looking. And then she said, "You should stay."

"Stay," I repeated.

"Here. With us."

The reality of her words filtered through, and the tingly magic of what had just happened between us numbed out.

"I want to, but I don't think I can."

"Why not?"

I considered the idea. The sun, the feasts, the friends . . . and the sameness, the perfect identical days. You can get sick of anything if you have too much of it, like all the petty luxuries my mother bought and quickly grew bored with.

But Emma. There was Emma. Maybe it wasn't so strange, what we could have. Maybe I could stay for a while and love her and then go home. But no. By the time I wanted to leave, it would be too late. She was a siren. I had to be strong.

"It's him you want, not me. I can't be him for you."

She looked away, stung. "That isn't why you should stay. You belong here, Jacob."

"I don't. I'm not like you."

"Yes, you are," she insisted.

"I'm not. I'm common, just like my grandfather."

Emma shook her head. "Is that really what you think?"

"If I could do something spectacular like you, don't you think I would've noticed by now?"

"I'm not meant to tell you this," she said, "but common people can't pass through time loops."

I considered this for a moment, but couldn't make sense of it. "There's nothing peculiar about me. I'm the most average person you'll ever meet."

"I doubt that very much," she replied. "Abe had a rare and peculiar talent, something almost no one else could do."

And then she met my eyes and said, "He could see the monsters."

CHAPTER NINE

He could see the monsters. The moment she said it, all the horrors I thought I'd put behind me came flooding back.

They were real. They were real and they'd killed my grandfather.

"I can see them, too," I told her, whispering it like a secret shame.

Her eyes welled and she embraced me. "I knew there was something peculiar about you," she said. "And I mean that as the highest compliment."

I'd always known I was strange. I never dreamed I was peculiar. But if I could see things almost no one else could, it explained why Ricky hadn't seen anything in the woods the night my grandfather was killed. It explained why everyone thought I was crazy. I wasn't crazy or seeing things or having a stress reaction; the panicky twist in my gut whenever they were close — that and the awful sight of them — that was my gift.

"And you can't see them at all?" I asked her.

"Only their shadows, which is why they hunt mainly at night."

"What's stopping them from coming after you right now?" I asked, then corrected myself. "All of us, I mean."

She turned serious. "They don't know where to find us. That and they can't enter loops. So we're safe on the island — but we can't leave."

"But Victor did."

She nodded sadly. "He said he was going mad here. Said he couldn't stand it any longer. Poor Bronwyn. My Abe left, too, but at least he wasn't murdered by hollows."

I forced myself to look at her. "I'm really sorry to have to tell you this . . ."

"What? Oh no."

"They convinced me it was wild animals. But if what you're saying is true, my grandfather was murdered by them, too. The first and only time I saw one was the night he died."

She hugged her knees to her chest and closed her eyes. I slid my arm around her, and she tilted her head against mine.

"I knew they'd get him eventually," she

whispered. "He promised me he'd be safe in America. That he could protect himself. But we're never safe — none of us — not really."

We sat talking on the wrecked ship until the moon got low and the water lapped at our throats and Emma began to shiver. Then we linked hands and waded back to the canoe. Paddling toward the beach, we heard voices calling our names, and then we came around a rock and saw Hugh and Fiona waving at us on the shore. Even from a distance, it was clear something was wrong.

We tied the canoe and ran to meet them. Hugh was out of breath, bees darting around him in a state of agitation. "Something's happened! You've got to come back with us!"

There was no time to argue. Emma pulled her clothes over her swimsuit and I tripped into my pants, all gritty with sand. Hugh regarded me uncertainly. "Not him, though," he said. "This is serious."

"No, Hugh," Emma said. "The Bird was right. He's one of us."

He gaped at her, then at me. "You *told* him?!"

"I had to. He'd practically worked it out for himself, anyway."

Hugh seemed taken aback for a moment but then turned and gave me a resolute handshake. "Then welcome to the family."

I didn't know what to say, so I just said, "Thanks."

On the way to the house, we gleaned sketchy bits of information from Hugh about what had happened, but mostly we just ran. When we stopped in the woods to catch our breath, he said, "It's one of the Bird's ymbryne friends. She winged in an hour ago in a terrible state, yelling blue murder and rousing everyone from their beds. Before we could understand what she was getting at she fainted dead off." He wrung his hands, looking miserable. "Oh, I just *know* something wicked's happened."

"I hope you're wrong," said Emma, and we ran on.

In the hall just outside the sitting room's closed door, children in rumpled night-clothes huddled around a kerosene lantern, trading rumors about what might have happened.

"Perhaps they forgot to reset their loop," said Claire.

"Bet you it was hollows," Enoch said. "Bet they ate the lot of 'em too, right down to their boots!"

Claire and Olive wailed and clapped their little hands over their faces. Horace knelt beside them and said in a comforting voice, "There, there. Don't let Enoch fill your heads with rubbish. Everyone knows hollows like young ones best. That's why they let Miss Peregrine's friend go — she tastes like old coffee grounds!"

Olive peeked out from between her fingers. "What do young ones taste like?"

"Lingonberries," he said matter-of-factly. The girls wailed again.

"Leave them alone!" Hugh shouted, and a squadron of bees sent Horace yelping down the hall.

"What's going on out there?" Miss Peregrine called from inside the sitting room. "Is that Mr. Apiston I hear? Where are Miss Bloom and Mr. Portman?"

Emma cringed and shot Hugh a nervous look. "She knows?"

"When she found out you were gone, she just about went off her chump. Thought you'd been abducted by wights or some barminess. Sorry, Em. I had to tell her."

Emma shook her head, but all we could do was go in and face the music. Fiona gave us a little salute — as if to wish us luck — and we opened the doors.

Inside the sitting room, the only light was

a hearth fire that threw our quivering shadows against the wall. Bronwyn hovered anxiously around an old woman who was teetering half-conscious in a chair, mummied up in a blanket. Miss Peregrine sat on an ottoman, feeding the woman spoonfuls of dark liquid.

When Emma saw her face, she froze. "Oh my God," she whispered. "It's Miss Avocet."

Only then did I recognize her, though just barely, from the photograph Miss Peregrine had shown me of herself as a young girl. Miss Avocet had seemed so indomitable then, but now she looked frail and weak.

As we stood watching, Miss Peregrine brought a silver flask to Miss Avocet's lips and tipped it, and for a moment the elder ymbryne seemed to revive, sitting forward with brightening eyes. But then her expression dulled again and she sank back into the chair.

"Miss Bruntley," said Miss Peregrine to Bronwyn, "go and make up the fainting couch for Miss Avocet and then fetch a bottle of coca wine and another flask of brandy."

Bronwyn trooped out, nodding solemnly as they passed. Next Miss Peregrine turned to us and said in a low voice, "I am tremendously disappointed in you, Miss Bloom.

Tremendously. And of all the nights to sneak away."

"I'm sorry, Miss. But how was I to know something bad would happen?"

"I should punish you. However, given the circumstances, it hardly seems worth the effort." She raised a hand and smoothed her mentor's white hair. "Miss Avocet would never have left her wards to come here unless something dire had taken place."

The roaring fire made beads of sweat break out on my forehead, but in her chair Miss Avocet lay shivering. Would she die? Was the tragic scene that had played out between my grandfather and me about to play out again, this time between Miss Peregrine and her teacher? I pictured it: me holding my grandfather's body, terrified and confused, never suspecting the truth about him or myself. What was happening now, I decided, was nothing like what had happened to me. Miss Peregrine had always known who she was.

It hardly seemed like the time to bring it up, but I was angry and couldn't help myself. "Miss Peregrine?" I began, and she looked up. "When were you going to tell me?"

She was about to ask *what,* but then her eyes went to Emma, and she seemed to read the answer on her face. For a moment she looked mad, but then she saw my anger, and her own faded. "Soon, lad. Please understand. To have laid the entire truth upon you at our first meeting would have been an awful shock. Your behavior was unpredictable. You might've fled, never to return. I could not take that risk."

"So instead you tried to seduce me with food and fun and girls while keeping all the bad things a secret?"

Emma gasped. "*Seduce?* Oh, please, don't think that of me, Jacob. I couldn't bear it."

"I fear you've badly misjudged us," said Miss Peregrine. "As for seducing you, what you've seen is how we live. There has been no deception, only the withholding of a few facts."

"Well here's a fact for you," I said. "One of those creatures killed my grandfather."

Miss Peregrine stared at the fire for a moment. "I am very sorry to hear that."

"I saw one with my own eyes. When I told people about it, they tried to convince me I was crazy. But I wasn't, and neither was my grandfather. His whole life he'd been telling me the truth, and I didn't believe him." Shame flooded over me. "If I had, maybe he'd still be alive."

Miss Peregrine saw that I was wobbling

and offered me the chair across from Miss Avocet.

I sat, and Emma knelt down beside me. "Abe must've known you were peculiar," she said. "And he must've had a good reason for not telling you."

"He did indeed know," replied Miss Peregrine. "He said as much in a letter."

"I don't understand, then. If it was all true — all his stories — and if he knew I was like him, why did he keep it a secret until the last minute of his life?"

Miss Peregrine spoon-fed more brandy to Miss Avocet, who groaned and sat up a little before settling back into the chair. "I can only imagine that he wanted to protect you," she said. "Ours can be a life of trials and deprivations. Abe's life was doubly so because he was born a Jew in the worst of times. He faced a double genocide, of Jews by the Nazis and of peculiars by the hollowgast. He was tormented by the idea that he was hiding here while his people, both Jews and peculiars, were being slaughtered."

"He used to say he'd gone to war to fight monsters," I said.

"He did," said Emma.

"The war ended the Nazis' rule, but the hollowgast emerged stronger than ever," Miss Peregrine continued. "So, like many peculiars, we remained in hiding. But your grandfather returned a changed man. He'd become a warrior, and he was determined to build a life for himself outside the loop. He refused to hide."

"I begged him not to go to America," Emma said. "We all did."

"Why did he choose America?" I asked.

"It had few hollowgast at that time," Miss Peregrine replied. "After the war there was a minor exodus of peculiars to America. For a while many were able to pass as common, as your grandfather did. It was his fondest wish to be common, to live a common life. He often mentioned it in his letters. I'm sure that's why he kept the truth from you for so long. He wanted for you what he could never have for himself."

"To be ordinary," I said.

Miss Peregrine nodded. "But he could never escape his peculiarity. His unique skill, coupled with the prowess he'd honed during the war as a hunter of hollows, made him too valuable. He was often pressed into service, asked to help eradicate troublesome pockets of hollows. His nature was such that he rarely refused."

I thought about all the long hunting trips Grandpa Portman used to go on. My family had a picture of him taken during one of these, though I don't know who took it or when since he almost always went alone. But when I was a kid I thought it was the funniest thing because, in the picture, he's wearing a suit. Who brings a suit on a hunting trip?

Now I knew: Someone who's hunting more than just animals.

I was moved by this new idea of my grandfather, not as a paranoiac gun nut or a secretive philanderer or a man who wasn't there for his family, but as a wandering knight who risked his life for others, living out of cars and cheap motels, stalking lethal shadows, coming home shy a few bullets and marked with bruises he could never quite explain and nightmares he couldn't talk about. For his many sacrifices, he received only scorn and suspicion from those he loved. I guess that's why he wrote so many letters to Emma and Miss Peregrine. They understood.

Bronwyn returned with a decanter of coca wine and another flask of brandy. Miss Peregrine sent her away and set about mixing them together in a teacup. Then she began to pat Miss Avocet gently on her blue-veined cheek.

"Esmerelda," she said, "Esmerelda, you must rouse yourself and drink this tonic I've

prepared."

Miss Avocet moaned, and Miss Peregrine raised the teacup to her lips. The old woman took a few sips and, though she sputtered and coughed, most of the purplish liquid disappeared down her throat. For a moment she stared as if about to sink back into her stupor, but then she sat forward, face brightening.

"Oh, my," she said, her voice a dry rasp. "Have I fallen asleep? How indecorous of me." She looked at us in mild surprise, as if we'd appeared out of nowhere. "Alma? Is that you?"

Miss Peregrine kneaded the old woman's bony hands. "Esmerelda, you've come a long way to see us in the dead of night. I'm afraid you've got us all terribly worked up."

"Have I?" Miss Avocet squinted and furrowed her brow, and her eyes seemed to fix on the opposite wall, alive with flickering shadows. Then a haunted expression stole across her face. "Yes," she said, "I've come to warn you, Alma. You must be on your guard. You mustn't allow yourselves to be taken by surprise, as I was."

Miss Peregrine stopped kneading. "By what?"

"They could only have been wights. A pair of them came in the night, disguised as council members. There are no male council members, of course, but it fooled my sleep-dazed wards just long enough for the wights to bind them and drag them away."

Miss Peregrine gasped. "Oh, Esmerelda . . ."

"Miss Bunting and I were awoken by their anguished cries," she explained, "but we found ourselves barricaded inside the house. It took some time to force the doors, but when we did and followed the wights' stink out of the loop, there was a gang of shadow-beasts lying in wait on the other side. They fell upon us, howling." She stopped, choking back tears.

"And the children?"

Miss Avocet shook her head. All the light seemed to have gone out of her eyes. "The children were merely bait," she said.

Emma slid her hand into mine and squeezed, and I saw Miss Peregrine's cheeks glisten in the firelight.

"It was Miss Bunting and myself whom they wanted. I was able to escape, but Miss Bunting was not so fortunate."

"She was killed?"

"No — abducted. Just as Miss Wren and Miss Treecreeper were when their loops were invaded a fortnight ago. They're taking ymbrynes, Alma. It's some sort of coordinated effort. For what purpose, I shudder to imagine."

"Then they'll come for us, too," Miss Peregrine said quietly.

"If they can find you," replied Miss Avocet. "You are better hidden than most, but you must be ready, Alma."

Miss Peregrine nodded. Miss Avocet looked helplessly at her hands, trembling in her lap like a broken-winged bird. Her voice began to hitch. "Oh, my dear children. Pray for them. They are all alone now." And she turned away and wept.

Miss Peregrine pulled the blanket around the old woman's shoulders and rose. We followed her out, leaving Miss Avocet to her grief.

We found the children huddled around the sitting-room door. If they hadn't heard everything Miss Avocet had said, they'd heard enough, and it showed on their anxious faces.

"Poor Miss Avocet," Claire whimpered, her bottom lip trembling.

"Poor Miss Avocet's children," said Olive.

"Are they coming for us now, Miss?" asked Horace.

"We'll need weapons!" cried Millard.

"Battle-axes!" said Enoch.

"Bombs!" said Hugh.

"Stop that at once!" Miss Peregrine shouted, raising her hands for quiet. "We must all remain calm. Yes, what happened to Miss Avocet was tragic — profoundly so — but it was a tragedy that need not be repeated here. However, we must be on watch. Henceforth, you will travel beyond the house only with my consent, and then only in pairs. Should you observe a person unknown to you, even if they appear to be peculiar, come immediately and inform me. We'll discuss these and other precautionary measures in the morning. Until then, to bed with you! This is no hour for a meeting."

"But Miss —" Enoch began.

"To bed!"

The children scurried off to their rooms. "As for you, Mr. Portman, I'm not terribly comfortable with you traveling alone. I think perhaps you should stay, at least until things calm a bit."

"I can't just disappear. My dad will flip out."

She frowned. "In that case, you must at least spend the night. I insist upon it."

"I will, but only if you'll tell me everything you know about the creatures that killed my grandfather."

She tilted her head, studying me with

something like amusement. "Very well, Mr. Portman, I won't argue with your need to know. Install yourself on the divan for the evening and we'll discuss it first thing."

"It has to be now." I'd waited ten years to hear the truth, and I couldn't wait another minute. "Please."

"At times, young man, you tread a precariously thin line between being charmingly headstrong and insufferably pigheaded." She turned to Emma. "Miss Bloom, would you fetch my flask of coca wine? It seems I won't be sleeping tonight, and I shall have to indulge if I am to keep awake."

The study was too close to the children's bedrooms for a late-night talk, so the headmistress and I adjourned to a little greenhouse that edged the woods. We sat on overturned planters among climbing roses, a kerosene lantern on the grass between us, dawn not yet broken beyond the glass walls. Miss Peregrine drew a pipe from her pocket, and bent to light it in the lamp flame. She drew a few thoughtful puffs, sending up wreaths of blue smoke, then began.

"In ancient times people mistook us for gods," she said, "but we peculiars are no less mortal than common folk. Time loops merely delay the inevitable, and the price we pay for using them is hefty — an irrevocable divorce from the ongoing present. As you know, long-term loop dwellers can but dip their toes into the present lest they wither and die. This has been the arrangement since time immemorial."

She took another puff, then continued.

"Some years ago, around the turn of the last century, a splinter faction emerged among our people — a coterie of disaffected peculiars with dangerous ideas. They believed they had discovered a method by which the function of time loops could be perverted to confer upon the user a kind of immortality; not merely the suspension of aging, but the reversal of it. They spoke of eternal youth enjoyed outside the confines of loops, of jumping back and forth from future to past with impunity, suffering none of the ill effects that have always prevented such recklessness — in other words, of mastering time without being mastered by death. The whole notion was mad — absolute bunkum — a refutation of the empirical laws that govern everything!"

She exhaled sharply, then paused for a moment to collect herself.

"In any case. My two brothers, technically brilliant but rather lacking in sense, were taken with the idea. They even had the audacity to request my assistance in making it a reality. You're talking about making yourselves into gods, I said. It can't be done. And even if it can, it shouldn't. But they would not be deterred. Having grown up among Miss Avocet's ymbrynes-in-training, they knew more about our unique art than most peculiar males — just enough, I'm afraid, to be dangerous. Despite warnings, even threats, from the Council, in the summer of 1908 my brothers and several hundred members of this renegade faction — a number of powerful ymbrynes among them, traitors every one — ventured into the Siberian tundra to conduct their hateful experiment. For the site they chose a nameless old loop unused for centuries. We expected them to return within a week, tails between their legs, humbled by the immutable nature of nature. Instead, their comeuppance was far more dramatic: a catastrophic explosion that rattled windows as far as the Azores. Anyone within five hundred kilometers surely thought it was the end of the world. We assumed they'd all been killed, that obscene world-cracking bang their last collective utterance."

"But they survived," I guessed.

"In a manner of speaking. Others might call the state of being they subsequently assumed a kind of living damnation. Weeks later there began a series of attacks upon peculiars by awful creatures who, apart from their shadows, could not be seen except by peculiars like yourself — our very first clashes with the hollowgast. It was some time before we realized that these tentacle-mawed abominations were in fact our wayward brothers, crawled from the smoking crater left behind by their experiment. Rather than becoming gods, they had transformed themselves into devils."

"What went wrong?"

"That is still a matter of debate. One theory is that they reverse-aged themselves to a time before even their souls had been conceived, which is why we call them *hollowgast* — because their hearts, their souls, are empty. In a cruel twist of irony, they achieved the immortality they'd been seeking. It's believed that the hollows can live thousands of years, but it is a life of constant physical torment, of humiliating debasement — feeding on stray animals, living in isolation — and of insatiable hunger for the flesh of their former kin, because our blood is their only hope for salvation. If a hollow gorges itself on enough peculiars, it becomes a wight."

"That word again," I said. "When we first

met, Emma accused me of being one."

"I might have thought the same thing, if I hadn't observed you beforehand."

"What are they?"

"If being a hollow is a living hell — and it most certainly is — then being a wight is akin to purgatory. Wights are almost common. They have no peculiar abilities. But because they can pass for human, they live in servitude to their hollow brethren, acting as scouts and spies and procurers of flesh. It's a hierarchy of the damned that aims someday to turn all hollows into wights and all peculiars into corpses."

"But what's stopping them?" I said. "If they used to be peculiar, don't they know all your hiding places?"

"Fortunately, they don't appear to retain any memory of their former lives. And though wights aren't as strong or as frightening as hollows, they're often just as dangerous. Unlike hollows, they're ruled by more than instinct, and are often able to blend into the general population. It can be difficult to distinguish them from common folk, though there are certain indicators. Their eyes, for instance. Curiously, wights lack pupils."

I broke out in goosebumps, remembering the white-eyed neighbor I'd seen watering

his overgrown lawn the night my grandfather was killed. "I think I've seen one. I
thought he was just an old blind man."

"Then you are more observant than
most," she said. "Wights are adept at passing unnoticed. They tend to adopt personas
invisible to society: the gray-suited man on
the train; the indigent begging for spare
coins; just faces in the crowd. Though some
have been known to risk exposure by plac-
ing themselves in more prominent positions
— physicians, politicians, clergymen — in
order to interact with a greater number of
people, or to have some measure of power
over them, so that they can more easily
discover peculiars who might be hiding
among common folk — as Abe was."

Miss Peregrine reached for a photo album
she'd brought from the house and began to
flip through it. "These have been repro-
duced and distributed to peculiars everywhere, rather like wanted posters. Look
here," she said, pointing to a picture of two
girls astride a fake reindeer, a chilling blank-
eyed Santa Claus peeping out through its
antlers. "This wight was discovered working
in an American department store at Christmas. He was able to interact with a great
many children in a remarkably short time
— touching them, interrogating them —

screening for signs of peculiarity."

She turned the page to reveal a photo of a sadistic-looking dentist. "This wight worked as an oral surgeon. It wouldn't surprise me to learn that the skull he's posing with belonged to one of his peculiar victims."

She flipped the page again, this time to a picture of a little girl cowering before a looming shadow. "This is Marcie. She left us thirty years ago to live with a common family in the countryside. I pleaded with her to stay, but she was determined. Not long after, she was snatched by a wight as she waited for the school bus. A camera was found at the scene with this undeveloped picture inside."

"Who took it?"

"The wight himself. They are fond of dramatic gestures, and invariably leave behind some taunting memento."

I studied the pictures, a small, familiar dread turning inside me.

When I couldn't bear to look at the pictures anymore, I shut the album.

"I tell you all this because to know it is your birthright," Miss Peregrine said, "but also because I need your help. You are the only one among us who can go outside the loop without arousing suspicion. So long as you're with us, and you insist upon travel-

346

ing back and forth, I need you to watch for new arrivals to the island and report them to me."

"There was one just the other day," I said, thinking of the birder who had upset my dad.

"Did you see his eyes?" she asked.

"Not really. It was dark, and he was wearing a big hat that hid part of his face."

Miss Peregrine chewed her knuckle, her brow furrowing.

"Why? Do you think he could be one of them?"

"It's impossible to be certain without seeing the eyes," she said, "but the possibility that you were followed to the island concerns me very much."

"What do you mean? By a wight?"

"Perhaps the very one you described seeing on the night of your grandfather's death. It would explain why they chose to spare your life — so that you could lead them to an even richer prize: this place."

"But how could they have known I was peculiar? *I* didn't even know!"

"If they knew about your grandfather, you can be certain they knew about you, as well."

I thought about all the chances they must've had to kill me. All the times I'd felt them nearby in the weeks after Grandpa Portman died. Had they been watching me? Waiting for me to do exactly what I did, and come here?

Feeling overwhelmed, I put my head down on my knees. "I don't suppose you could let me have a sip of that wine," I said.

"Absolutely not."

All of the sudden I felt my chest clench up. "Will I ever be safe anywhere?" I asked her.

Miss Peregrine touched my shoulder. "You're safe here," she said. "And you may live with us as long as you like."

I tried to speak, but all that came out was little stutters. "But I — I can't — my parents."

"They may love you," she whispered, "but they'll never understand."

By the time I got back to town, the sun was casting its first long shadows across the streets, all-night drinkers were wheeling around lampposts on their reluctant journeys home, fishermen were trudging soberly to the harbor in great black boots, and my father was just beginning to stir from a heavy sleep. As he rolled out of his bed I was crawling into mine, pulling the covers over my sandy clothes only seconds before

349

he opened the door to check on me.

"Feeling okay?"

I groaned and rolled away from him, and he went out. Late that afternoon I woke to find a sympathetic note and a packet of flu pills on the common room table. I smiled and felt briefly guilty for lying to him. Then I began to worry about him, out there wandering across the headlands with his binoculars and little notebook, possibly in the company of a sheep-murdering madman.

Rubbing the sleep from my eyes and throwing on a rain jacket, I walked a circuit around the village and then around the nearby cliffs and beaches, hoping to see either my father or the strange ornithologist — and get a good look at his eyes — but I didn't find either of them. It was nearing dusk when I finally gave up and returned to the Priest Hole, where I found my father at the bar, tipping back a beer with the regulars. Judging from the empty bottles around him, he'd been there a while.

I sat down next to him and asked if he'd seen the bearded birder. He said he hadn't.

"Well, if you do," I said, "do me a favor and keep your distance, okay?"

He looked at me strangely. "Why?"

"He just rubs me the wrong way. What if

he's some nutcase? What if *he's* the one who killed those sheep?"

"Where do you get these bizarre ideas?"

I wanted to tell him. I wanted to explain everything, and for him to tell me he understood and offer some tidbit of parental advice. I wanted, in that moment, for everything to go back to the way it had been before we came here; before I ever found that letter from Miss Peregrine, back when I was just a sort-of-normal messed-up rich kid in the suburbs. Instead, I sat next to my dad for awhile and talked about nothing, and I tried to remember what my life had been like in that unfathomably distant era that was four weeks ago, or imagine what it might be like four weeks from now — but I couldn't. Eventually we ran out of nothing to talk about, and I excused myself and went upstairs to be alone.

CHAPTER TEN

On Tuesday night, most of what I thought I understood about myself had turned out to be wrong. On Sunday morning, my dad and I were supposed to pack our things and go home. I had just a few days to decide what to do. Stay or go — neither option seemed good. How could I possibly stay here and leave behind everthing I'd known? But after all I'd learned, how could I go home?

Even worse, there was no one I could talk to about it. Dad was out of the question. Emma made frequent and passionate arguments as to why I should stay, none of which acknowledged the life I would be abandoning (however meager it seemed), or how the sudden inexplicable disappearance of their only child might affect my parents, or the stifling suffocation that Emma herself had admitted feeling inside the loop. She would only say, "With you here, it'll be better."

Miss Peregrine was even less helpful. Her only answer was that she couldn't make such a decision for me, even though I only wanted to talk it through. Still, it was obvious she wanted me to stay; beyond my own safety, my presence in the loop would make everyone else safer. But I didn't relish the idea of spending my life as their watchdog. (I was beginning to suspect my grandfather had felt the same way, and it was part of the reason he'd refused to return after the war.)

Joining the peculiar children would also mean I wouldn't finish high school or go to college or do any of the normal growing-up things people do. Then again, I had to keep reminding myself, I *wasn't* normal; and as long as hollows were hunting me, any life lived outside the loop would almost certainly be cut short. I'd spend the rest of my days living in fear, looking over my shoulder, tormented by nightmares, waiting for them to finally come back and punch my ticket. That sounded a lot worse than missing out on college.

Then I thought: Isn't there a third option? Couldn't I be like Grandpa Portman, who for fifty years had lived and thrived and fended off hollows outside the loop? That's when the self-deprecating voice in my head kicked in.

He was military-trained, dummy. A stone-cold badass. He had a walk-in closet full of sawed-off shotguns. The man was Rambo compared to you.

I could sign up for a class at the gun range, the optimistic part of me would think. *Take Karate. Work out.*

Are you joking? You couldn't even protect yourself in high school! You had to bribe that redneck to be your bodyguard. And you'd wet your pants if you so much as pointed a real gun at anyone.

No, I wouldn't.

You're weak. You're a loser. That's why he never told you who you really were. He knew you couldn't handle it.

Shut up. Shut up.

For days I went back and forth like this. Stay or go. I obsessed constantly without resolution. Meanwhile, Dad completely lost steam on his book. The less he worked, the more discouraged he got, and the more discouraged he got, the more time he spent in the bar. I'd never seen him drink that way — six, seven beers a night — and I didn't want to be around him when he was like that. He was dark, and when he wasn't sulking in silence he would tell me things I really didn't want to know.

"One of these days your mother's gonna

leave me," he said one night. "If I don't make something happen pretty soon, I really think she might."

I started avoiding him. I'm not sure he even noticed. It became depressingly easy to lie about my comings and goings.

Meanwhile, at the home for peculiar children, Miss Peregrine instituted a near-lockdown. It was like martial law had been declared: The smaller kids couldn't go anywhere without an escort, the older ones traveled in pairs, and Miss Peregrine had to know where everyone was at all times. Just getting permission to go outside was an ordeal.

Sentries were drafted into rotating shifts to watch the front and rear of the house. At all times of the day and most of the night you could see bored faces peeping out of windows. If they spotted someone approaching, they yanked a pull-chain that rang a bell in Miss Peregrine's room, which meant that whenever I arrived she'd be waiting inside the door to interrogate me. What was happening outside the loop? Had I seen anything strange? Was I sure I hadn't been followed?

Not surprisingly, the kids began to go a little nuts. The little ones got rambunctious while the older ones moped, complaining about the new rules in voices just loud enough to be overheard. Dramatic sighs erupted out of thin air, often the only cue that Millard had wandered into a room. Hugh's insects swarmed and stung people until they were banished from the house, after which Hugh spent all his time at the window, his bees screening the other side of the glass.

Olive, claiming she had misplaced her leaden shoes, took to crawling around the ceiling like a fly, dropping grains of rice on people's heads until they looked up and noticed her, at which point she'd burst into laughter so all-consuming that her levitation would falter and she'd have to grab onto a chandelier or curtain rod just to keep from falling. Strangest of all was Enoch, who disappeared into his basement laboratory to perform experimental surgeries on his clay soldiers that would've made Dr. Frankenstein cringe: amputating the limbs from two to make a hideous spider-man of a third, or cramming four chicken hearts into a single chest cavity in an attempt to create a super-clay-man who would never run out of energy. One by one their little gray bodies failed under the strain, and the basement came to resemble a Civil War field hospital.

For her part, Miss Peregrine remained in a constant state of motion, chain-smoking pipes while limping from room to room to check on the children, as if they might disappear the moment they left her sight. Miss Avocet stayed on, emerging from her torpor now and then to wander the halls, calling out forlornly for her poor abandoned wards before slumping into someone's arms to be taken back to bed. There followed a great deal of paranoid speculation about Miss Avocet's tragic ordeal and why hollows would want to kidnap ymbrynes, with theories ranging from the bizarre (to create the biggest time loop in history, large enough to swallow the whole planet) to the ridiculously optimistic (to keep the hollows company; being a horrible soul-eating monster can get pretty lonely).

Eventually, a morbid quiet settled over the house. Two days of confinement had made everyone lethargic. Believing that routine was the best defense against depression, Miss Peregrine tried to keep everyone interested in her daily lessons, in preparing the daily meals, and in keeping the house spic and span. But whenever they weren't under direct orders to do something, the children sank heavily into chairs, stared listlessly out locked windows, paged through dog-eared books they'd read a hundred times before, or slept.

I'd never seen Horace's peculiar talent in action until, one evening, he began to scream. A bunch of us rushed upstairs to the garret where he'd been on sentry duty to find him rigid in a chair, in the grips of what seemed to be a waking nightmare, clawing at the air in horror. At first his screaming was just that, but then he began to babble, yelling about the seas boiling and ash raining from the sky and an endless blanket of smoke smothering the earth. After a few minutes of these apocalyptic pronouncements, he seemed to wear himself out and fell into an uneasy sleep.

The others had seen this happen before — often enough that there were photos of his episodes in Miss Peregrine's album — and they knew what to do. Under the headmistress's direction, they carried him by the arms and legs to bed, and when he woke a few hours later he claimed he couldn't remember the dream and that dreams he couldn't remember rarely came true. The others accepted this because they already had too much else to worry about. I sensed he was holding something back.

When someone goes missing in a town as small as Cairnholm, it doesn't go unnoticed.

That's why on Wednesday, when Martin failed to open his museum or stop by the Priest Hole for his customary nightcap, people began to wonder if he was sick, and when Kev's wife went to check on him and found his front door hanging open and his wallet and glasses on the kitchen counter but no one at home, people began to wonder if he was dead. When he still hadn't turned up the next day, a gang of men was dispatched to open sheds and peer beneath overturned boats, searching anywhere a wifeless man who loved whiskey might sleep off a binge. But they'd only just begun when a call came in over the short-band radio: Martin's body had been fished out of the ocean.

I was in the pub with my dad when the fisherman who'd found him came in. It was hardly past noon but he was issued a beer on principle, and within minutes the man was telling his story.

"I was up Gannet's Point reelin' in my nets," he began. "They was heavy as anything, which was odd since all's I generally catch out thatways is just tidy little nothins, shrimps and such. Thought I'd got snagged on a crab trap, so I grab for the gaff and poke around under the boat till it hooks on something." We all scooted closer on our stools, like it was story-time in some morbid kindergarten. "It was Martin all right. Looked like he'd taken a quick trip down a cliffside and got nibbled by sharks. Lord knows what business he had bein' out by them cliffs in the dead of night in just his robe and trolleys."

"He weren't dressed?" Kev asked.

"Dressed for bed, maybe," said the fisherman. "Not for a walk in the wet."

Brief prayers were muttered for Martin's soul, and then people began trading theories. Within minutes the place was a smoke-filled den of tipsy Sherlock Holmeses.

"He coulda been drunk," one man ventured.

"Or if he was out by the cliffs, maybe he seen the sheep killer and was chasin' after," said another.

"What about that squirrely new fella?" the fisherman said. "The one who's camping."

My father straightened on his barstool. "I ran into him," he said. "Two nights ago."

I turned to him in surprise. "You didn't tell me."

"I was going to the chemist, trying to catch him before he closed, and this guy's headed the other way, out of town. In a huge hurry. I bump his shoulder as he passes, just to ruffle him. He stops and stares at me. Trying to be intimidating. I get in his face, tell him I want to know what he's doing here, what he's working on. Because people here talk about themselves, I say."

Kev leaned across the bar. "And?"

"He looks like he's about to take a swing at me, but then just walks off."

A lot of the men had questions — what an ornithologist does, why the guy was camping, and other things I already knew. I had only one question, which I'd been itching to ask. "Did you notice anything strange about him? About his face?"

My father thought for a second. "Yeah, actually. He had on sunglasses."

"At *night?*"

"Weirdest damn thing."

A sick feeling came over me, and I wondered how close my father had come to something far worse than a fistfight. I knew I had to tell Miss Peregrine about this — and soon.

"Ah, bollocks," said Kev. "There ain't been a murder on Cairnholm in a hundred years. Why would anyone want to kill old Martin, anyway? It don't make sense. I'll bet you all a round that when his autopsy comes back, it says he was arseholed right into the next century."

"Could be a tidy spell before that happens," the fisherman said. "Storm that's rollin' in now, weatherman says it's gonna be a right bomper. Worst we've had all year."

"Weatherman says," Kev scoffed. "I wouldn't trust that silly bugger to know if it's raining *now*."

The islanders often made gloomy predictions about what Mother Nature had in store for Cairnholm — they were at the mercy of the elements, after all, and pessimistic by default — but this time their worst fears were confirmed. The wind and rain that had pelted the island all week strengthened that night into a vicious band of storms that closed blackly over the sky and whipped the sea into foam. Between rumors about Martin having been murdered and the weather, the town went into lockdown much as the children's home had. People stayed in their houses. Windows were shuttered and doors bolted tight. Boats clattered against their moorings in the heavy chop but none left the harbor; to take one out in such a gale would've been suicidal. And because the mainland police couldn't collect Martin's body until the seas calmed, the townspeople were left with the nettlesome question of what to do with his body.

It was finally decided that the fishmonger, who had the island's largest stockpile of ice, would keep him cool in the back of his shop, among salmon and cod and other things. Which, like Martin, had been pulled from the sea.

I was under strict instructions from my father not to leave the Priest Hole, but I was also under instructions to report any strange goings-on to Miss Peregrine — and if a suspicious death didn't qualify, nothing did. So that night I feigned a flulike illness and locked myself in my room, then slipped out the window and climbed down a drainpipe to the ground. No one else was foolish enough to be outside, so I ran straight down the main path without fear of being spotted, the hood of my jacket scrunched tight against the whipping rain.

When I got to the children's home, Miss Peregrine took one look at me and knew something was wrong. "What's happened?" she said, her bloodshot eyes ranging over me.

I told her everything, all the sketchy facts and rumors I'd overheard, and she blanched. She hurried me into the sitting room, where in a panic she gathered all the kids she could find and then stomped off to find a few who had ignored her shouts. The rest were left to stand around, anxious and confused.

Emma and Millard cornered me. "What's she in such a tiff about?" Millard asked.

I quietly told them about Martin. Millard sucked in his breath and Emma crossed her arms, looking worried.

"Is it really that bad?" I said. "I mean, it can't have been hollows. They only hunt peculiars, right?"

Emma groaned. "Do you want to tell him, or shall I?"

"Hollows vastly prefer peculiars over common folk," Millard explained, "but they'll eat just about anything to sustain themselves, so long as it's fresh and meaty."

"It's one of the ways you know there might be a hollow hanging about," said Emma. "The bodies pile up. That's why they're mostly nomads. If they didn't move from place to place so often, they'd be simple to track down."

"How often?" I asked, a shiver tracing my spine. "Do they need to eat, I mean?"

"Oh, pretty often," said Millard. "Arranging the hollows' meals is what wights spend most of their time doing. They look for peculiars when they can, but a gobsmacking portion of their energy and effort is spent tracking down common victims for the hollows, animal and human, and then hiding the mess." His tone was academic, as if discussing the breeding patterns of a mildly interesting species of rodent.

"But don't the wights get caught?" I said. "I mean, if they're helping *murder* people, you'd think —"

"Some do," Emma said. "Wager you've heard of a few, if you follow the news. There was one fellow, they found him with human heads in the icebox and gibletty goodies in a stock pot over a low boil, like he was making Christmas dinner. In your time this wouldn't have been so very long ago."

I remembered — vaguely — a sensationalized late-night TV special about a cannibalistic serial killer from Milwaukee who'd been apprehended in similarly gruesome circumstances.

"You mean . . . Jeffrey Dahmer?"

"I believe that was the gentleman's name, yes," said Millard. "Fascinating case. Seems he never lost his taste for the fresh stuff, though he'd not been a hollow for many years."

"I thought you guys weren't supposed to know about the future," I said.

Emma flashed a canny smile. "The bird only keeps *good* things about the future to herself, but you can bet we hear all the brown-trouser bits."

Then Miss Peregrine returned, pulling Enoch and Horace behind her by their shirtsleeves. Everyone came to attention.

"We've just had word of a new threat," she announced, giving me an appreciative nod. "A man outside our loop has died under suspicious circumstances. We can't be certain of the cause or whether it represents a true threat to our security, but we must conduct ourselves as if it did. Until further notice, no one may leave the house, not even to collect vegetables or bring in a goose for the evening meal."

A collective groan arose, over which Miss Peregrine raised her voice. "This has been a challenging few days for us all. I beg your continued patience."

Hands shot up around the room, but she rebuffed all questions and marched off to secure the doors. I ran after her in a panic. If there really was something dangerous on the island, it might kill me the minute I set foot outside the loop. But if I stayed here, I'd be leaving my father defenseless, not to mention worried sick about me. Somehow, that seemed even worse.

"I need to go," I said, catching up to Miss Peregrine.

She pulled me into an empty room and

closed the door. "You will keep your voice down," she commanded, "and you will respect my rules. What I said applies to you as well. No one leaves this house."

"But —"

"Thus far I have allowed you an unprecedented measure of autonomy to come and go as you please, out of respect for your unique position. But you may have already been followed here, and that puts my wards' lives in jeopardy. I will not permit you to endanger them — or yourself — any further."

"Don't you understand?" I said angrily. "Boats aren't running. Those people in town are stuck. My *father* is stuck. If there really is a wight, and it's who I think it is, he and my dad have almost gotten into one fight already. If he just fed a total stranger to a hollow, who do you think he's going after next?"

Her face was like stone. "The welfare of the townspeople is none of my concern," she said. "I won't endanger my wards. Not for anyone."

"It isn't just townspeople. It's my *father*. Do you really think a couple of locked doors will stop me from going?"

"Perhaps not. But if you insist on leaving here, then I insist you never return."

I was so shocked I had to laugh. "But you *need* me," I said.

"Yes, we do," she replied. "We do very much."

I stormed upstairs to Emma's room. Inside was a tableau of frustration that might've been straight out of Norman Rockwell, if Norman Rockwell had painted people doing hard time in jail. Bronwyn stared woodenly out the window. Enoch sat on the floor, whittling a piece of hard clay. Emma was perched on the edge of her bed, elbows on knees, tearing sheets of paper from a notebook and igniting them between her fingers.

"You're back!" she said when I came in.

"I never left," I replied. "Miss Peregrine wouldn't let me." Everyone listened as I explained my dilemma. "I'm banished if I try to leave."

Emma's entire notebook ignited. "She can't do that!" she cried, oblivious to the flames licking her hand.

"She can do what she likes," said Bronwyn. "She's the Bird."

Emma threw down her book and stamped out the fire.

"I just came to tell you I'm going, whether she wants me to or not. I won't be held prisoner, and I won't bury my head in the

369

sand while my own father might be in real danger."

"Then I'm coming with you," Emma said.

"You ain't serious," replied Bronwyn.

"I am."

"What you are is three-quarters stupid," said Enoch. "You'll turn into a wrinkled old prune, and for what? Him?"

"I won't," said Emma. "You've got to be out of the loop for hours and hours before time starts to catch up with you, and it won't take nearly that long, will it, Jacob?"

"It's a bad idea," I said.

"*What's* a bad idea?" said Enoch. "She don't even know what she's risking her life to do."

"Headmistress won't like it," said Bronwyn, stating the obvious. "She'll *kill* us, Em."

Emma stood up and shut the door. "*She* won't kill us," she said, "those *things* will. And if they don't, living like this might just be worse than dying. The Bird's got us cooped up so tight we can hardly breathe, and all because she doesn't have the spleen to face whatever's out there!"

"Or not out there," said Millard, who I hadn't realized was in the room with us.

"But she won't like it," Bronwyn repeated.

Emma took a combative step toward her friend. "How long can you hide under the hem of that woman's skirt?"

"Have you already forgotten what happened to Miss Avocet?" said Millard. "It was only when her wards left the loop that they were killed and Miss Bunting kidnapped. If they'd only stayed put, nothing bad would've happened."

"Nothing bad?" Emma said dubiously. "Yes, it's true that hollows can't go through loops. But wights can, which is just how those kids were tricked into leaving. Should we sit on our bums and wait for them to come through our front door? What if rather than clever disguises, this time they bring guns?"

"That's what I'd do," Enoch said. "Wait till everyone's asleep and then slide down the chimney like Santa Claus and BLAM!" He fired an imaginary pistol at Emma's pillow. "Brains on the wall."

"Thank you for that," Millard said, sighing.

"We've got to hit them before they know we know they're there," said Emma, "while we've still got the element of surprise."

"But we *don't* know they're there!" said Millard.

"We'll find out."

"And how do you propose to do that? Wander around until you see a hollow?

What then? 'Excuse me, we were wondering what your intentions might be, vis à vis eating us.' "

"We've got Jacob," said Bronwyn. "He can see them."

I felt my throat tighten, aware that if this hunting party formed, I would be in some way responsible for everyone's safety.

"I've only ever seen *one*," I warned them. "So I wouldn't exactly call myself an expert."

"And if he shouldn't happen to see one?" said Millard. "It could either mean that there are none to be seen or that they're hiding. You'd still be clueless, as you so clearly are now."

Furrowed brows all around. Millard had a point.

"Well, it appears that logic has prevailed yet again," he said. "I'm off to fetch some porridge for supper, if any of you would-be mutineers would like to join me."

The bedsprings creaked as he got up and moved toward the door. But before he could leave, Enoch leapt to his feet and cried, "I've got it!"

Millard stopped. "Got what?"

Enoch turned to me. "The bloke who may or may not have been eaten by a hollow — do you know where they're keeping him?"

"At the fishmonger's."

He rubbed his hands together. "Then I know how we can be sure."

"And how's that?" said Millard.

"We'll ask him."

An expeditionary team was assembled. Joining me would be Emma, who flatly refused to let me go alone, Bronwyn, who was loath to anger Miss Peregrine but insisted that we needed her protection, and Enoch, whose plan we were to carry out. Millard, whose invisibility might have come in handy, would have no part of it, and he had to be bribed just to keep from ratting us out.

"If we all go," Emma reasoned, "the Bird won't be able to banish Jacob. She'll have to banish all four of us."

"But I don't want to be banished!" said Bronwyn.

"She'd never do it, Wyn. That's the point. And if we can make it back before lights-out, she may not even realize we were gone."

I had my doubts about that, but we all agreed it was worth a shot.

It went down like a jailbreak. After dinner, when the house was at its most chaotic and Miss Peregrine at her most distracted, Emma pretended to head for the sitting room and I for the study. We met a few minutes later at the end of the upstairs hallway, where a rectangle of ceiling pulled down to reveal a ladder. Emma climbed it and I followed, pulling it closed after us, and we found ourselves in a tiny, dark attic space. At one end was a vent, easily unscrewed, that led out onto a flat section of roof.

We stepped into the night air to find the others already waiting. Bronwyn gave us each a crushing hug and handed out black rain slickers she'd snagged, which I'd suggested we wear to provide some measure of protection from the storm raging outside the loop. I was about to ask how we were planning to reach the ground when I saw Olive float into view past the edge of the roof.

"Who's keen for a game of parachute?" she said, smiling broadly. She was barefoot and wore a rope knotted around her waist. Curious what she was attached to, I peeked over the roof to see Fiona, rope in hand, hanging out a window and waving up at me. Apparently, we had accomplices.

"You first," Enoch barked.

"Me?" I said, backing nervously away from the edge.

"Grab hold of Olive and jump," Emma said.

"I don't remember this plan involving me shattering my pelvis."

"You won't, dummy, if you just hang on to Olive. It's great fun. We've done it loads of times." She thought for a moment, "Well, one time."

There seemed to be no alternative, so I steeled myself and approached the roof's edge. "Don't be frightened!" Olive said.

"Easy for you to say," I replied. "You can't fall."

She reached out her arms and bear-hugged me and I hugged her back, and she whispered, "Okay, go." I closed my eyes and stepped into the void. Instead of the drop I'd feared, we drifted slowly to the ground like a balloon leaking helium.

"That was fun," Olive said. "Now let go!"

I did, and she went rocketing back up to the roof, saying *"Wheeeee!"* all the way. The others shushed her and then, one after another, they hugged her and floated down to join me. When we were all together we began sneaking toward the moon-capped woods, Fiona and Olive waving behind us. Maybe it was my imagination, but the breeze-blown topiary creatures seemed to wave at us, too, with Adam nodding a somber farewell.

When we stopped at the bog's edge to catch our breath, Enoch reached into his bulging coat and handed out packages wrapped in cheesecloth. "Take these," he said. "I ain't carryin' em all."

"What are they?" asked Bronwyn, undoing the cloth to reveal a hunk of brownish meat with little tubes shunting out of it. "Ugh, it *stinks!*" she cried, holding it away from her.

"Calm down, it's only a sheep heart," he said, thrusting something of roughly the same dimensions into my hands. It stank of formaldehyde and, even through the cloth, felt unpleasantly moist.

"I'll chuck my guts if I have to carry this," Bronwyn said.

"I'd like to see that," Enoch grumbled, sounding offended. "Stash it in your slicker and let's get on with it."

We followed the hidden ribbon of solid ground through the bog. I'd been over it so many times now, I'd almost forgotten how dangerous it could be, how many lives it had swallowed over the centuries. Stepping onto the cairn mound, I told everyone to button up their coats.

"What if we see someone?" asked Enoch.

"Just act normal," I said. "I'll tell them you're my friends from America."

"What if we see a wight?" asked Bronwyn.

"Run."

"And if Jacob sees a hollow?"

"In that case," Emma said, "run like the devil's after you."

One by one we ducked into the cairn, disappearing from that calm summer night. All was quiet until we reached the end chamber, and then the air pressure dropped and the temperature fell and the storm screamed into full-throated being. We spun toward the sound, rattled, and for a moment just stood listening as it seethed and howled at the mouth of the tunnel. It sounded like a caged animal that had just been shown its dinner. There was nothing to do but offer ourselves up to it.

We fell to our knees and crawled into what seemed like a black hole, the stars lost behind a mountain of thunderheads, whipping rain and freezing wind rifling through our coats, wires of lightning bleaching us bone white and making the dark that followed seem darker still. Emma tried to make a flame but she looked like a broken cigarette lighter, every sparking flick of her wrist hissing out before it could catch, so we shrugged up our coats and ran bent against the gale and the swollen bog that sucked at our legs, navigating as much by memory as by sight.

In the town, rain drummed on every door and window, but everyone stayed locked and shuttered inside their cottages as we ran unnoticed through the flooding streets, past scattered roof tiles torn away by the wind, past a single rain-blinded sheep lost and crying, past a tipped outhouse disgorging itself into the road, to the fishmonger's shop. The door was locked, but with two thudding kicks Bronwyn flung it in. Drying her hand inside her coat, Emma was finally able to make a flame. As wide-eyed sturgeon stared from glass cases, I led us into the shop, around the counter where Dylan spent his days mumbling curses and scaling fish, through a rust-pocked door. On the other side was a little icehouse, just a lean-to shed floored with dirt and roofed with tin, its walls made from rough-cut planks, rain weeping through where they had shivered apart like bad teeth. Crowding the room were a dozen rectangular troughs raised on sawhorses and filled with ice.

"Which one's he in?" Enoch asked.

"I don't know," I said.

Emma shone her flame around as we

walked among the troughs, trying to guess which might hold more than just the corpses of fish — but they all looked the same, just lidless coffins of ice. We would have to search every one until we found him.

"Not me," Bronwyn said, "I don't want to see him. I don't like dead things."

"Neither do I, but we have to," said Emma. "We're all in this together."

Each of us chose a trough and dug into it like a dog excavating a prized bed of flowers, our cupped hands scooping mounds of ice onto the floor. I'd emptied half of one and was losing feeling in my fingers when I heard Bronwyn shriek. I turned to see her stumble away from a trough, her hands across her mouth.

We crowded around to see what she'd uncovered. Jutting from the ice was a frozen, hairy-knuckled hand. "I daresay you found our man," Enoch said, and through split fingers the rest of us watched as he scraped away more ice, slowly revealing an arm, then a torso, and finally Martin's entire wrecked body.

It was an awful sight. His limbs were twisted in improbable directions. His trunk had been scissored open and emptied out, ice filling the cavity where his vitals had been. When his face appeared, there was a collective intake of breath. Half was a purple contusion that hung in strips like a shredded mask. The other was just undamaged enough to recognize him by: a jaw stippled with beard, a jig-sawed section of cheek and brow, and one green eye, filmed over and gazing emptily. He wore only boxers and ragged scraps of a terrycloth robe. There was no way he'd walked by himself out to the cliffs at night dressed like that. Someone — or something — had dragged him there.

"He's pretty far gone," said Enoch, appraising Martin as a surgeon might assess an all-but-hopeless patient. "I'm telling you now, this might not work."

"We got to try," Bronwyn said, stepping bravely to the trough with the rest of us. "We come all this way, we at least got to try."

Enoch opened his slicker and pulled one of the wrapped hearts from an interior pocket. It looked like a maroon catcher's mitt folded in on itself. "If he wakes up," Enoch said, "he ain't gonna be happy. So just stand back and don't say I didn't warn you."

All of us took a generous step back except Enoch, who bellied up to the trough and plunged his arm into the ice that filled Martin's chest, swirling it around like he was fishing for a can of soda in a cooler. After a moment he seemed to latch onto something, and with his other hand he raised the sheep heart above his head.

A sudden convulsion passed through Enoch's body and the sheep heart started to beat, spraying out a fine mist of bloody pickling solution. Enoch took fast, shallow breaths. He seemed to be channeling something. I studied Martin's body for any hint of movement, but he lay still.

Gradually the heart in Enoch's hand began to slow and shrink, its color fading to a blackish gray, like meat left too long in the freezer. Enoch threw it on the ground and thrust his empty hand at me. I pulled out the heart I'd been keeping in my pocket and gave it to him. He repeated the same process, the heart pumping and sputtering for a while before faltering like the last one. Then he did it a third time, using the heart he'd given to Emma.

Bronwyn's heart was the only one left — Enoch's last chance. His face took on a new intensity as he raised it above Martin's rude coffin, squeezing it like he meant to drive his fingers through. As the heart began to shake and tremble like an overcranked motor, Enoch shouted, "Rise up, dead man. Rise up!"

I saw a flicker of movement. Something had shifted beneath the ice. I leaned as close as I could stand to, watching for any sign of life. For a long moment there was nothing, but then the body wrenched as suddenly and forcefully as if it had been shocked with a thousand volts. Emma screamed, and we all jumped back. When I lowered my arms to look again, Martin's head had turned in my direction, one cataracted eye wheeling crazily before fixing, it seemed, on me.

"He sees you!" Enoch cried.

I leaned in. The dead man smelled of turned earth and brine and something worse. Ice fell away from his hand, which rose up to tremble in the air for a moment, afflicted and blue, before coming to rest on my arm. I fought the urge to throw it off.

His lips fell apart and his jaw hinged open. I bent down to hear him, but there was nothing to hear. *Of course there isn't,* I thought, *his lungs have burst* — but then a tiny sound leaked out, and I leaned closer, my ear almost to his freezing lips. I thought, strangely, of the rain gutter by my house, where if you put your head to the bars and wait for a break in traffic, you can just make out the whisper of an underground stream, buried when the town was first built but still flowing, imprisoned in a world a permanent night.

The others crowded around, but I was the only one who could hear the dead man. The first thing he said was my name.

"Jacob."

Fear shot through me. "Yes."

"I was dead." The words came slowly, dripping like molasses. He corrected himself. "Am dead."

"Tell me what happened," I said. "Can you remember?"

There was a pause. The wind whistled through the gaps in the walls. He said something and I missed it.

"Say it again. Please, Martin."

"He killed me," the dead man whispered.

"Who."

"My old man."

"You mean Oggie? Your uncle?"

"My old man," he said again. "He got big. And strong, so strong."

"Who did, Martin?"

His eye closed, and I feared he was gone for good. I looked at Enoch. He nodded. The heart in his hand was still beating.

Martin's eye flicked beneath its lid. He began to speak again, slowly but evenly, as if reciting something. "For a hundred generations he slept, curled like a fetus in the earth's mysterious womb, digested by

383

roots, fermenting in the dark, summer fruits canned and forgotten in the larder until a farmer's spade bore him out, rough midwife to a strange harvest."

Martin paused, his lips trembling, and in the brief silence Emma looked at me and whispered, "What's he saying?"

"I don't know," I said. "But it sounds like a poem."

He continued, his voice wavering but loud enough now that everyone could hear — "Blackly he reposes, tender face the color of soot, withered limbs like veins of coal, feet lumps of driftwood hung with shriveled grapes" — and finally I recognized the poem. It was the one he'd written about the bog boy.

"Oh Jacob, I took such good careful care of him!" he said. "Dusted the glass and changed the soil and made him a home — like my own big bruised baby. I took such careful care, but —" He began to shake, and a tear ran down his cheek and froze there. "But he killed me."

"Do you mean the bog boy? The Old Man?"

"Send me back," he pleaded. "It hurts." His cold hand kneaded my shoulder, his voice fading again.

I looked to Enoch for help. He tightened

his grip on the heart and shook his head. "Quick now, mate," he said.

Then I realized something. Though he was describing the bog boy, it wasn't the bog boy who had killed him. *They only become visible to the rest of us when they're eating,* Miss Peregrine had told me, *which is to say, when it's too late.* Martin had seen a hollowgast — at night, in the rain, as it was tearing him to shreds — and had mistaken it for his most prized exhibit.

The old fear began to pump, coating my insides with heat. I turned to the others. "A hollowgast did this to him," I said. "It's somewhere on the island."

"Ask him where," said Enoch.

"Martin, where. I need to know where you saw it."

"Please. It hurts."

"Where did you see it?"

"He came to my door."

"The old man did?"

His breath hitched strangely. He was hard to look at but I made myself do it, following his eye as it shifted and focused on something behind me.

"No," he said. "*He* did."

And then a light swept over us and a loud voice barked, *"Who's there!"*

Emma closed her hand and the flame

hissed out, and we all spun to see a man standing in the doorway, holding a flashlight in one hand and a pistol in the other.

Enoch yanked his arm out of the ice while Emma and Bronwyn closed ranks around the trough to block Martin from view. "We didn't mean to break in," Bronwyn said. "We was just leaving, honest!"

"Stay where you are!" the man shouted. His voice was flat, accentless. I couldn't see his face through the beam of light, but the layered jackets he wore were an instant giveaway. It was the ornithologist.

"Mister, we ain't had nothing to eat all day," Enoch whined, for once sounding like a twelve-year-old. "All we come for was a fish or two, swear!"

"Is that so?" said the man. "Looks like you've picked one out. Let's see what kind." He waved his flashlight back and forth as if to part us with the beam. "Step aside!"

We did, and he swept the light over Martin's body, a landscape of garish ruin. "Goodness, that's an odd-looking fish, isn't it?" he said, entirely unfazed. "Must be a fresh one. He's still moving!" The beam came to rest on Martin's face. His eye rolled back and his lips moved soundlessly, just a reflex as the life Enoch had given him drained away.

"Who are you?" Bronwyn demanded.

"That depends on whom you ask," the man replied, "and it isn't nearly as important as the fact that I know who *you* are." He pointed the flashlight at each of us and spoke as if quoting some secret dossier. "Emma Bloom, a spark, abandoned at a circus when her parents couldn't sell her to one. Bronwyn Bruntley, berserker, taster of blood, didn't know her own strength until the night she snapped her rotten stepfather's neck. Enoch O'Connor, dead-riser, born to a family of undertakers who couldn't understand why their clients kept walking away." I saw each of them shrink away from him. Then he shone the light at me. "And Jacob. Such peculiar company you're keeping these days."

"How do you know my name?"

He cleared his throat, and when he spoke again his voice had changed radically. "Did you forget me so quick?" he said in a New England accent. "But then I'm just a poor old bus driver, guess you wouldn't remember."

It seemed impossible, but somehow this man was doing a dead-on impression of my middle school bus driver, Mr. Barron. A man so despised, so foul tempered, so robotically inflexible that on the last day of

387

eighth grade we defaced his yearbook picture with staples and left it like an effigy
behind his seat. I was just remembering
what he used to say as I got off the bus every
afternoon when the man before me sang it
out:

"End of the line, Portman!"

"Mr. Barron?" I asked doubtfully, struggling to see his face through the flashlight
beam.

The man laughed and cleared his throat,
his accent changing again. "Either him or
the yard man," he said in a deep Florida
drawl. "Yon trees need a haircut. Give yah
good price!" It was the pitch-perfect voice
of the man who for years had maintained
my family's lawn and cleaned our pool.

"How are you doing that?" I said. "How
do you know those people?"

"Because I *am* those people," he said, his
accent flat again. He laughed, relishing my
baffled horror.

Something occurred to me. Had I ever
seen Mr. Barron's eyes? Not really. He was
always wearing these giant, old-man sunglasses that wrapped around his face. The
yard man wore sunglasses, too, and a wide-
brimmed hat. Had I ever given either of
them a hard look? How many other roles in
my life had this chameleon played?

"What's happening?" Emma said. "Who is this man?"

"Shut up!" he snapped. "You'll get your turn."

"You've been watching me," I said. "You killed those sheep. You killed Martin."

"Who, me?" he said innocently. "*I* didn't kill anyone."

"But you're a wight, aren't you?"

"That's *their* word," he said.

I couldn't understand it. I hadn't seen the yard man since my mother replaced him three years ago, and Mr. Barron had vanished from my life after eighth grade. Had they — he — really been following me?

"How'd you know where to find me?"

"Why, Jacob," he said, his voice changing yet again, "you told me yourself. In confidence, of course." It was a middle-American accent now, soft and educated. He tipped the flashlight up so that its glow spilled onto his face.

The beard I'd seen him wearing the other day was gone. Now there was no mistaking him.

"Dr. Golan," I said, my voice a whisper swallowed by the drumming rain.

I thought back to our telephone conversation a few days ago. The noise in the background — he'd said he was at the airport.

But he wasn't picking up his sister. He was coming after me.

I backed against Martin's trough, reeling, numbness spreading through me. "The neighbor," I said. "The old man watering his lawn the night my grandfather died. That was you, too."

He smiled.

"But your eyes," I said.

"Contact lenses," he replied. He popped one out with his thumb, revealing a blank orb. "Amazing what they can fabricate these days. And if I may anticipate a few more of your questions, yes, I am a licensed therapist — the minds of common people have long fascinated me — and no, despite the fact that our sessions were predicated on a lie, I don't think they were a complete waste of time. In fact, I may be able to continue helping you — or, rather, we may be able to help each other."

"Please, Jacob," Emma said, "don't listen to him."

"Don't worry," I said. "I trusted him once. I won't make that mistake again."

Golan continued as though he hadn't heard me. "I can offer you safety, money. I can give you your life back, Jacob. All you have to do is work with us."

"Us?"

"Malthus and me," he said, turning to call over his shoulder. "Come and say hello, Malthus."

A shadow appeared in the doorway behind him, and a moment later we were overcome by a noxious wave of stench. Bronwyn gagged and fell back a step, and I saw Emma's fists clench, as if she were thinking about charging it. I touched her arm and mouthed, *Wait.*

"This is all I'm proposing," Golan continued, trying to sound reasonable. "Help us find more people like you. In return, you'll have nothing to fear from Malthus or his kind. You can live at home. In your free time you'll come with me and see the world, and we'll pay you handsomely. We'll tell your parents you're my research assistant."

"If I agree," I said, "what happens to my friends?"

He made a dismissive gesture with his gun. "They made their choice long ago. What's important is that there's a grand plan in motion, Jacob, and you'll be part of it."

Did I consider it? I suppose I must have, if only for a moment. Dr. Golan was offering me exactly what I'd been looking for: a third option. A future that was neither *stay here forever* nor *leave and die.* But one look at my friends, their faces etched with worry, banished any temptation.

"Well?" said Golan. "What's your answer?"

"I'd die before I did anything to help you."

"Ah," he said, "but you already have helped me." He began to back toward the door. "It's a pity we won't have any more sessions together, Jacob. Though it isn't a total loss, I suppose. The four of you together might be enough to finally shift old Malthus out of the debased form he's been stuck in so long."

"Oh, no," Enoch whimpered, "I don't want to be eaten!"

"Don't cry, it's degrading," snapped Bronwyn. "We'll just have to kill them, that's all."

"Wish I could stay and watch," Golan said from the doorway. "I do love to watch!"

And then he was gone, and we were alone with it. I could hear the creature breathing in the dark, a viscid leaking like faulty pipeworks. We each took a step back, then another, until our shoulders met the wall, and we stood together like condemned prisoners before a firing squad.

"I need a light," I whispered to Emma, who was in such shock that she seemed to have forgotten her own power.

Her hand came ablaze, and among the

flickering shadows I saw it, lurking among the troughs. My nightmare. It stooped there, hairless and naked, mottled gray-black skin hanging off its frame in loose folds, its eyes collared in dripping putrefaction, legs bowed and feet clubbed and hands gnarled into useless claws — every part looking withered and wasted like the body of an impossibly old man — save one. Its outsized jaws were its main feature, a bulging enclosure of teeth as tall and sharp as little steak knives that the flesh of its mouth was hopeless to contain, so that its lips were perpetually drawn back in a deranged smile.

And then those awful teeth came unlocked, its mouth reeling open to admit three wiry tongues into the air, each as thick as my wrist. They unspooled across half the room's length, ten feet or more, and then hung there, wriggling, the creature breathing raggedly through a pair of leprous holes in its face as if tasting our scent, considering how best to devour us. That we would be so easy to kill was the only reason we weren't dead already; like a gourmand about to enjoy a fine meal, there was no reason to rush things.

The others couldn't see it in the way I did but recognized its shadow projected on the wall and that of its ropelike tongues. Emma flexed her arm, and her flame burned brighter. "What's it doing?" she whispered. "Why hasn't it come at us?"

"It's playing with us," I said. "It knows we're trapped."

"We ain't any such thing," Bronwyn muttered. "Just gimme one square go at its face. I'll punch its bloody teeth in."

"I wouldn't get anywhere near those teeth if I were you," I said.

The hollow took a few lumbering steps forward to match the ones we'd taken back, its tongues unfurling more and then splitting apart, one coming toward me, another toward Enoch, and the third toward Emma.

"Leave us be!" Emma yelled, lashing out with her hand like a torch. The tongue twisted away from her flame, then inched back like a snake preparing to strike.

"We've got to try for the door!" I yelled. "The hollow's by the third trough from the left, so keep to the right!"

"We'll never make it!" Enoch cried. One of the tongues touched him on the cheek, and he screamed.

"We'll go on three!" Emma shouted. "One —"

And then Bronwyn launched herself toward the creature, howling like a banshee. The creature shrieked and reared up, its bunched skin pulling tight. Just as it was about to lash its trident of tongues at her, she rammed Martin's ice trough with the full weight of her body and levered her arms under it as it tipped and then heaved it and the whole huge thing, full of ice and fish and Martin's body, careened through the air and fell upon the hollow with a terrific crash.

Bronwyn spun and bounded back in our direction. "MOVE!" she cried, and I leapt away as she collided with the wall beside me, kicking a hole through the rotten planks. Enoch, the smallest of us, dove through first, followed by Emma, and before I could protest Bronwyn had grabbed me by the shoulders and tossed me out into the wet night. I landed chest-first in a puddle. The cold was shocking, but I was elated to feel anything other than the hollow's tongue wrapping around my throat.

Emma and Enoch hauled me to my feet, and we took off running. A moment later Emma shouted Bronwyn's name and stopped. We turned, realizing she hadn't come with us.

We called for her and scanned the dark, not quite brave enough to run back, and then Enoch shouted, "There!" and we saw Bronwyn leaning against a corner of the icehouse.

"What's she doing?!" cried Emma. "BRONWYN! RUN!"

It looked as though she was hugging the building. Then she stepped back and took a running start and rammed her shoulder into its corner support, and like a house made of matchsticks the whole thing tumbled in on itself, a cloud of pulverized ice and splintered wood puffing out and blowing down the street in a gust of wind.

We all hollered and cheered as Bronwyn sprinted toward us with a manic grin on her face, then stood in the pelting rain hugging her and laughing. It didn't take long for our moods to darken, though, as the shock of what had just happened set in, and then Emma turned to me and asked the question that must've been on all their minds.

"Jacob, how did that wight know so much about you? And us?"

"You called him doctor," said Enoch.

"He was my psychiatrist."

"Psychiatrist!" Enoch said. "That's just grand! Not only did he betray us to a wight, he's mad to boot!"

"Take it back!" Emma yelled, shoving him hard. He was about to shove back when I stepped between them.

"Stop!" I said, pushing them apart. I faced

Enoch. "You're wrong. I'm not crazy. He let me think I was, though all along he must've known I was peculiar. You're right about one thing, though. I did betray you. I told my grandfather's stories to a stranger."

"It's not your fault," Emma said. "You couldn't have known we were real."

"Of course he could've!" shouted Enoch. "Abe told him everything. Even showed him bloody pictures of us!"

"Golan knew everything but how to find you," I said. "And I led him straight here."

"But he tricked you," said Bronwyn.

"I just want you to know that I'm sorry."

Emma hugged me. "It's all right. We're alive."

"For now," said Enoch. "But that maniac is still out there, and considering how willing he was to feed us all to his pet hollowgast, it's a good bet he's figured out how to get into the loop on his own."

"Oh god, you're right," said Emma.

"Well then," I said, "we'd better get there before he does."

"And before *it* does," Bronwyn added. We turned to see her pointing at the wrecked icehouse, where broken boards had begun to shift in the collapsed pile. "I imagine he'll be coming for us directly, and I'm fresh out of houses to drop on him."

Someone shouted *Run!* but we already were, tearing down the path toward the one place the hollow couldn't reach us — the loop. We raced out of town in the spitting dark, vague blue outlines of cottages giving way to sloping fields, then charged up the ridge, sheets of water streaming over our feet, making the path treacherous.

Enoch slipped and fell. We hauled him up and ran on. As we were about to crest the ridge, Bronwyn's feet went out from under her, too, and she slid down twenty feet before she could stop herself. Emma and I ran back to help, and as we took her arms I turned to look behind us, hoping to catch a glimpse of the creature. But there was only inky, swirling rain. My talent for spotting hollows wasn't much good without light to see them by. But then, as we made it back to the top, chests heaving, a long flash of lightning lit up the night and I turned and saw it. It was off below us a ways but climbing fast, its muscular tongues punching into the mud and propelling it up the ridge like a spider.

"*Go!*" I shouted, and we all bolted down the far side, the four of us sliding on our butts until we hit level ground and could run again.

There was another flash of lightning. It

was even closer than before. At this rate there was no way we'd be able to outrun it. Our only hope was to outmaneuver it.

"If it catches us, it'll kill us all," I shouted, "but if we split up, it'll have to choose. I'll lead it around the long way and try to lose it in the bog. The rest of you get to the loop as quick you can!"

"You're mad!" shouted Emma. "If anyone stays behind it should be me! I can fight it with fire!"

"Not in this rain," I said, "and not if you can't see it!"

"I won't let you kill yourself!" she shouted.

There was no time to argue, so Bronwyn and Enoch ran ahead while Emma and I veered off the path, hoping the creature would follow, and it did. It was close enough now that I didn't need a lightning flash to know where it was; the twist in my gut was enough.

We ran arm in arm, tripping through a field rent with furrows and ditches, falling and catching each other in an epileptic dance. I was scanning the ground for rocks to use as weapons when, out of the darkness ahead, there appeared a structure — a small sagging shack with broken windows and missing doors, which in my panic I failed to recognize.

"We have to hide!" I said between gasping breaths.

Please let this creature be stupid, I prayed as we sprinted toward the house, *please, please let it be stupid.* We made a wide arc, hoping to enter it unseen.

"Wait!" Emma cried as we rounded the back of it. She pulled one of Enoch's cheesecloths from her coat and quickly tied it around a stone plucked from the ground, making a kind of slingshot. She cradled it in her hands until it caught fire and then hurled it away from us. It landed in the boggy distance, glowing weakly in the dark.

"Misdirection," she explained, and we turned and committed ourselves to the shack's concealing gloom.

We slipped through a door that was hanging off its hinges and stepped down into a sea of dark, aromatic muck. As our feet sank with a nauseating squelch, I realized where we were.

"What *is* this?" Emma whispered, and then a sudden exhalation of animal breath made us both jump. The house was crowded with sheep taking shelter from the unfriendly night, just as we were. As our eyes adjusted, we caught the dull gleam of theirs staring back at us — dozens and dozens of them.

"It's what I think it is, isn't it," she said, lifting one foot gingerly.

"Don't think about it," I replied. "Come on, we need to get away from this door."

I took her hand and we pushed into the house, snaking through a maze of skittish animals that shied from our touch. We threaded a narrow hall and came into a room with one high window and a door that was still in its frame and closed against the night, which was more than could be said for the other rooms. Squeezing into the far corner, we knelt down to wait and listen, hidden behind a wall of nervous sheep.

We tried not to sit too deeply in the muck but there was really no helping it. After a minute of staring blindly into the dark, I began to make out shapes in the room. There were crates and boxes stacked in one corner, and along the wall behind us hung rusted tools. I looked for anything that might be sharp enough to serve as a weapon. Seeing something that looked like a pair of giant scissors, I stood up to grab it.

"Planning on shearing some sheep?" said Emma.

"It's better than nothing."

Just as I was taking the shears down from

the wall, a noise came from outside the window. The sheep bleated anxiously, and then a long black tongue drifted through the glassless enclosure. I sank back to the floor as quietly as I could. Emma put her hand over her mouth to silence her breathing.

The tongue poked around the room like a periscope, seeming to be testing the air. Luckily, we'd taken refuge in the most fragrant room on the island. All that sheep aroma must've masked our scent, because after a minute the creature seemed to give up and reeled out the window. We heard its retreating steps.

Emma's hand came away from her mouth and she let out a shuddering breath. "I think it's taking the bait," she whispered.

"I want you to know something," I said. "If we make it through this, I'm staying."

She grabbed my hand. "Do you mean it?"

"I can't go home. Not after all that's happened. Anyway, whatever help I can be, I owe you that and a lot more. You were all perfectly safe until I got here."

"If we make it through this," she said, leaning into me, "then I don't regret one thing."

And then some strange magnet was pulling our heads together, but just as our lips were about to touch, the quiet was shattered by terrified, bleating shrieks from the next room. We pulled apart as the awful noise set the sheep around us into frantic motion, bounding off one another and pushing us into the wall.

The beast was not as dumb as I'd hoped.

We could hear it coming toward us through the house. If there was a time to run it had already passed, so we screwed ourselves into the reeking soil and prayed it would pass us by.

And then I could smell it, even more pungent than the house's other stinks, and I could feel it at the threshold of the room. All the sheep pushed away from the door at once, herding together like a school of fish and pinning us against the wall so hard the breath was pressed out of us. We gripped each other but didn't dare make a sound, and for an unbearably tense moment we heard only the bleating of sheep and the clop of staggering hooves. Then another hoarse scream erupted, sudden and desperate and just as suddenly silenced, broken off by lurid, ripping bone snap. I knew without looking that a sheep had just been torn apart.

Chaos broke out. Panicked animals ricocheted off one another, throwing us against the wall so many times I got dizzy. The hollow let out an ear-splitting screech and began to lift sheep to its slavering jaws one after another, taking a blood-spurting bite from each and then tossing it aside like a gluttonous king gorging at a medieval feast. It did this again and again — killing its way toward us. I was paralyzed with fear. That's why I can't quite explain what happened next.

My every instinct screamed to stay hidden, to dig myself even deeper into the muck, but then one clear thought cut through all the static — *I won't let us die in this shit-house* — and I pushed Emma behind the biggest sheep I could see and bolted for the door.

The door was closed and ten feet away, and a lot of animals stood between it and me, but I plowed through them like a linebacker. I hit the door with my shoulder and it flung open.

I tumbled outside into the rain and screamed "Come get me, you ugly bastard!" I knew I had its attention because it let out a terrifying howl and sheep came flushing out the door past me. I scrambled to my feet and when I was sure it was coming after me and not Emma, I took off toward the bog.

I could feel it behind me. I might've run faster but I was still holding the shears — I couldn't seem to make myself let go — and then the ground went soft beneath me and I knew I'd reached the bog.

Twice the hollow was close enough for its tongues to lash my back, and twice, just as I was certain one was about to lasso my neck and squeeze until my head popped, it stumbled and fell back. The only reason I made it to the cairn with my head still attached was that I knew exactly where to put my feet; thanks to Emma, I could run that route on a moonless night in half a hurricane.

Clambering onto the cairn-mound, I tore around to the stone entrance and dove in. It was black as tar inside but it didn't matter — I only had to reach the chamber to be safe. I scrambled on my hands and knees, because even standing would've cost time I didn't have to waste, and I was halfway to the end and feeling cautiously optimistic about my chances for survival when suddenly I could crawl no more. One of the tongues had caught my ankle.

The hollow had used two of its tongues to grapple onto the capstones around the tunnel's mouth as leverage against the mud, and it covered the entrance with its body like a lid on a jar. The third tongue was reeling me toward it, I was a fish on a hook.

I scrabbled at the ground, but it was all gravel and my fingers slid right through. I flipped onto my back and clawed at the stones with my free hand, but I was sliding too quickly. I tried hacking at the tongue with my shears, but it was too sinewy and tough, a rope of undulating muscle, and my shears too dull. So I squeezed my eyes shut, because I didn't want its gaping jaws to be the last thing I'd ever see, and gripped the shears in front of me with both hands. Time seemed to stretch out, like they say it does in car crashes and train accidents and free-falls from airplanes, and the next thing I felt was a bone-jarring collision as I slammed into the hollow.

All the breath rushed out of me and I heard it scream. We flew out of the tunnel together and rolled down the cairn mound into the bog, and when I opened my eyes again, I saw my shears buried to the hilt in the beast's eye sockets. It howled like ten pigs being gelded, rolling and thrashing in the rain-swollen mud, weeping a black river of itself, viscous fluid pumping over the blades' rusted handle.

I could feel it dying, the life draining out of it, its tongue loosening around my ankle.

I could feel the difference in me, too, the panicky clutch in my stomach slowly coming undone. Finally, the creature stiffened and sank from view, slime closing over its head, a slick of dark blood the only sign it had ever been there.

I could feel the bog sucking me down with it. The more I struggled, the more it seemed to want me. What a strange find the two of us would make a thousand years from now, I thought, preserved together in the peat.

I tried to paddle toward solid ground but succeeded only in pushing myself deeper. The muck seemed to climb me, rising up my arms, my chest, collaring my throat like a noose.

I screamed for help — and miraculously, help came, in the form of what I thought at first was a firefly, flashing as it flew toward me. Then I heard Emma call out, and I answered.

A tree branch landed in the water. I grabbed it and Emma pulled, and when I finally came out of the bog I was shaking too hard to stand. Emma sank down beside me and I fell into her arms.

I killed it, I thought. *I really killed it.* All the time I'd spent being afraid, I never dreamed I could actually *kill* one!

It made me feel powerful. Now I could

defend myself. I knew I'd never be as strong as my grandfather, but I wasn't a gutless weakling, either. I could *kill* them.

I tested out the words. "It's dead. I *killed* it."

I laughed. Emma hugged me, pressing her cheek against mine. "I know he would've been proud of you," she said.

We kissed, and it was gentle and nice, rain dripping from our noses and running warm into our just-open mouths. Too soon she broke away and whispered, "What you said before — did you mean it?"

"I'll stay," I said. "If Miss Peregrine will let me."

"She will. I'll make certain of it."

"Before we worry about that, we'd better find my psychiatrist and take away his gun."

"Right," she said, her expression hardening. "No time to waste, then."

We left the rain behind and emerged into a landscape of smoke and noise. The loop hadn't yet reset, and the bog was pocked with bomb holes, the sky buzzing with planes, walls of orange flame marching against the distant tree line. I was about to suggest we wait until today became yesterday and all this disappeared before trying to cross to the house when a set of brawny arms clapped around me.

"You're alive!" Bronwyn cried. Enoch and Hugh were with her, and when she pulled away they moved in to shake my hand and look me over.

"I'm sorry I called you a traitor," Enoch said. "I'm glad you're not dead."

"Me, too," I replied.

"All in one piece?" Hugh asked, looking me over.

"Two arms and two legs," I said, kicking out my limbs to demonstrate their wholeness. "And you won't have to worry about that hollow anymore. We killed it."

"Oh, stuff the modesty!" Emma said proudly. "*You* killed it."

"That's brilliant," Hugh said, but neither he nor the other two could muster a smile.

"What's the matter?" I asked. "Wait. Why aren't you three at the house? Where's Miss Peregrine?"

"She's gone," said Bronwyn, her lip trembling. "Miss Avocet, too. He took them."

"Oh God," said Emma. We were too late.

"He come in with a gun," Hugh said, studying the dirt. "Tried to take Claire hostage, but she chomped him with her backmouth, so he grabbed me instead. I tried to fight, but he knocked me upside the skull with his gun." He touched the back of his ear and his fingers came away spotted with blood. "Locked everyone in the basement and said if Headmistress and Miss Avocet didn't change into birds he'd put an extra hole in my head. So they did, and he stuffed 'em both into a cage."

"He had a cage?" Emma said.

Hugh nodded. "Little one, too, so they didn't have room to do nothing, like change back or fly off. I reckoned I was good as shot, but then he pushed me down the basement with the others and run off with the birds."

"That's how we found 'em when we come in," Enoch said bitterly. "Hiding down there like a lot of cowards."

"We wasn't hiding!" Hugh cried. "He locked us in! He would've shot us!"

"Forget that," snapped Emma. "Where'd he run off to? Why didn't you go after him?!"

"We don't know where he went," said Bronwyn. "We was hoping you'd seen him."

"No, we haven't seen him!" Emma said, kicking a cairn stone in frustration.

Hugh drew something out of his shirt. It was a little photograph. "He stuffed this in my pocket before he went. Said if we tried to come after him, this is what would happen."

Bronwyn snatched the photo from Hugh.

CAW CAW CAW

"Oh," she gasped. "Is that Miss Raven?"

"I think it's Miss Crow," said Hugh, rubbing his face with his hands.

"That's it, they're good as dead," Enoch moaned. "I knew this day would come!"

"We should never have left the house," Emma said miserably. "Millard was right."

At the far edge of the bog a bomb fell, its muted blast followed by a distant rain of excavated glop.

"Wait a minute," I said. "First of all, we don't know that this is Miss Crow or Miss Raven. It could just as easily be a picture of a regular crow. And if Golan was going to kill Miss Peregrine and Miss Avocet, why would he go to all the trouble of kidnapping them? If he wanted them dead, they'd be dead already." I turned to Emma. "And if we hadn't left, we'd be locked in the basement with everybody else, and there'd still be a hollowgast wandering around!"

"Don't try to make me feel better!" she said. "It's *your* fault this is happening!"

"Ten minutes ago you said you were *glad!*"

"Ten minutes ago Miss Peregrine wasn't kidnapped!"

"Will you stop!" said Hugh. "All that matters now is that the Bird's gone and we've got to get her back!"

"Fine," I said, "so let's think. If you were

a wight, where would you take a couple of kidnapped ymbrynes?"

"Depends on what's to be done with 'em," Enoch said. "And that, we don't know."

"You'd have to get them off the island first," Emma said. "So you'd need a boat."

"But *which* island?" asked Hugh. "In the loop or out of it?"

"The outside's getting torn apart by a storm," I said. "Nobody's getting far in a boat over there."

"Then he's got to be on our side," Emma said, beginning to sound hopeful. "So what are we larking about here for? Let's get to the docks!"

"*Maybe* he's at the docks," Enoch said. "That is, if he ain't gone yet. And even if he ain't and we somehow manage to find him in all this dark, and without getting holes ripped through our guts by shrapnel on the way, there's still his gun to worry about. Have you all gone mad? Would you rather have the Bird kidnapped — or shot right in front of us?"

"Fine, then!" Hugh shouted. "Let's just give up and go home then, shall we? Who'd like a nice hot cup of tea before bed? Hell, as long as the Bird ain't around, make it a toddy!" He was crying, wiping angrily at his eyes. "How can you not even *try,* after all she's done for us?"

Before Enoch could answer, we heard a voice calling us from the path. Hugh stepped forward, squinting, and after a moment his face went strange. "It's Fiona," he said. Before that moment I'd never heard Fiona utter so much as a peep. It was impossible to make out what she was saying over the sound of planes and distant concussions, so we took off running across the bog.

When we got to the path, we were breathing hard and Fiona was hoarse from shouting, her eyes as wild as her hair. Immediately she began to pull at us, to drag and push us down the path toward town, yelling so frantically in her thick Irish accent that none of us could understand. Hugh caught her by the shoulders and told her to slow down.

She took a deep breath, shaking like a leaf, then pointed behind her. "Millard followed him!" she said. "He was hiding when the man shut us all in the basement, and when he lit out Millard followed!"

"Where to?" I said.

"He had a boat."

"See!" cried Emma. "The docks!"

"No," said Fiona, "it was *your* boat, Emma. The one you think nobody knows about, that you keep stowed on that wee strand of yours. He launched off with the cage and was just goin' in circles, but then the tide got too rough, so he pulled onto the lighthouse rock, and that's where he still is."

We made for the lighthouse in a dead run. When we reached the cliffs overlooking it, we found the rest of the children in a thick patch of sawgrass near the edge.

"Get down!" Millard hissed.

We dropped to our knees and crawled over to them. They were crouched in a loose huddle behind the grass, taking turns peeking at the lighthouse. They looked shell-shocked — the younger ones especially — as if they hadn't fully grasped the unfolding nightmare. That we'd just survived a nightmare of our own barely registered.

I crawled through the grass to the edge of the cliff and peered out. Past where the shipwreck lay submerged I could see Emma's canoe tied to the rocks. Golan and the ymbrynes were out of sight.

"What's he doing out there?" I said.

"It's anyone's guess," Millard answered. "Waiting for someone to pick him up, or for the tide to settle so he can row out."

"In my little boat?" Emma said doubtfully.

"As I said, we don't know."

Three deafening cracks sounded in quick succession, and we all ducked as the sky

416

flashed orange.

"Do any bombs fall 'round here, Millard?" asked Emma.

"My research concerns only the behavior of humans and animals," he replied. "Not bombs."

"Fat lot of good that does us now," said Enoch.

"Do you have any more boats hidden around here?" I asked Emma.

"I'm afraid not," she said. "We'll just have to swim across."

"Swim across and what?" said Millard. "Get shot to pieces?"

"We'll figure something out," she replied.

Millard sighed. "Oh, lovely. Improvised suicide."

"Well?" Emma looked at each of us. "Does anyone have a better idea?"

"If I had my soldiers . . ." Enoch began.

"They'd fall to bits in the water," said Millard.

Enoch hung his head. The others were quiet.

"Then it's decided," said Emma. "Who's in?"

I raised my hand. So did Bronwyn. "You'll need someone the wight can't see," Millard said. "Take me along, if you must."

"Four's enough," Emma said. "Hope

you're all strong swimmers."

There was no time for second thoughts or long goodbyes. The others wished us luck, and we were on our way.

We shed our black coats and loped through the grass, doubled-over like commandos, until we came to the path that led to the beach. We slid down on our behinds, little avalanches of sand pouring around our feet and down our pants.

Suddenly, there was a noise like fifty chainsaws over our heads, and we ducked as a plane roared by, the wind whipping our hair and blowing up a sandstorm. I clenched my teeth, waiting for a bomb blast to tear us apart. None came.

We kept moving. When we hit the beach, Emma gathered us in a tight huddle.

"There's a shipwreck between here and the lighthouse," she said. "Follow me out to it. Stay low in the water. Don't let him see you. When we reach the wreck, we'll look for our man and decide what's next."

"Let's get our ymbrynes back," Bronwyn said.

We crawled down to the surf and slid into the cold water on our bellies. It was easy going at first, but the farther we swam from shore, the more the current tried to push us back. Another plane buzzed overhead, kicking up a stinging spray of water.

We were breathing hard by the time we reached the shipwreck. Clinging to its rusted hull, just our heads poking out of the water, we stared at the lighthouse and the barren little island that anchored it, but saw no sign of my wayward therapist. A full moon hovered low in the sky, breaking through reefs of bomb smoke now and then to shine like the lighthouse's ghostly double.

We pushed ourselves along the wreck until we reached the end, just a fifty-yard swim in open water to the lighthouse rocks.

"Here's what I reckon we should do," Emma said. "He's seen how strong Wyn is, so she's in the most danger. Jacob and I find Golan and get his attention while Wyn sneaks up from behind and gives him a belter over the head. Meantime, Millard makes a grab for the birdcage. Any objections?"

As if in answer, a shot rang out. At first we didn't realize what it was — it didn't sound like the gunshots we'd been hearing, distant and powerful. This was small caliber — a *pop* rather than a *bang* — and it wasn't until we heard a second one, accompanied by a nearby splash, that we knew it was Golan.

"Fall back!" Emma shouted, and we stood

out of the water and sprinted across the hull until it dropped out from beneath us, then dove into the open water beyond it. A moment later we all came up in a cluster, panting for air.

"So much for getting the drop on him!" Millard said.

Golan had stopped shooting, but we could see him standing guard by the lighthouse door, gun in hand.

"He may be an evil bastard, but he ain't stupid," Bronwyn said. "He knew we'd come after him."

"Not now we can't!" Emma said, slapping the water. "He'll shoot us to bits!"

Millard stepped up onto the wreck. "He can't shoot what he can't see. I'll go."

"You're not invisible in the ocean, dummy," Emma said, and it was true — a torso-shaped negative space bobbed in the water where he stood.

"More than you are," he replied. "Anyhow, I followed him all the way across the island and he was none the wiser. I think I can manage a few hundred meters more."

It was difficult to argue, since our only remaining options were either giving up or running into a hail of gunfire.

"Fine," Emma said. "If you really think you can make it."

"Someone's got to be the hero," he replied, and walked off across the hull.

"Famous last words," I muttered.

In the smoky distance, I saw Golan in the lighthouse doorway kneel down and take aim, leveling his arm across a railing.

"Look out!" I shouted, but it was too late.

A shot rang out. Millard screamed.

We all clambered onto the wreck and raced toward him. I felt absolutely certain I was about to be shot, and for a moment I thought the splashes of our feet in the water were bullets raining down on us. But then the shooting stopped — *reloading,* I thought — and we had a brief window of time.

Millard was kneeling in the water, dazed, blood running down his torso. For the first time I could see the true shape of his body, painted red.

Emma took him by the arm. "Millard! Are you all right? Say something!"

"I must apologize," he said. "It seems I've gone and gotten myself shot."

"We have to stop the bleeding!" said Emma. "We've got to take him back to shore!"

"Nonsense," Millard said. "That man will never let you get this close to him again. Turn back now, and we'll certainly lose Miss Peregrine."

More shots rang out. I felt a bullet zip past my ear.

"This way!" Emma shouted. "Dive!"

I didn't know what she meant at first — we were a hundred feet from the end of the wreck — but then I saw what she was running toward. It was the black hole in the hull, the door to the cargo hold.

Bronwyn and I lifted Millard and ran after her. Metal slugs clanged into the hull around us. It sounded like someone kicking a trash can.

"Hold your breath," I told Millard, and we came to the hold and dove in feet-first.

We pulled ourselves down the ladder a few rungs and hung there. I tried to keep my eyes open but the saltwater stung too much. I could taste Millard's blood in the water.

Emma handed me the breathing tube, and we passed it among us. I was winded from running, and the single breath it allowed me every few seconds wasn't enough. My lungs hurt, and I began to feel light-headed.

Someone tugged at my shirt. *Come up.* I pulled myself slowly up the ladder, and then Bronwyn, Emma and I broke the surface just enough to breathe and talk while Millard stayed safe a few feet below, the tube all to himself.

We spoke in whispers and kept our eyes

on the lighthouse.

"We can't stay here," Emma said. "Millard will bleed to death."

"It could take twenty minutes to get him back to shore," I said. "He could just as easily die on the way."

"I don't know what else to do!"

"The lighthouse is close," Bronwyn said. "We'll take him there."

"Then Golan will make us *all* bleed to death!" I said.

"No, he won't," replied Bronwyn.

"Why not? Are you bullet-proof?"

"Maybe," Bronwyn replied mysteriously, then took a breath and disappeared down the ladder.

"What's she talking about?" I said.

Emma looked worried. "I haven't a clue. But whatever it is, she'd better hurry." I looked down to see what Bronwyn was doing but instead caught a glimpse of Millard on the ladder below us, surrounded by curious flashlight fish. Then I felt the hull vibrate against my feet, and a moment later Bronwyn surfaced holding a rectangular piece of metal about six feet by four, with a riveted round hole in the top. She had wrenched the cargo hold's door from its hinges.

"And what are you going to do with that?"

Emma said.

"Go to the lighthouse," she replied. Then she stood up and held the door in front of her.

"Wyn, he'll shoot you!" Emma cried, and then a shot rang out — and caromed right off the door.

"That's amazing!" I said. "It's a shield!"

Emma laughed. "Wyn, you're a genius!"

"Millard can ride my back," she said. "The rest of you, fall in behind."

Emma brought Millard out of the water and hung his arms around Bronwyn's neck. "It's magnificent down there," he said. "Emma, why did you never tell me about the angels?"

"What angels?"

"The lovely green angels who live just below." He was shivering, his voice dreamy. "They kindly offered to take me to heaven."

"No one's going to heaven just yet," Emma said, looking worried. "You just hang on to Bronwyn, all right?"

"Very well," he said vacantly.

Emma stood behind Millard, pressing him into Bronwyn's back so he wouldn't slide off. I stood behind Emma, taking up the rear of our strange little conga line, and we began to plod forward across the wreck toward the lighthouse.

We were a big target, and right away Golan began to empty his gun at us. The sound of his bullets bouncing off the door was deafening — but somehow reassuring — but after about a dozen shots he stopped. I wasn't optimistic enough to think he'd run out of bullets, though.

Reaching the end of the wreck, Bronwyn guided us carefully into open water, always keeping the massive door held out in front of us. Our conga line became a chain of dog-paddlers swimming in a knot behind her. Emma talked to Millard as we paddled, making him answer questions so he wouldn't drift into unconsciousness.

"Millard! Who's the prime minister?"

"Winston Churchhill," he said. "Have you gone daft?"

"What's the capital of Burma?"

"Lord, I've no idea. Rangoon."

"Good! When's your birthday?"

"Will you quit shouting and let me bleed in peace!"

It didn't take long to cross the short distance between the wreck and the lighthouse. As Bronwyn shouldered our shield and climbed onto the rocks, Golan fired a few more shots, and their impact threw her off balance. As we cowered behind her, she wobbled and nearly slipped backward off the rocks, which between her weight and the door's would've crushed us all. Emma planted her hands on the small of Bronwyn's back and pushed, and finally both Bronwyn and the door tottered forward onto dry land. We scrambled after her in a pack, shivering in the crisp night air.

Fifty yards across at its widest, the lighthouse rocks were technically a tiny island. At the lighthouse's rusted base were a dozen stone steps leading to an open door, where Golan stood with his pistol aimed squarely in our direction.

I risked a peek through the porthole. He held a small cage in one hand, and inside were two flapping birds mashed so close together I could hardly tell one from the other.

A shot whizzed past and I ducked.

"Come any closer and I'll shoot them both!" Golan shouted, rattling the cage.

"He's lying," I said. "He needs them."

"You don't know that," said Emma. "He's a madman, after all."

"Well we can't just do *nothing*."

"Rush him!" Bronwyn said. "He won't know what to do. But if it's going to work we've got to go NOW!"

And before we had a chance to weigh in, Bronwyn was running toward the lighthouse. We had no choice but to follow — she was carrying our protection, after all — and a moment later bullets were clanging against the door and chipping at the rocks around our feet.

It was like hanging from the back of a speeding train. Bronwyn was terrifying: She bellowed like a barbarian, the veins in her neck bulging, with Millard's blood smeared all over her arms and back. I was very glad, in that moment, not to be on the other side of the door.

As we neared the lighthouse, Bronwyn shouted, "Get behind the wall!" Emma and I grabbed Millard and cut left to take cover behind the far side of the lighthouse. As we ran, I saw Bronwyn lift the door above her head and hurl it toward Golan.

There was a thunderous crash quickly followed by a scream, and moments later Bronwyn joined us behind the wall, flushed and panting.

"I think I hit him!" she said excitedly.

"What about the birds?" Emma said. "Did you even think about them?"

"He dropped 'em. They're fine."

"Well, you might've asked us before you went berserk and risked all our lives!" Emma cried.

"Quiet," I hissed. We heard the faint

sound of creaking metal. "What *is* that?"

"He's climbing the stairs," Emma replied.

"You'd better get after him," croaked Millard. We looked at him, surprised. He was slumped against the wall.

"Not before we take care of you," I said. "Who knows how to make a tourniquet?"

Bronwyn reached down and tore the leg of her pants. "I do," she said. "I'll stop his bleeding; you get the wight. I knocked him pretty good, but not good enough. Don't give him a chance to get his wind back."

I turned to Emma. "You up for this?"

"If it means I get to melt that wight's face off," she said, little arcs of flame pulsing between her hands, "then absolutely."

Emma and I clambered over the ship's door, which lay bent on the steps where it had landed, and entered the lighthouse. The building consisted mainly of one narrow and profoundly vertical room — a giant stairwell, essentially — dominated by a skeletal staircase that corkscrewed from the floor to a stone landing, more than a hundred feet up. We could hear Golan's footsteps as he bounded up the stairs, but it was too dark to tell how far he was from the top.

"Can you see him?" I said, peering up the

stairwell's dizzying height.

My answer was a gunshot ricocheting off a wall nearby, followed by another that slammed into the floor at my feet. I jumped back, heart hammering.

"Over here!" Emma cried. She grabbed my arm and pulled me farther inside, to the one place Golan's gunshots couldn't reach us — directly under the stairs.

We climbed a few steps, which were already swaying like a boat in bad weather. "These are frightful!" Emma exclaimed, her fingers white-knuckled as they gripped the rail. "Even if we make it to the top without falling, he'll only shoot us!"

"If we can't go up," I said, "maybe we can bring him down." I began to rock back and forth where I stood, yanking on the railing and stomping my feet, sending shockwaves up the stairs. Emma looked at me like I was nuts for a second, but then got the idea and began to stomp and sway along with me. Pretty soon the staircase was rocking like crazy.

"What if the whole thing comes down?" Emma shouted.

"Let's hope it doesn't!"

We shook harder. Screws and bolts began to rain down. The rail was lurching so violently, I could hardly keep hold of it. I heard Golan scream a spectacular array of curses, and then something clattered down the stairs, landing nearby.

The first thing I thought was, *Oh God, what if that was the birdcage* — and I dashed down the stairs past Emma and ran out on the floor to check.

"What are you doing?!" Emma shouted. "He'll shoot you!"

"No, he won't!" I said, holding up Golan's handgun in triumph. It felt warm from all the firing he'd done and heavy in my hand, and I had no idea if it still had bullets or even how, in the near darkness, to check. I tried in vain to remember something useful from the few shooting lessons Grandpa had been allowed to give me, but finally I just ran back up the steps to Emma.

"He's trapped at the top," I said. "We've got to take it slow, try to reason with him, or who knows what he'll do to the birds."

"I'll reason him right over the side," Emma replied through her teeth.

We began to climb. The staircase swayed terribly and was so narrow that we could only proceed in single-file, crouching so our heads wouldn't hit the steps above. I prayed that none of the fasteners we'd shaken loose had secured anything crucial.

We slowed as we neared the top. I didn't

dare look down; there were only my feet on the steps, my hand sliding along the shivering rail and my other hand holding the gun. Nothing else existed.

I steeled myself for a surprise attack, but none came. The stairs ended at an opening in the stone landing above our heads, through which I could feel the snapping chill of night air and hear the whistle of wind. I stuck the gun through, followed by my head. I was tense and ready to fight, but I didn't see Golan. On one side of me spun the massive light, housed behind thick glass — this close it was blinding, forcing me to shut my eyes as it swung past — and on the other side was a spindly rail. Beyond that was a void: ten stories of empty air and then rocks and churning sea.

I stepped onto the narrow walkway and turned to give Emma a hand up. We stood with our backs pressed again the lamp's warm housing and our fronts to the wind's chill. "The Bird's close," Emma whispered. "I can feel her."

She flicked her wrist and a ball of angry red flame sprang to life. Something about its color and intensity made it clear that this time she hadn't summoned a light, but a weapon.

"We should split up," I said. "You go

around one side and I'll take the other. That way he won't be able to sneak past us."

"I'm scared, Jacob."

"Me, too. But he's hurt, and we have his gun."

She nodded and touched my arm, then turned away.

I circled the lamp slowly, clenching the maybe-loaded gun, and gradually the view around the other side began to peel back.

I found Golan sitting on his haunches with his head down and his back against the railing, the birdcage between his knees. He was bleeding badly from a cut on the bridge of his nose, rivulets of red streaking his face like tears.

Clipped to the bars of the cage was a small red light. Every few seconds it blinked.

I took another step forward, and he raised his head to look at me. His face was a stubble of caked blood, his one white eye shot through with red, spit flecking the corners of his mouth.

He rose unsteadily, the cage in one hand.

"Put it down."

He bent over as if to comply but faked away from me and tried to run. I shouted and gave chase, but as soon as he disappeared around the lamp housing I saw the glow of Emma's fire flare across the concrete. Golan came howling back toward me, his hair smoking and one arm covering his face.

"Stop!" I screamed at him, and he realized he was trapped. He raised the cage, shielding himself, and gave it a vicious shake. The birds screeched and nipped at his hand through the bars.

"Is this what you want?" Golan shouted. "Go ahead, burn me! The birds will burn, too! Shoot me and I'll throw them over the side!"

"Not if I shoot you in the head!"

He laughed. "You couldn't fire a gun if you wanted to. You forget, I'm intimately familiar with your poor, fragile psyche. It'd give you nightmares."

I tried to imagine it: curling my finger around the trigger and squeezing; the recoil and the awful report. What was so hard about that? Why did my hand shake just thinking about it? How many wights had my grandfather killed? Dozens? Hundreds? If he were here instead of me, Golan would be dead already, laid out while he'd been squatting against the rail in a daze. It was an opportunity I'd already wasted; a split-second of gutless indecision that might've cost the ymbrynes their lives.

The giant lamp spun past, blasting us with

light, turning us into glowing white cutouts. Golan, who was facing it, grimaced and looked away. *Another wasted opportunity,* I thought.

"Just put it down and come with us," I said. "Nobody else has to get hurt."

"I don't know," Emma said. "If Millard doesn't make it, I might reconsider that."

"You want to kill me?" Golan said. "Fine, get it over with. But you'll only be delaying the inevitable, not to mention making things worse for yourselves. We know how to find you now. More like me are coming, and I can guarantee the collateral damage they do will make what I did to your friend seem downright charitable."

"Get it *over* with?" Emma said, her flame sending a little pulse of sparks skyward. "Who said it would be quick?"

"I told you, I'll kill them," he said, drawing the cage to his chest.

She took a step toward him. "I'm eighty-eight years old," she said. "Do I look like I need a pair of babysitters?" Her expression was steely, unreadable. "I can't tell you how long we've been dying to get out from under that woman's wing. I swear, you'd be doing us a favor."

Golan swiveled his head back and forth, nervously sizing us up. *Is she serious?* For a moment he seemed genuinely frightened, but then he said, "You're full of shit."

Emma rubbed her palms together and pulled them slowly apart, drawing out a noose of flame. "Let's find out."

I wasn't sure how far Emma would take this, but I had to step in before the birds went up in flames or were sent tumbling over the rail.

"Tell us what you want with those ymbrynes, and maybe she'll go easy on you," I said.

"We only want to finish what we started," Golan said. "That's all we've ever wanted."

"You mean the experiment," Emma said. "You tried it once, and look what happened. You turned yourselves into monsters!"

"Yes," he said, "but what an unchallenging life it would be if we always got things right on the first go." He smiled. "This time we'll be harnessing the talents of all the world's best time manipulators, like these two ladies here. We won't fail again. We've had a hundred years to figure out what went wrong. Turns out all we needed was a bigger reaction!"

"A *bigger* reaction?" I said. "Last time you blew up half of Siberia!"

"If you must fail," he said grandly, "fail spectacularly!"

I remembered Horace's prophetic dream of ash clouds and scorched earth, and I realized what he'd been seeing. If the wights and hollows failed again, this time they'd destroy a lot more than five hundred miles of empty forest. And if they succeeded, and turned themselves into the deathless demigods they'd always dreamed of becoming . . . I shuddered to imagine it. Living under them would be a hell all its own.

The light came around and blinded Golan again — I tensed, ready to lunge — but the moment sped by too quickly.

"It doesn't matter," Emma said. "Kidnap all the ymbrynes you want. They'll never help you."

"Yes, they will. They'll do it or we'll kill them one by one. And if that doesn't work, we'll kill *you* one by one, and make them watch."

"You're insane," I told him.

The birds began to panic and screech. Golan shouted over them.

"No! What's *really* insane is how you peculiars hide from the world when you could rule it — succumb to death when you could dominate it — and let the common genetic trash of the human race drive you underground when you could so easily make them your slaves, as they rightly should be!" He drove home every sentence with another shake of the cage. "*That's* insane!"

"Stop it!" Emma shouted.

"So you *do* care!" He shook the cage even harder. Suddenly, the little red light attached to its bars began to glow twice as bright, and Golan whipped his head around and searched the darkness behind him. Then he looked back at Emma and said, "You want them? Here!" and he pulled back and swung the cage at her face.

She cried out and ducked. Like a discus thrower, Golan continued the swing until the cage sailed over her head, then released. It flew out of his hands and over the rail, tumbling end over end into the night.

I cursed and Emma screamed and threw herself against the rail, clawing at the air as the cage fell toward the sea. In that moment of confusion, Golan leapt and knocked me to the ground. He slammed a fist into my stomach and another into my chin.

I was dizzy and couldn't breathe. He grabbed for the gun, and it took every bit of my strength to keep him from snatching it. Because he wanted it so badly, I knew it must've been loaded. I would've thrown it over the rail, but he almost had it and I couldn't let go. Emma was screaming *bas-*

tard, you bastard, and then her hands, gloved in flame, came from behind and seized him around the neck.

I heard Golan's flesh singe like a cold steak on a hot grill. He howled and rolled off me, his thin hair going up in flame, and then his hands were around Emma's throat, as though he didn't mind burning as long as he could choke the life out of her. I jumped to my feet, held the gun in both hands, and pointed it.

I had, just for a moment, a clear shot. I tried to empty my mind and focus on steadying my arm, creating an imaginary line that extended from my shoulder through the sight to my target — a man's head. No, not a man, but a corruption of one. A thing. A force that had arranged the murder of my grandfather and exploded all that I'd humbly called a life, poorly lived though it may have been, and carried me here to this place and this moment, in much the way less corrupt and violent forces had done my living and deciding for me since I was old enough to decide anything. *Relax your hands, breathe in, hold it.* But now I had a chance to force back, a slim nothing of a chance that I could already feel slipping away.

Now squeeze.

The pistol bucked in my hands and its report sounded like the earth breaking open, so tremendous and sudden that I shut my eyes. When I opened them again, everything seemed strangely frozen. Though Golan stood behind Emma with her arms locked in a hold, wrestling her toward the railing, it was as if they'd been cast in bronze. Had the ymbrynes turned human again and worked their magic on us? But then everything came unstuck and Emma wrenched her arms away and Golan began to totter backward, and he stumbled and sat heavily on the rail.

Gaping at me in surprise, he opened his mouth to speak but found he could not. He clapped his hands over the penny-sized hole I'd made in his throat, blood lacing through his fingers and running down his arms, and then the strength went out of him and he fell back, and he was gone.

The moment Golan disappeared from view, he was forgotten. Emma pointed out to sea and shouted, "There, there!" Following her finger and squinting into the distance I could barely pick out the pulse of a red LED bobbing on the waves. Then we were scrambling to the hatch and sprinting down and down the endless seesawing staircase, hopeless that we could reach the cage before it sank but hysterical to try to anyway.

We tore outside to find Millard wearing a tourniquet and Bronwyn by his side. He shouted something I didn't quite hear, but it was enough to assure me he was alive. I grabbed Emma's shoulder and said, "The boat!" pointing to where the stolen canoe had been lashed to a rock, but it was too far away, on the wrong side of the lighthouse, and there was no time. Emma pulled me instead toward the open sea, and, running, we dashed ourselves into it.

I hardly felt the cold. All I could think about was reaching the cage before it disappeared beneath the waves. We tore at the water and sputtered and choked as black swells slapped our faces. It was difficult to tell how far away the beacon was, just a single point of light in a surging ocean of dark. It bobbed and fell and came and went, and twice we lost sight of it and had to stop, searching frantically before spotting it again.

The strong current was carrying the cage out to sea, and us with it. If we didn't reach it soon, our muscles would fail and we'd drown. I kept this morbid thought to myself for as long as I could, but when the beacon disappeared a third time and we looked for it so long we couldn't even be sure what section of the rolling black sea it had disappeared from, I shouted, "We have to go back!"

Emma wouldn't listen. She swam ahead of me, farther out to sea. I grasped at her scissoring feet but she kicked me off.

"It's gone! We aren't going to find them!"

"Shut up, shut up!" she cried, and I could tell from her labored breaths that she was as exhausted as I was. "Just shut up and look!"

I grabbed her and shouted in her face and she kicked at me, and when I wouldn't let go and she couldn't force me to, she began to cry, just wordless howls of despair.

I tried to drag her back toward the lighthouse, but she was like a stone in the water, pulling me down. "You have to swim!" I shouted. "Swim or we'll drown!"

And then I saw it — the faintest blink of red light. It was close, just below the surface. At first I didn't say anything, afraid I'd imagined it, but then it blinked a second time.

Emma whooped and shouted. It looked like the cage had landed on another wreck — how else could it have come to rest so shallowly? — and because it had only just sunk, I told myself it was possible the birds were still alive.

We swam and prepared to dive for the cage, though I didn't know where the breath would come from, we had so little left. Then, strangely, the cage seemed to rise toward us.

"What's happening?" I shouted. "Is that a wreck?"

"Can't be. There are none over here!"

"Then what the hell is *that?*"

It looked like a whale about to surface, long and massive and gray, or some ghost ship rising from its grave, and there erupted a sudden and powerful swell that came up from below and pushed us away. We tried to paddle against it but had no more luck than flotsam caught in a tidal wave, and then it thudded against our feet and we were rising, too, riding its back.

It came out of the water beneath us, hissing and clanking like some giant mechanical monster. We were caught in a sudden rush of foaming surf that raced off it in every direction, thrown hard onto a surface of metal grates. We hooked our fingers through the grates to keep from being washed into the sea. I squinted through the salt spray and saw that the cage had come to rest between what looked like two fins jutting from the monster's back, one smaller and one larger. And then the lighthouse beam swept past, and in its gleam I realized they weren't fins at all but a conning tower and a giant bolted-down gun. This thing we were riding wasn't a monster or a wreck or a whale —

"It's a U-boat!" I shouted. That it had risen right beneath our feet was no coincidence. It had to be what Golan was waiting for.

Emma was already on her feet and sprinting across the rolling deck toward the cage. I scrambled to stand. As I began to run a wave flashed over the deck and knocked us both down.

I heard a shout and looked up to see a man in a gray uniform rise from a hatch in the conning tower and level a gun at us.

Bullets rained down, hammering the deck. The cage was too far away — we'd be torn to pieces before we could reach it — but I could see that Emma was about to try anyway.

I ran and tackled her and we tumbled sideways off the deck and into the water. The black sea closed above us. Bullets peppered the water, leaving trails of bubbles in their wake.

When we surfaced again, she grabbed me and screamed, "Why did you do that? I nearly had them!"

"He was about to kill you!" I said, wrestling away — and then it occurred to me that she hadn't even seen him, she'd been so focused on the cage, so I pointed up at the deck, where the gunner was striding toward it. He picked the cage up and rattled it. Its door hung open, and I thought I saw movement inside — some reason for hope — and then the lighthouse beam washed over everything. I saw the gunner's face full in the light, his mouth curled into a leering grin, his eyes depthless and blank. He was a wight.

He reached into the cage and pulled out a single sodden bird. From the conning tower, another soldier whistled to him, and he ran back toward the hatch with it.

The sub began to rattle and hiss. The water around us churned as if boiling.

"Swim or it'll suck us down with it!" I shouted to Emma. But she hadn't heard me — her eyes were locked elsewhere, on a patch of dark water near the stern of the boat.

She swam for it. I tried to stop her but she fought me off. Then, over the whine of the sub, I heard it — a high, shrieking call. Miss Peregrine!

We found her bobbing in the waves, struggling to keep her head above water, one wing flapping, the other broken looking. Emma scooped her up. I screamed that we had to go.

We swam away with what little strength we had. Behind us, a whirlpool was opening up, all the water displaced by the sub rushing back to fill the void as it sank. The sea was consuming itself and trying to consume us, too, but we had with us now a screeching winged symbol of victory, or half a victory at least, and she gave us the strength to fight the unnatural current. Then we heard Bronwyn shouting our names, and our brawny friend came crashing through the waves to tow us back to safety.

We lay on the rocks beneath the clearing sky, gasping for air and trembling with exhaustion. Millard and Bronwyn had so many questions, but we had no breath to answer them. They had seen Golan's body fall and the submarine rise and sink and Miss Peregrine come out of the water but not Miss Avocet; they understood what they needed to. They hugged us until we stopped shaking, and Bronwyn tucked the headmistress under her shirt for warmth. Once we'd recovered a little, we retrieved Emma's canoe and pushed off toward the shore.

When we got there, the children all waded

into the shallows to meet us.

"We heard shooting!"

"What was that strange boat?"

"Where's Miss Peregrine?"

We climbed out of the rowboat, and Bronwyn raised her shirt to reveal the bird nuzzled there. The children crowded around, and Miss Peregrine lifted her beak and crowed at them to show that she was tired but all right. A cheer went up.

"You did it!" Hugh shouted.

Olive danced a little jig and sang, "The Bird, the Bird, the Bird! Emma and Jacob saved the Bird!"

But the celebration was brief. Miss Avocet's absence was quickly noted, as was Millard's alarming condition. His tourniquet was tight, but he'd lost a lot of blood and was weakening. Enoch gave him his coat, Fiona offered her woolen hat.

"We'll take you to see the doctor in town," Emma said to him.

"Nonsense," Millard replied. "The man's never laid eyes on an invisible boy, and he wouldn't know what to do with one if he did. He'd either treat the wrong limb or run away screaming."

"It doesn't matter if he runs away screaming," Emma said. "Once the loop resets he won't remember a thing."

"Look around you. The loop should've reset an hour ago."

Millard was right — the skies were quiet, the battle had ended, but rolling drifts of bomb smoke still mixed with the clouds.

"That's not good," Enoch said, and everyone got quiet.

"In any case," Millard continued, "all the supplies I need are in the house. Just give me a bolt of Laudanum and swab the wound with alcohol. It's only the fleshy part anyway. In three days I'll be right as rain."

"But it's still bleeding," Bronwyn said, pointing out red droplets that dotted the sand beneath him.

"Then tie the damn tourniquet tighter!"

She did, and Millard gasped in a way that made everyone cringe, then fainted into her arms.

"Is he all right?" Claire asked.

"Just blacked out is all," said Enoch. "He ain't as fit as he pretends to be."

"What do we do now?"

"Ask Miss Peregrine!" Olive said.

"Right. Put her down so she can change back," said Enoch. "She can't very well tell us what to do while she's still a bird."

So Bronwyn set her on a dry patch of sand, and we all stood back and waited. Miss Peregrine hopped a few times and flapped her good wing and then swiveled her feathered head around and blinked at us — but that was it. She remained a bird.

"Maybe she wants a little privacy," Emma suggested. "Let's turn our backs."

So we did, forming a ring around her. "It's safe now, Miss P," said Olive. "No one's looking!"

After a minute, Hugh snuck a peek and said, "Nope, still a bird."

"Maybe she's too tired and cold," Claire said, and enough of the others agreed this was plausible that it was decided we would go back to the house, treat Millard with what supplies we had, and hope that with some time to rest, both the headmistress and her loop would return to normal.

CHAPTER ELEVEN

We marched up the steep trail and across the ridge like a company of war-weary veterans, single file, heads down, Bronwyn carrying Millard in her arms and Miss Peregrine riding the nestlike crown of Fiona's hair. The landscape was gouged with smoking craters, fresh-turned earth thrown everywhere as if some giant dog had been digging at it. We all wondered what awaited us back at the house, but no one dared to ask.

We had our answer even before clearing the forest. Enoch's foot kicked something, and he bent down to look. It was half a charred brick.

Panic broke out. The children began to sprint down the path. When they reached the lawn, the younger ones broke out in tears. There was smoke everywhere. The bomb had not come to rest atop Adam's finger, as it usually did, but had split him straight down the middle and exploded. The back corner of the house had been reduced to a slumped and smoking ruin. Small fires burned in the charred shell of two rooms. Where Adam had been was a raw crater deep enough to bury a person upright. It was easy now to picture what this place would one day become: that sad and desecrated wreck I had first discovered weeks ago. The nightmare house.

Miss Peregrine leapt from Fiona's hair and began to race around on the scorched grass, squawking in alarm.

"Headmistress, what happened?" Olive said. "Why hasn't the changeover come?"

Miss Peregrine could only screech in reply. She seemed as confused and frightened as the rest of us.

"Please turn back!" begged Claire, kneeling before her.

Miss Peregrine flapped and jumped and seemed to be straining herself, but still couldn't shift her shape. The children crowded around in concern.

"Something's wrong," Emma said. "If she could turn human, she would've done it by now."

"Perhaps that's why the loop slipped," Enoch suggested. "Remember that old story about Miss Kestrel, when she was thrown

450

from her bicycle in a road accident? She knocked her head and stayed a kestrel for a whole entire week. That's when her loop slipped."

"What's that got to do with Miss Peregrine?"

Enoch sighed. "Maybe she's only injured her head and we just need to wait a week for her to come to her senses."

"A speeding lorry's one thing," Emma said. "Being abused by wights is quite another. There's no knowing what that bastard did to Miss Peregrine before we got to her."

"Wights? As in plural?"

"It was wights who took Miss Avocet," I said.

"How do you know that?" demanded Enoch.

"They were working with Golan, weren't they? And I saw the eyes of the one who shot at us. There's no question."

"Then Miss Avocet's as good as dead," said Hugh. "They'll kill her for sure."

"Maybe not," I replied. "At least not right away."

"If there's one thing I know about wights," said Enoch, "it's that they kill peculiars. It's their nature. It's what they do."

"No, Jacob's right," said Emma. "Before

that wight died, he told us why they've been abducting so many ymbrynes. They're going to force them to re-create the reaction that made the hollows in the first place — only bigger. Much bigger."

I heard someone gasp. Everyone else fell silent. I looked around for Miss Peregrine and saw her perched forlornly on the edge of Adam's crater.

"We've got to stop them," Hugh said. "We've got to find out where they're taking the ymbrynes."

"How?" said Enoch. "Follow a submarine?"

Behind me a throat cleared loudly, and we turned to see Horace sitting cross-legged on the ground. "I know where they're going," he said quietly.

"What do you mean, you know?"

"Never mind how he knows, he *knows*," said Emma. "Where are they taking her, Horace?"

He shook his head. "I don't know the name," he said, "but I've seen it."

"Then draw it," I said.

He thought for a moment and then rose stiffly. Looking like a beggar evangelist in his torn black suit, he shuffled to an ash pile that had spilled from the cracked-open house and bent to gather a palm full of soot.

Then, in the soft light of the moon, he began to paint on a broken wall with broad strokes.

We gathered around to watch. He made a row of bold vertical stripes topped with thin loops, like bars and razor wire. To one side was a dark forest. There was snow on the ground, rendered in black. And that was all.

When it was done, he staggered back and sat down hard in the grass, a dull distant look in his eyes. Emma took him gently by the shoulder and said, "Horace, what more do you know about this place?"

"It's somewhere cold."

Bronwyn stepped forward to study the marks Horace had made. She held Olive in the crook of her arm, the little girl's head resting sweetly on her shoulder. "Looks like a jail to me," said Bronwyn.

Olive raised her head. "Well?" came her small voice. "When do we go?"

"Go where?" Enoch said, tossing up his hands. "That's just a lot of squiggles!"

"It's *somewhere,*" Emma said, turning to face him.

"We can't simply go someplace snowy and look for a prison."

"And we can't very well stay here."

"Why not?"

"Look at the state of this place. Look at

453

the headmistress. We had a damn good run here, but it's over."

Enoch and Emma went back and forth for a while. People took sides. Enoch argued that they'd been too long out of the world, that they'd get snared in the war or caught by hollows if they left, that it was better to take their chances here, where at least they knew the territory. The others insisted that the war and the hollows had come to *them* now, and they had no choice. The hollows and wights would return for Miss Peregrine, and in ever-greater numbers. And there was Miss Peregrine herself to consider.

"We'll find another ymbryne," Emma suggested. "If anyone will know how to help the headmistress, it'll be one of her friends."

"But what if all the other loops have slipped too?" said Hugh. "What if all the ymbrynes have already been kidnapped?"

"We can't think that way. There must be *some* left."

"Emma's right," Millard said, lying on the ground with a chunk of broken masonry under his head for a pillow. "If the alternative is to wait and just hope — that no more hollows come, that the headmistress gets better — I say that's no alternative at all."

The dissenters were finally shamed into

agreement. The house would be abandoned. Belongings would be packed. A few boats would be requisitioned from the harbor and pressed into service, and in the morning everyone would go.

I asked Emma how they were going to navigate. After all, none of the children had been off the island in nearly eighty years, and Miss Peregrine couldn't speak or fly.

"There's a map," she told me, turning her head slowly to look at the smoking house. "If it hasn't burned, that is."

I volunteered to help her find it. Wrapping wet cloths over our faces, we ventured into the house, entering through the collapsed wall. The windows were shattered, the air hung with smoke, but by the bright light of Emma's hand-flame we found our way to the study. All the shelves had fallen like dominoes, but we shoved them aside and searched through the books spilled across the floor, crouching low. As luck would have it, the book was easy to find: it was the largest one in the library. Emma yelped with joy and held it up.

On the way out, we found alcohol and Laudanum and proper bandages for Millard. Once we'd helped clean and dress his wound, we sat down to examine the book. It was more atlas than map, bound in quilted leather dyed a deep burgundy, each page drawn carefully on what looked like parchment. It was very fine and very old, and big enough to fill Emma's lap.

"It's called the Map of Days," she said. "It's got every loop ever known to exist." The page she'd opened to appeared to be a map of Turkey, though no roads were marked and no borders indicated. Instead, the map was scattered with tiny spirals, which I took to be the location of loops. At the center of each was a unique symbol that corresponded to a legend at the bottom of the page, where the symbols reappeared next to a list of numbers separated by dashes. I pointed to one that read *29-3-316/?-?-399* and said, "What is this, some kind of code?"

Emma traced it with her finger. "This loop was the twenty-ninth of March, 316 A.D. It existed until sometime in the year 399, though the day and month are unknown."

"What happened in 399?"

She shrugged. "It doesn't say."

I reached across her and turned to a map of Greece, even more clustered with spirals and numbers. "But what's the point of listing all these?" I said. "How would you even get to these ancient loops?"

"By leapfrogging," said Millard. "It's a

highly complex and dangerous undertaking, but by leapfrogging from one loop to an- other — a day fifty years in the past, for instance — then you'll find you have access to a whole range of loops that have ceased to exist in the last fifty years. Should you have the wherewithal to travel to them, within those you'll find still other loops, and so on exponentially."

"That's time travel," I said, astonished. "*Real* time travel."

"I suppose so, yes."

"So this place," I said, pointing to Hor- ace's ash painting on the wall. "We wouldn't just have to figure out *where* it is, but *when,* too?"

"I'm afraid so. And if Miss Avocet is indeed being held by wights, who are noto- riously adept at leapfrogging, then it's extremely likely that the place she and the other ymbrynes are being taken is some- where in the past. That will make them all the more difficult to find, and getting there all the more dangerous. The locations of historical loops are well known to our enemies, who tend to lurk near the en- trances."

"Well then," I said, "it's a good thing I'm coming with you."

Emma spun to look at me. "Oh, that's

wonderful!" she cried, and hugged me. "Are you certain?"

I told her I was. Tired as they were, the children whistled and clapped. Some embraced me. Even Enoch shook my hand. But when I looked at Emma again, her smile had faded.

"What's the matter?" I said.

She shifted uncomfortably. "There's something you should know," she said, "and I'm afraid it'll make you not want to come with us."

"It won't," I assured her.

"When we leave here, this loop will close behind us. It's possible you may never be able to return to the time you came from. At least, not easily."

"There's nothing for me there," I said quickly. "Even if I could go back, I'm not sure I'd want to."

"You say that now. I need you to be sure."

I nodded, then stood.

"Where are you going?" she asked.

"For a walk."

I didn't go far, just around the perimeter of the neat yard in a slow shuffle, watching the sky, clear now, a billion stars spread across it. Stars, too, were time travelers. How many of those ancient points of light were the last echoes of suns now dead? How many had been born but their light not yet come this far? If all the suns but ours collapsed tonight, how many lifetimes would it take us to realize that we were alone? I had always known the sky was full of mysteries — but not until now had I realized how full of them the earth was.

I came to the place where the path emerged from the woods. In one direction lay home and everything I knew, unmysterious and ordinary and safe.

Except it *wasn't.* Not really. Not any more. The monsters had murdered Grandpa Portman, and they had come after me. Sooner or later, they would again. Would I come home one day to find my dad bleeding to death on the floor? My mom? In the other direction, the children were gathering in excited little knots, plotting and planning, for the first time any of them could remember, for the future.

I walked back to Emma, still poring over her massive book. Miss Peregrine was perched next to her, tapping with her beak here and there on the map. Emma looked up as I approached.

"I'm sure," I said.

She smiled. "I'm glad."

"There's just one thing I have to do before I go."

■ ■ ■ ■

I made it back to town just before dawn. The rain had finally eased, and the beginning of a blue day was percolating on the horizon. The main path looked like an arm with the veins stripped out, long slashes where flooding had washed the gravel away.

I walked into the pub and through the empty bar and up to our rooms. The shades were drawn and my father's door was closed, which was a relief because I hadn't yet figured out how to say what I needed to tell him. Instead I sat down with pen and paper and wrote him a letter.

I tried to explain everything. I wrote about the peculiar children and the hollows and how all of Grandpa Portman's stories had turned out to be true. I told him what had happened to Miss Peregrine and Miss Avocet and tried to make him understand why I had to go. I begged him not to worry.

Then I stopped and read over what I'd written. It was no good. He would never believe it. He'd think I'd lost my mind the way Grandpa had, or that I'd run away or been abducted or taken a nosedive off the cliffs. Either way, I was about to ruin his life. I wadded up the paper and threw it in

461

the trash.

"Jacob?"

I turned to see my father leaning in the doorjamb, bleary-eyed, hair tangled, dressed in a mud-splashed shirt and jeans.

"Hi, Dad."

"I'm going to ask you a simple, straightforward question," he said, "and I'd like a simple, straightforward answer. Where were you last night?" I could tell he was struggling to maintain his composure.

I decided I was done lying. "I'm fine, Dad. I was with my friends."

It was like I'd pulled the pin on a grenade. "YOUR FRIENDS ARE IMAGINARY!" he shouted. He came toward me, his face turning red. "I wish your mother and I had never let that crackpot therapist talk us into bringing you out here, because it has been an unmitigated *disaster!* You just lied to me for the last time! Now get in your room and start packing. We're on the next ferry!"

"Dad?"

"And when we get home, you're not leaving the house until we find a psychiatrist who's not a complete *jackass!*"

"Dad!"

I wondered for a moment if I would have to run from him. I pictured my dad holding me down, calling for help, loading me onto the ferry with my arms locked in a straight-jacket.

"I'm not coming with you," I said.

His eyes narrowed and he cocked his head, as if he hadn't heard properly. I was about to repeat myself when there was a knock at the door.

"Go away!" my dad shouted.

The knock came again, more insistent this time. He stormed over and flung it open, and there at the top of the stairs stood Emma, a tiny ball of blue flame dancing above her hand. Next to her was Olive.

"Hullo," Olive said. "We're here to see Jacob."

He stared at them, baffled. "What is this . . ."

The girls edged past him into the room.

"What are you *doing* here?" I hissed at them.

"We only wanted to introduce ourselves," Emma replied, flashing a big smile at my dad. "We've come to know your son rather well of late, so we thought it only proper that we should pay a friendly call."

"Okay," my father said, his eyes darting between them.

"He's really a fine boy," said Olive. "So brave!"

"And handsome!" Emma added, winking

at me. She began to roll the flame between her hands like a toy. My father stared at it, hypnotized.

"Y-yes," he stammered. "He sure is."

"Do you mind if I slip off my shoes?" Olive asked, and without waiting for an answer she did, and promptly floated to the ceiling. "Thanks. That's much more comfortable!"

"These are my friends, Dad. The ones I was telling you about. This is Emma, and that's Olive, on the ceiling."

He staggered back a step. "I'm still sleeping," he said vaguely. "I'm so tired . . ."

A chair lifted off the floor and floated over to him, followed by an expertly wrapped medical bandage bobbing through the air. "Then please, have a seat," Millard said.

"Okay," my dad replied, and he did.

"What are you doing here?" I whispered to Millard. "Shouldn't you be lying down?"

"I was in the neighborhood." He held up a modern-looking pill bottle. "I must say, they make some marvelously effective pain tablets in the future!"

"Dad, this is Millard," I said. "You can't see him because he's invisible."

"Nice to meet you."

"Likewise," said Millard.

I went over to my father and knelt down

beside his chair. His head bobbed slightly. "I'm going away, Dad. You might not see me for a while."

"Oh, yeah? Where are you going?"

"On a trip."

"A trip," he repeated. "When will you be back?"

"I don't really know."

He shook his head. "Just like your grandfather." Millard ran tap water into a glass and brought it to him, and Dad reached out and took it, as though floating glasses weren't at all unusual. I guess he really thought he was dreaming. "Well, goodnight," he said and then stood up, steadied himself on the chair, and stumbled back into his bedroom. Stopping at the door, he turned to face me.

"Jake?"

"Yeah, Dad?"

"Be careful, okay?"

I nodded. He closed the door. A moment later I heard him fall into bed.

I sat down and rubbed my face. I didn't know how to feel.

"Did we help?" Olive asked from her perch on the ceiling.

"I'm not sure," I said. "I don't think so. He'll just wake up later thinking he dreamed all of you."

"You could write a letter," Millard suggested. "Tell him anything you like — it's not as if he'll be able to follow us."

"I did write a letter. But it's not *proof*."

"Ah," he replied. "Yes, I see your problem."

"Nice problem to have," said Olive. "Wish *my* mum and dad had loved me enough to worry when I left home."

Emma reached up and squeezed her hand. Then she said, "I might have proof."

She pulled a small wallet from the waistband of her dress and took out a snapshot. She handed it to me. It was a picture of her and my grandfather when my grandfather was young. All her attention was focused on him, but he seemed elsewhere. It was sad and beautiful and encapsulated what little I knew about their relationship.

"It was taken just before Abe left for the war," Emma said. "Your dad'll recognize me, won't he?"

I smiled at her. "You look like you haven't aged a day."

"Marvelous!" said Millard. "There's your proof."

"Do you always keep this with you?" I asked, handing it back to her.

"Yes. But I don't need it anymore." She went to the table and took my pen and began to write on the back of the photo. "What's your father's name?"

"Franklin."

When she finished writing, she gave it to me. I looked at both sides and then fished my letter from the trash, smoothed it, and left it on the table with the photo.

"Ready to go?" I said.

My friends were standing in the doorway, waiting for me.

"Only if you are," Emma replied.

Dear Franklin,

It was a great pleasure meeting you. This is a photograph of your father and me taken when he lived here. I hope it will be sufficient to convince you that I am still among the living, and that Jacob's stories are no fantasy.

Jacob will be traveling with my friends and me for a time. We will keep one another as safe as anyone like us can be. One day, when the danger has passed, he will come back to you. You have my word.

Very sincerely yours,
Emma Bloom

P.S. I understand you may have discovered a letter I sent your father many years ago. It was inappropriate, and I assure you

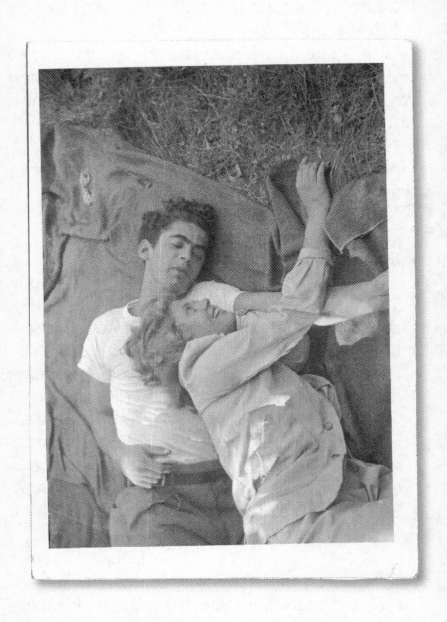

unsolicited; he did not respond in kind. He was one of the most honorable men I have ever known.

We set out for the ridge. At the spot near the crest where I always stopped to see how far I'd come, this time I kept walking. Sometimes it's better not to look back.

When we reached the cairn, Olive patted the stones like a beloved old pet. "Goodbye, old loop," she said. "You've been such a good loop, and we'll miss you ever so much." Emma squeezed her shoulder, and they both crouched down and went inside.

In the rear chamber, Emma held her flame to the wall and showed me something I'd never noticed before: a long list of dates and initials carved into the rocks. "It's all the other times people have used this loop," she explained. "All the other days the loop's been looped."

Peering at it, I made out a *P.M. 3-2-1853* and a *J.R.R. 1-4-1797* and a barely-legible *X.J. 1580.* Near the bottom were some strange markings I couldn't decipher.

"Runic inscriptions," Emma said. "Quite ancient."

Millard searched through the gravel until he found a sharpened stone, and, using another stone as a hammer, he chipped an inscription of his own below the others. It read *A.P. 3-9-1940.*

"Who's AP?" asked Olive.

"Alma Peregrine," said Millard, and then he sighed. "It should be her carving this, not me."

Olive ran her hand over the rough markings. "Do you think another ymbryne will come along to make a loop here someday?"

"I hope so," he said. "I dearly hope so."

We buried Victor. Bronwyn lifted his whole bed and carried it outside with Victor still in it, and with all the children assembled on the grass she pulled back the sheets and tucked him in, planting one last kiss on his forehead. We boys lifted the corners of his bed like pallbearers and walked him down into the crater that the bomb had made. Then all of us climbed out but Enoch, who took a clay man from his pocket and laid it gently on the boy's chest.

"This is my very best man," he said. "To keep you company." The clay man sat up and Enoch pushed it back down with his thumb. The man rolled over with one arm under his head and seemed to go to sleep.

When the crater had been filled, Fiona dragged some shrubs and vines over the raw soil and began to grow them. By the time the rest of us had finished packing for the journey, Adam was back in his old spot, only now he was marking Victor's grave.

Once the children had said goodbye to their house, some taking chips of brick or flowers from the garden as forget-me-nots, we made one last trip across the island: through the smoking charred woods and the flat bog dug with bomb holes, over the ridge and down through the little town hung with peat smoke, where the townspeople lingered on porches and in doorways, so tired and numb with shock that they hardly seemed to notice the small parade of peculiar-looking children passing them by.

We were quiet but excited. The children hadn't slept, but you wouldn't have known it to look at them. It was September fourth, and for the first time in a very long time, the days were moving again. Some of them claimed they could feel the difference; the air in their lungs was fuller, the race of blood through their veins faster. They felt more vital, more real.

I did, too.

I used to dream about escaping my ordinary life, but my life was never ordinary. I had simply failed to notice how extraordinary it was. Likewise, I never imagined that home might be something I would miss. Yet as we stood loading our boats in the breaking dawn, on a brand new precipice of Before and After, I thought of everything I was about to leave behind — my parents, my town, my once-best-and-only friend — and I realized that leaving wouldn't be like I had imagined, like casting off a weight. Their memory was something tangible and heavy, and I would carry it with me.

And yet my old life was as impossible to return to as the children's bombed house. The doors had been blown off our cages.

Ten peculiar children and one peculiar bird were made to fit in just three stout rowboats, with much being jettisoned and left behind on the dock. When we'd finished, Emma suggested that one of us say something — make a speech to dedicate the journey ahead — but no one seemed ready with words. And so Enoch held up Miss Peregrine's cage and she let out a great screeching cry. We answered with a cry of our own, both a victory yell and a lament, for everything lost and yet to be gained.

Hugh and I rowed the first boat. Enoch sat watching us from the bow, ready to take his turn, while Emma in a sunhat studied the receding island. The sea was a pane of rippled glass spreading endlessly before us.

The day was warm, but a cool breeze came off the water, and I could've happily rowed for hours. I wondered how such calm could belong to a world at war.

In the next boat, I saw Bronwyn wave and raise Miss Peregrine's camera to her eye. I smiled back. We'd brought none of the old photo albums with us; maybe this would be the first picture in a brand new one. It was strange to think that one day I might have my own stack of yellowed photos to show skeptical grandchildren — and my own fantastic stories to share.

Then Bronwyn lowered the camera and raised her arm, pointing at something beyond us. In the distance, black against the rising sun, a silent procession of battle-ships punctuated the horizon.

We rowed faster.

All the pictures in this book are authentic, vintage found photographs, and with the exception of a few that have undergone minimal postprocessing, they are unaltered. They were lent from the personal archives of ten collectors, people who have spent years and countless hours hunting through giant bins of unsorted snapshots at flea markets and antiques malls and yard sales to find a transcendent few, rescuing images of historical significance and arresting beauty from obscurity — and, most likely, the dump. Their work is an unglamorous labor of love, and I think they are the unsung heroes of the photography world.

ACKNOWLEDGMENTS

I would like to thank:

Everyone at Quirk, especially Jason Rekulak, for his seemingly endless patience and many excellent ideas; Stephen Segal, for his close readings and sharp insights; and Doogie Horner, certainly the most talented book designer/stand-up comic working today.

My wonderful and tenacious agent, Kate Shafer Testerman.

My wife Abbi, for cheerfully enduring long months of nervous pacing and beard growth on my part, and her parents, Barry and Phyllis, for their support, and Barry's parents, Gladys and Abraham, whose story of survival inspired me.

Mom, to whom I owe everything, obviously.

All my photo collector friends: the very generous Peter Cohen; Leonard Lightfoot, who introduced me around; Roselyn Leibowitz; Jack Mord of the Thanatos Archive;

Steve Bannos; John Van Noate; David Bass; Martin Isaac; Muriel Moutet; Julia Lauren; Yefim Tovbis; and especially Robert Jackson, in whose living room I spent many pleasant hours looking at peculiar photographs.

Chris Higgins, whom I consider a leading authority on time travel, for always taking my calls.

Laurie Porter, who took the photo of me that appears on the jacket of this book while we were exploring some weird abandoned shacks in the Mojave desert.

ABOUT THE AUTHOR

Ransom Riggs grew up in Florida but now makes his home in the land of peculiar children — Los Angeles. Along the way he earned degrees from Kenyon College and the University of Southern California's School of Cinema-Television, got married, and made some award-winning short films. He moonlights as a blogger and travel writer, and his series of travel essays, *Strange Geographies,* can be found at mentalfloss.com or via ransomriggs.com. This is his first novel.